MANAGING INTERACTIVE VIDEO/ MULTIMEDIA PROJECTS

MANAGING INTERACTIVE VIDEO/ MULTIMEDIA PROJECTS

ROBERT E. BERGMAN & THOMAS V. MOORE

EDUCATIONAL TECHNOLOGY PUBLICATIONS
ENGLEWOOD CLIFFS, NEW JERSEY 07632

Library of Congress Cataloging-in-Publication Data

Bergman, Robert E.
  Managing interactive video/multimedia projects / Robert E.
Bergman, Thomas V. Moore.
      p.   cm.
  Includes bibliographical references.
  ISBN 0-87778-209-1
  1. Interactive video—Planning. 2. Video recordings—Production
and direction. 3. Educational technology. I. Moore, Thomas V.
II. Title.
LB1028.75.B47   1990
371.3'078—dc20
                                                    89-77528
                                                        CIP

Printed in the United States of America.

Library of Congress Catalog Card Number:
89-77528.

International Standard Book Number:
0-87778-209-1.

First Printing: June, 1990.
Second Printing: September, 1991.

ACKNOWLEDGMENTS

Writing a book is lonely work, but it's never done alone. Many people contribute their time, energy, and ideas to produce the finished text. This effort was no different. Our families, colleagues, and organizations all played a significant part in this project.

We are indebted to the IBM Corporation for their generous support of publication of this book about interactive video and multimedia projects. Their contributions of class materials, copyrighted forms, and time allowed us to incorporate examples from hundreds of actual projects. Many of the concepts and procedures in this book were originally designed, developed, and delivered in IBM's seven day IVD Project Manager's Workshop.

Our colleagues in the field have helped refine our tools and techniques. Their ideas are spread throughout the book; we appreciate their willingness to share. A special note of thanks to Dr. Elizabeth Wright and to Bill Mauger, president of Sunbreak Productions. They were part of each IVD workshop and thereby influenced much of its content. Their management and production ideas are reflected in several chapters.

Many IVD vendors have contributed to the methods we have presented in this book. They have helped us test our model and refine our documentation. The professionals at Crawford Communications Co. played a critical role in the success of the IVD workshops; their creative techniques are incorporated into the book.

Our thanks also go to Rockley Miller for providing the introduction, photographs and insight regarding the present and future state of our industry.

We must acknowledge the contribution of our editor, Lawrence Lipsitz, in helping us to refine and clarify our ideas and words through many drafts. His diligent efforts and cogent suggestions have made a vital difference in the final product.

Finally, and most importantly, we want to thank our families, and especially our wives, Joan and Judy, for their patience and support each time we cancelled personal plans to "work on the book."

Contents

SECTION ONE: THE PROJECT MANAGER'S GUIDE

PART ONE: Orientation

Chapter One   Defining Multimedia Applications

Chapter Two   Understanding the Development Model

Chapter Three   Building the Project Team

PART TWO: Preparation

Chapter Four Planning the Project

Chapter Five Analyzing the Application

PART THREE: Construction

Chapter Six Designing the Application

Chapter Seven Developing and Documenting the Design

Chapter Eight Producing the Media

Chapter Nine   Authoring

Chapter Ten Validating the Application

PART FOUR: Implementation and Management

Chapter Eleven **The Implementation Phase**

Chapter Twelve Managing the Project

SECTION TWO: THE PROJECT MANAGER'S RESOURCES

Appendix A Checklists

Introduction

by Rockley Miller

After more than ten years in the marketplace, the results are in. It's a proven fact that interactive video systems (most typically those which use videodisc) can be used effectively to improve the learning process. Students regularly learn more in half the time with interactive video — and at much lower cost than traditional alternatives.

In retail environments, such interactive systems dramatically increase sales. In public access environments, they deliver personalized information in a highly efficient manner to thousands of users every day. In museums, they engage the visitor as never before. Interactive video combines the unparalleled data management power of the computer and the compelling audio-visual experience of television. The combination is truly a Gestalt phenomenon in which the whole of the experience is significantly greater than the sum of its component parts.

To realize this potentially powerful result, the art and science of each technology are placed in the hands of a project manager, who in turn must orchestrate the complete interactive experience for the final user. This represents a vast opportunity and significant responsibility. It also poses a difficult problem, for as with your local Philharmonic, many can play the instruments but few can conduct the entire ensemble.

To further compound the challenge, imagine that each musician not only plays a different instrument, but also speaks a different language. Such is the case with interactive video, where the assembled team includes instructional designers who speak of authoring, pedagogics and remediation; graphic artists who talk of drop shadows, GUI's, and animated sprites; video producers who think in terms of wipes, fades, pictures, plots, scenes, and storylines; and computer specialists who deal in bits and bytes, images and data, icons, picons, micons, and programming languages all their own.

Add a systems person who wants to integrate LDs and CD-ROMs with DVI and Windows via SCSI or RS-232 ports, and then telecommunicate the whole mess to a host; an accountant who wants to estimate the cost per instructional seat-minute or unit of customer interaction; and of course, don't forget the subject expert who may know nothing about anything but hydraulic engineering.

The management challenge is obvious.

There have been many books written on the musicians and instruments in the interactive multimedia orchestra: instructional design, system integration, graphics, video techniques, hardware, authoring packages, courseware and more. And there have been many papers written and models developed on the "why" of multimedia applications: learning effectiveness, cost justification, retail impact, etc.

Managing Interactive Video/Multimedia Projects is the first book that puts it all together for the new project manager from the manager's perspective. It is written by managers who have been there — managers who have made the mistakes, learned the lessons, and successfully taught many others the brand-new tricks of a brand-new trade. It has codified the collective interactive management wisdom gathered in a ten-year climb up the learning curve and gives the reader a real head start on the management process. With processes, forms, checklists and worksheets, it's all right there.

I have little advice of my own to add. But if you have been handed an in-house project or must deal with outside vendors, have just gotten into interactive video/multimedia or consider yourself an old pro, are responsible for the effort or just a participant — you can't help but benefit from this book. Just as I've often told developers not to recreate the wheel, I am happy now to tell managers that they don't have to make the same old mistakes in order to learn their own lessons. The trail is finally blazed. The map is drawn. Start with this book and forge on from there.

Rockley Miller is editor and publisher of *The Videodisc Monitor* and president of the Interactive Video Industry Association.

Preface

The time is not yet here, but soon will be, when interactive video and multimedia play a major role in the communications of our society. It will deliver inexpensive, high quality, consistent messages to wide audiences who can actively participate in acquiring the information. The technology will affect all aspects of human activity from how we market our products to how we educate our children. The project managers in this field have arrived early enough on the scene to have a direct effect on how fast and how well the technology achieves its promise. Yet they are also early enough to have to face many valid concerns that abound at every turn. Consider the following statements:

- "Interactive multimedia is too difficult and costly to produce."

- "There's not enough application software to justify a system."

- "Every application I look at requires a different system to run it."

- "The technology is changing too fast to make a decision now."

These statements express very real problems. They often reflect the tempered experience of former enthusiastic proponents who underestimated the difficulties, complexities and dynamics of this emerging medium. These problems are not, however, insurmountable.

The statements above represent issues of substance that project managers should take into consideration along with all of the other problems that they face. Those who are deterred from pressing on by such problems will lose the opportunity to participate in the formative stages of this medium, and will leave the rewards of leadership to others. It is a goal of this book to provide a base of knowledge that will help avoid such unfortunate and unnecessary decisions.

On the other hand, this book does not deal directly with these problems. The authors have assumed that you're going to develop an application that has been justified and approved, and we've focused our attention on the activities required to manage the project. Before we start this discussion, however, we'll present our perspective on the major problem areas that could inhibit the growth of multimedia technology in these early years. Overall, our perspective is that the problems should be given serious attention,

but they should **not** be allowed to get in the way of worthwhile development efforts.

Let's consider the problems one at a time.

Problem 1: The High Cost of Development

There's no question that interactive videodisc (IVD) and multimedia development is complex and costly. As project managers, our challenge is to make that complexity more understandable to more people, and to reduce those costs to more reasonable levels. We can do that if we use the knowledge we gain by participating in multimedia development wisely, and apply sound principles of project management. If we can then keep our experienced teams together, the development of subsequent applications will be markedly more efficient.

The problems of complexity and cost stem from a single cause: our development teams lack experience in the medium. All the disciplines that contribute to IVD are complex in and of themselves. Shelves of books have been written about each; programs of graduate study are taught about each. The complexity is compounded by the difficulty of communications between the disciplines, and the cost is high because of the additional time and effort required to achieve clear communications. Too often, we incur unnecessary expense to redevelop or rework mistakes that happened due to lack of understanding of the problem.

As a project manager in this new medium, here is where you can make a vital contribution. With your own background of experience, hopefully well augmented by the material in this book, you can select and build a team that can work together and communicate effectively. Over time, this capability will result in more effective applications, completed in less time at more reasonable costs.

Once your team members have developed a complete application, they and you will have a more secure sense of where they are heading in the next project. Designers will understand what they must provide to the programmers; graphic artists and video producers will understand how they affect one another. It will be easier to visualize the final product early in the project, and to avoid expensive redevelopment work. The learning curve will be in full ascendency, and the problem of high costs will diminish accordingly.

Problem 2: The Lack of Applications

The growth of multimedia technology will depend on the availability of applications that address real problems. To justify a large number of systems, we'll need a large number of applications. We'll need so many applications that it will take entire industries to produce them — and today, those industries are only beginning to develop.

One such industry is starting to be called by the name "Electronic Publishing." The products of this industry are generic applications, with most of the first efforts being devoted to training. Electronic Publishers will perform the same functions as print-oriented publishers. They will acquire titles and authors, edit the material, replicate and manufacture the product, market and distribute the applications, and account for the royalties. The only difference will be that they will distribute the applications on optical and magnetic media rather than in print. Most Electronic Publishers will probably start up as divisions of major publishing firms. A fair amount of activity in this area is already underway.

A second industry will be formed by firms that use multimedia technology for innovative marketing programs. For want of a better name, let's call them "Interactive Media Marketing Agencies," as opposed to "Broadcast Advertising Agencies." Mass media advertising agencies appeared as a new industry in the late twenties and thirties in response to the new technology of radio. These firms could create and produce broadcast programming, acquire time from the stations and networks, and sell the programs to clients for advertising. The advertising was suited to the one-way medium and ranged from early innovations such as the singing commercial to the electronic extravaganzas seen today on network television.

Multimedia marketing applications in public access environments will need a different kind of programming. The applications will have to be high in information content, and responsive to individual needs and interests. There is solid evidence building up that such applications will have high effectiveness, and more and more dollars will be diverted from broadcast advertising into multimedia presentations.

As these industries grow, the economics of multimedia will change. Costs will decline and delivery systems will proliferate. The result will be that all users of the technology will benefit. The consumer/entertainment explosion in video cassette technology made that medium viable for all sorts of industrial and institutional uses. Likewise, the growth of Electronic Publishing and Interactive Media Marketing will provide the application base that will support the use of multimedia in many diverse areas of communications in our society. As this base grows, the technology will become more affordable for all of us, no matter how we use it.

Problem 3: The Lack of Standards

There is no more frustrating problem for a potential multimedia user than to find that one needed application will run only on System A, and another will only run on System B. Attempts to promulgate standards that will avoid this problem have to date been only marginally successful. In a field where technology is advancing so rapidly, standardization is often seen as an agent to hobble progress. Without it, however, there never seems to be enough software accumulated on one system to justify its purchase.

In the area of custom applications for large institutions and corporations, it is likely that the use of the latest technology will continue without regard for standards. If your applications only need to run on your own system, it is tempting and often justified to use the latest graphic mode, digital audio technique or video format. If the use of generic courseware is not an issue, there is no reason not to consider state-of-the-art technology.

On the other hand, economics will eventually force the development of system standards that will allow producers to develop applications that can be purchased by a wide base of users. These standards will probably be based on software packages that can run on systems of different manufacturers. The key factor in determining the standards will be the wide acceptance of a few media formats that can deliver basic functions with economy and reliability.

As a project manager, what should be your attitude toward standards? If you are working on a large custom application, you have the flexibility to use the most effective functions technology can provide. There is a danger, however, that you may end up putting a lot of effort toward the testing and proving of new technology instead of concentrating on meeting the goals of your sponsoring executive. There may be enough challenge in the development of the application itself, so that you don't really need to take on the additional problem of breaking in new technology.

If you need to be sure that your system will work with applications and software being developed by the rest of the industry, you should probably not attempt to use exotic technology of any kind. Select a system from a reliable manufacturer, and be sure that service will be available. Use the smallest set of hardware functions that will do your job, and stick to formats that are widely used and accepted. Use a high level authoring facility that you expect to keep up with new hardware and software releases.

In other words, keep your application and your system as simple as possible. This approach will help you avoid the problems that come with the general lack of standards; and keep your operation in the mainstream as standards for multimedia applications continue to develop.

Problem 4: The Changing Technology

Hardly a month goes by without an announcement of a new breakthrough in technology that promises to have a profound effect on multimedia applications at some time in the future. New graphics formats and processors, new approaches to improving the video signal, new ways to store data at higher and higher densities — the list never seems to end.

A case in point is the many formats being talked about in optical discs. Using the phenomenal success of compact discs in the consumer audio market as a springboard, several new formats have been developed to support multimedia applications on the same physical disc. These formats provide several ways to store large amounts of data, video pictures and audio tracks in various combinations. They are called by a bewildering set of alphabet soup names like CD-ROM, DVI, CDI, CD-V and so on. Many potential users of multimedia technology have decided to wait until one or the other of these becomes available, or simply to wait until the whole mess gets straightened out.

The authors are painfully aware of the effects of changing technology. When this book was begun, the term "multimedia application" was used to describe presentations made with multiple slide projectors and audio players controlled with a computer. The term most commonly used to describe the kind of application we address in this book is "interactive videodisc," or "IVD." It is still widely used, whether or not the video component is actually delivered from a videodisc. The term "IVD" is often used interchangeably with "multimedia."

However, the latter term has come into use to reflect the advent of many new technologies that extend the capability of systems beyond traditional audio/video presentations. These include more sophisticated touch screens and other pointing devices, digitized video that can be stored in data files and manipulated by computer, compressed audio that offers hours of sound track on single discs,

and so on. Keeping the material in the book up to date as it was written has been a real challenge.

Despite the promise of many new technologies, the medium most commonly used today for video recording is the optical videodisc that has become a standard in the last few years. There are good reasons for this. Most importantly, it is cheaper to use than compact digital video formats at present, and it promises to stay ahead in the next few years at least. Videodisc is beginning to move into the consumer market, and the cost of discs and players should decrease. The capacity and quality of the videodisc can be achieved without expensive electronics to decode the compressed signals of compact formats. Video production for videodisc is relatively simple and well-understood. Computer electronics are now available that achieve the same effects using the analog videodisc that digital formats offer (such as squeezing a picture into a corner of a screen). Some day, one or more of the compact digital formats will become as viable as videodisc, but that day is not yet here.

With this in mind, we have referred to video-based presentations in this book as "Interactive Video" or "IVD" applications. It should be noted that many IVD projects are implemented with **both** a videodisc player **and** a CD-ROM. The use of the large capacity of CD-ROM for data storage, digital audio and high-quality graphics makes it a natural partner for the videodisc, and it is quite inexpensive to use it for these purposes. The combination provides designers with the capability to implement true "multimedia" applications. Thus, we often use the term "IVD/multimedia" as a generic term. Technology has made this not a mere matter of semantics, but an actuality.

The question remains, however, how should this changing technology be dealt with in a practical program of using multimedia applications to solve business or educational problems? It is certainly fascinating, and indeed, many people are drawn to this field by an interest in the technology itself. They are very welcome, because they are the ones that will work out the bugs in new devices and software, and provide practical, usable technologies in the future. This is not, however, the direction that will be followed in this book.

The focus of this book is on the **fundamentals** of interactive video/multimedia application development — for you and each member of your project team. We plan to concentrate on: cogent analysis, creative design, comprehensive development, quality production, and meticulous project management. We will discuss how to evaluate good design, and how to recognize effective graphics and well-written scripts regardless of the way they are recorded and played back. It is our belief that quality content comes from human intelligence and imagination, and is independent of whether it is recorded on a laser beam or a cave wall.

We are not suggesting that new technology is not important. Project managers must keep up with this aspect of their job along with everything else. Often, a new function has a profound effect on the way applications are designed. Recent examples include the ability to overlay graphics on video, the touch screen, and the significant increase in audio capacity. The ability to digitize video frames and display them in small windows on the screen provides an exciting new function. Such advances provide new power to the designer to deliver the application's message. However, the purpose of new technology should not be to dazzle the user, or to maintain a short-lived interest through cheap electronic tricks. Technology should be used to make the machine invisible, and to remove all possible distractions that intervene between the user and the message you want to deliver.

There is no reason, then, to let the rapid change of technology affect your plans to get involved in interactive media. There are many new electronic innovations and computer software tools created each year; up to now, however, there are few interactive presentations that are worthy of more than a passing interest. The conclusion is that building new technology is easy, but building teams that can develop effective multimedia applications is a real challenge.

George Bernard Shaw said, "The true joy in life is being used for a purpose recognized by yourself as a mighty one." Today, our family, our friends, our managers are only dimly aware of the great promise of this technology, and what role as project managers we play in it. It is up to us, however, to find ways to realize the promise, and to overcome the problems inherent in implementing a new medium. As long as we ourselves know what we are setting out to achieve, our work and our dedication to our team members will be worth our best efforts.

How to Manage This Book

During our initial planning for this book, we tried to focus on the real needs of a project manager who had just been assigned to develop a large Interactive Videodisc application. We identified a variety of those needs: sample documentation, estimating tools, checklists, models and guidelines, problems to watch for, and a realistic approach to the whole project. From this list we experimented with several structures before settling on the following two-section format:

- Section I . The Project Manager's Guide

This section takes you phase-by-phase, step-by-step through a complete IVD/multimedia project — its activities, guidelines, deliverables, and evaluation methods. The Guide is divided into four parts: Orientation, Preparation, Construction, and Implementation. Within each part, individual chapters focus on one of the key activities that must be managed.

- Section II . The Project Manager's Resources

This section contains a collection of checklists, sample forms, and worksheets to complement the material in the Guide Book. A separate tutorial on IVD documentation techniques is included for the application developers. These resources serve as examples when you're reading the Guide Section, but they also stand alone as tools for your future project management efforts.

Alternative Approaches

Given this material and the varied needs of an IVD team, there are several study options for the book. Here are four suggestions:

SURVEY MODE

You may want to skim all the sections for an overview, then focus on one or more specific areas of interest. We've written section introductions, chapter previews, and graphic road maps at the beginning of each chapter to help you get the big picture. Skimming the chapters and the checklists will give you a flavor for the type, variety, and extent of IVD documentation. After surveying these sections, you can choose another alternative.

STUDY MODE

Starting with the first chapter, you can study the book proactively. Keeping your application in mind, become the project manager. As we introduce each new phase, assume your new roles, assess the examples, apply the tools, and evaluate the deliverables with our checklists. As each phase ends, reflect and record: which activities need more study, what techniques fit your style and organization, and how the work in one phase influences the others.

PROJECT MODE

After studying our project model, guidelines, documentation methods, and evaluation techniques in each chapter, you can re-employ the book as a true project management tool. Copy our checklists and worksheets, follow our agendas and estimates, apply our phase-by-phase procedures to your actual project. Personalize these elements as you proceed; make our methods your methods.

DEVELOPMENT MODE

Individual parts of the book may be valuable for training strategies, documentation methods, or analysis techniques. Select the appropriate chapters, sections, or resources for study; adopt those same strategies or techniques as part of your project standards. For example, our "Components of Multimedia Documentation" could serve as a tutorial for developers, then those same forms could be employed during the project.

The Development Model

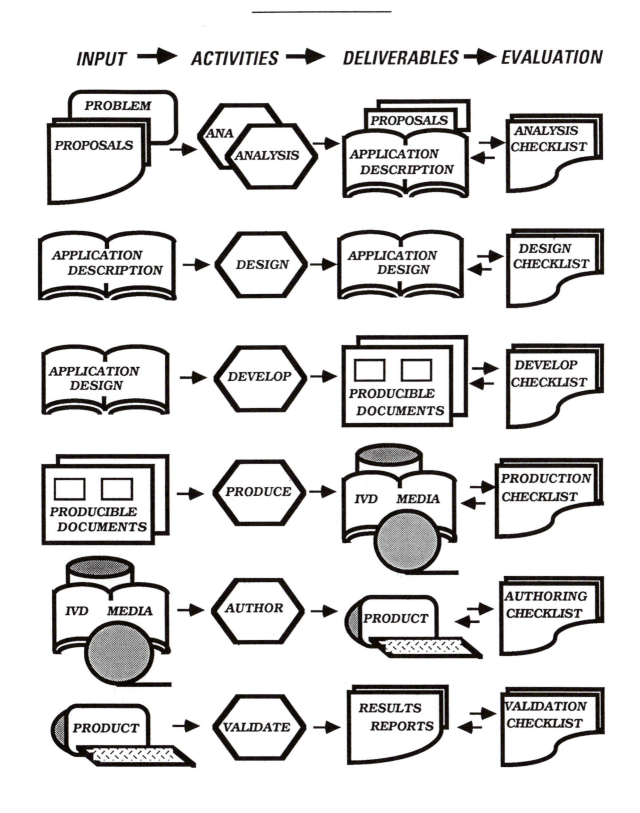

SECTION ONE
THE PROJECT MANAGER'S GUIDE

PART ONE

Orientation

Interactive video and multimedia projects are new, different, and challenging. They involve more resources, more factors, longer development times, and larger budgets. Managing the development of a multimedia application is likewise a challenging undertaking. The sheer number and variety of activities, people, schedules, and documentation can be overwhelming. Just knowing where to begin among these diverse factors can be difficult. But it can be done. Part of it is understanding the technology; part is understanding the development process; part is understanding the roles and responsibilities of your vendors and project team members.

Terminology presents another major challenge. These projects involve different professional disciplines, each with its own specialized vocabulary. The terms sometimes conflict with each other, and the rapid evolution of technology brings new words into play all the time. Even the words "interactive video" and "multimedia" can cause confusion. For several years, the videodisc was the only source of motion video segments that could be accessed rapidly enough to support effective interactivity. Hence, the term applied to these applications came to be "interactive videodisc," or more commonly, "IVD." Recently, digital technology has made it possible to provide motion video using other devices, especially the small optical discs called CD-ROM. Another factor has been the development of image-based applications that use graphic pictures and digital audio, and no motion video at all. The term "multimedia" has been adapted as a generic reference to all such image-based applications. We have tried to be fairly consistent in the way we use these terms. We have followed the convention of the industry and used the abbreviation "IVD" to stand for interactive video, recognizing that a videodisc may or may not be used in the final delivery system. (This usually has little effect on project management considerations anyway.) If we are specifically addressing topics that apply only in non-video applications, we use the term "multimedia" alone. In most cases, however, the project management and development considerations are applicable to any image-based application, and we use the term "IVD/multimedia" to cover the entire range of technologies now becoming available.

This book is designed to help you sort through the factors, reduce the complexity, and meet the challenge. Our goal is to provide a project management perspective for interactive video/multimedia applications. To achieve that goal, we have:

- isolated critical documents and activities,

- organized them into a step-by-step model,

- identified who is responsible for each step, and

- created new tools and checklists to support the process.

This orientation section introduces the technology and its key variables; it is divided into three chapters:

Chapter 1 ... describes IVD/multimedia applications by looking at them from several different viewpoints.

Chapter 2 ... re-creates our development model to highlight each activity, end product, and checkpoint.

Chapter 3 ... identifies the skills required at each stage of the application so you can build a project team.

From this basic orientation, you (and the team) should be ready to begin the project planning and analysis activities.

Chapter One

Defining Multimedia Applications

Preview

Just what is an interactive video/multimedia application? It depends on who you ask. A user's definition will differ from a designer's; a script writer's view will differ from the sponsoring executive's. Here are some descriptions—all accurate:

- It's how we train our new marketing representatives.

- It's television with a touch screen.

- It's a personal computer with a videodisc or CD-ROM attached.

- It's part of our promotional display in the mall.

- It's mixing graphics, video, audio, and text.

- It's expensive.

- It's exciting!

IVD/multimedia is all this — and more. In fact, it's those multiple descriptions, viewpoints, and factors that make interactive multimedia applications unique, complex, and challenging. But managing all the different facets can be overwhelming unless you can place them into some meaningful framework or unifying context. In this chapter, we'll begin to build that framework (and reduce some of the complexity) by picturing IVD/multimedia from several perspectives. By merging these different viewpoints, you can start to visualize the components, the concepts, and the possible combinations. From these initial "pictures," we can then begin to answer some fundamental questions: What is IVD/multimedia? Why is it different? How can you make a difference?

Looking Over the Territory

In this chapter we want to begin the definition process — to introduce the technology from an application point of view: not all the detailed procedures, they'll come later in the book; not all the technical specifications, they'll be the province of your media specialists or application designers. Our initial description focuses on the underlying concep-

tual views of the technology — the ones that will help you "see" the critical pieces, their relationships, and help you with the management process. We'll look at IVD/multimedia from four general viewpoints:

- the hardware components and their functions,

- the software tools, packages, or systems,

- the different disciplines on a project team,

- the multiple design options for your message.

From these initial perspectives, you can start to develop a personal picture of these applications. The rest of the book extends, explains, and elaborates on these different facets to fill in more detail. Then, as you participate in an actual project, you'll gain your own personal, comprehensive, realistic definition.

A Marketing Application for City Services and Attractions
Courtesy TouchTel, Inc. Atlanta, Georgia

7

Rather than begin with some traditional explanations, let's explore some typical applications in our mind's eye. We'll consider two points of view—the user's perception, and the underlying techniques that the project developers employed to create that perception.

A Sampling of Techniques

ATTRACT ROUTINES

"Attract routines" are usually used with applications that are located in areas where the general public has access to the presentation screen. You may have seen them in lobbies, grocery stores, malls or information centers. They often employ striking video or graphic effects to attract your attention, and to let you know what kind of information is available. The visual must stand alone, because the attract routine plays over and over, and a sound track would be highly annoying, especially to persons who had to work near the machine. The attract routine also provides an invitation and instruction for activating the presentation. In a public access setting, this is usually done by requesting the user to touch the screen to begin.

To grab and hold the user's attention, some project requirements include:

- designing, manufacturing, and positioning the kiosk,

- creating an eye-catching opener,

- drawing and sequencing individual art segments,

- digitizing and animating the art onto a videotape,

- coding to time and repeat the animation sequence,

- coding to recognize any touch interruption.

VIDEO SEGMENTS

Video segments are the most powerful presentation technique available to the IVD/multimedia developer. Using the senses of seeing and hearing together, video can be used to illustrate a complex procedure, or display a product in use. The pictures can be taken with a telescope, a microscope, or a camera in any location on earth (or for that matter, outer space as well.) Video segments created for IVD use all of the effective techniques employed in linear video or film, but they are generally more condensed, address a single idea, and last less than a minute. To create effective video segments and maintain user interest, your development decisions include:

- selecting a location—or—building a realistic set,

- scripting the audio and video content,

- auditioning actors, rehearsing lines,

- directing scenes during video production,

- creating video graphics to enhance the message,

- editing the graphics and pictures into a single segment.

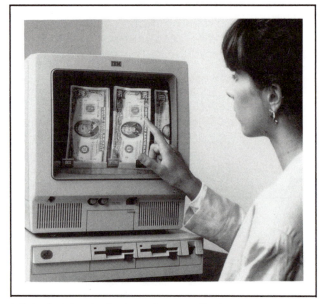

A Teller Training Application   Courtesy The Videodisc Monitor

CHOICE FRAMES OR MENUS

Choice frames and "menus" are single screen displays that allow the user to indicate what he or she wants the program to do next. They can also be used to ask questions, and allow the user to choose an answer from a list provided. The user may choose by pointing at the selected area on the screen with a finger or a mouse, or by entering the number of a choice from a keyboard. It is this technique that differentiates interactive presentations from less powerful media. Menus allow the user to tailor the presentation to individual interests and needs. Question/answer screens allow the user to check progress, and to be sure the lessons of a training program are being mastered. Wrong answers may be remediated by appropriate feedback. Choice frames promote the user from spectator to an actively involved participant in the presentation.

To provide a manageable number of options and ease of selection, some development activities include:

- designing the menu's appearance,

- designating each of the touch areas on the screen,

- displaying user guidance and directions,

- coding a path for each possible selection,

- providing a return to the opening if no selection is made within a specified time period.

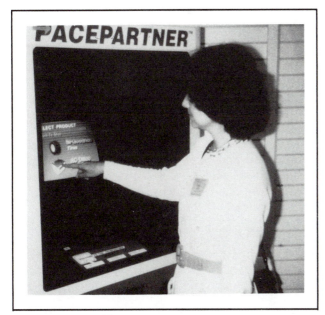

A Marketing Application for Automobile Products
Courtesy The Videodisc Monitor

PROVIDING USER CONTROL

User control options are the most important factor in making interactive applications "user friendly." These techniques allow the user to interrupt the presentation at any time, go back to a previous point, skip ahead or start over. Often, the developer will provide "icons" on the screen that the user can select at any time; typical examples are [PAUSE], [RESUME] or [MAIN MENU]. (They are called "icons" because some designers use pictorial representations such as stop signs or arrows to depict the functions.) These options permit the user to control the pace of the presentation, correct mistakes, escape from uninteresting segments or go back and try a completely different part of the presentation. To give the user control over the presentation sequence and its pace, some design decisions include:

- providing an adequate set of control options,

- making sure the icons' functions are clear,

- enabling the user to interrupt at appropriate times,

- coding a path for each possible selection,

- providing operational directions when needed.

As we consider these techniques, it's clear that there are two perspectives: the users' view— their perceptions, actions, feelings, and involvement; the developers' view— the events, sequences, media, actors, and controls. Both perspectives are needed to create an effective presentation.

How Do We Get There?

As with any professional, artistic event, the finished product looks easy and obvious. To achieve that "look" requires painstaking attention to every detail. With an IVD/multimedia application those details include a myriad of interwoven decisions on hardware, software, media, messages, and people. What makes an application interesting, inviting, and intriguing for the user demands a tight integration of all the components, disciplines, and objectives. What makes an application look easy and obvious on the surface demands careful management of the complexity underneath. That's your primary task—managing and coordinating the myriad factors that contribute to success.

Public Information Kiosks at the Smithsonian Institute's
Visitor Center   Courtesy T. C. Moore

One way of reducing the complexity is to group these factors into logical chunks. By temporarily isolating and studying the components that make IVD possible, you can begin to determine their functions. If you can start to categorize the pieces, you can see their individual roles and how they can be combined. In this chapter, we'll divide applications into hardware, software, disciplines, and design components.

So What's New?

As we've illustrated, we are dealing with a combination of many media. Each component medium already exists, and each one has a discipline associated with it that could literally take a lifetime to learn. The main components include computer technology, video and audio production, and instructional design. The chances are that since you're reading this book, you're already familiar with one or more of these disciplines, but it's equally likely that you aren't expert in all of them.

Our objective in the book, then, will be to concentrate on two areas. First, we'll try to cover the essentials of each discipline so you'll know what you need even if you haven't worked with it before. If you're already familiar with a medium, you can skip through that area quickly.

Secondly, and more importantly, we'll try to describe the **differences** that will affect the media when they are integrated into an interactive application. Experience shows that project managers tend to encounter trouble more often in areas in which they are familiar than those in which they are not. Expert linear video producers are comfortable with video production, but may fail to take account of the special requirements imposed by the videodisc. Those who have worked with computers for years may not realize how minor design improvements made to the program logic may adversely affect other media components. These differences are sometimes small and subtle, but failure to recognize and deal with them can lead to costly re-work in the production schedule. As we look at each phase of the project, then, we'll devote a section to the differences, and highlight what's new about an interactive video/multimedia project.

Components of IVD Projects

Hardware Components and Media

Simply stated, the purpose of the hardware is to deliver your message—the graphics, motion, and audio segments stored on various media. You can start to see some of the complexity with the number of different devices and their possible combinations. A conceptual view of a typical hardware configuration is shown in Figure 1-1. Your system may have other devices or combinations of equipment, but the basic functions are similar:

- Videodisc Player

  The most common devices used to provide motion video material are videodisc players that play 12" LaserVision discs. This format will provide 30 or 60 minutes of motion video, additional sound tracks for audio, and thousands of still frame pictures. Other formats are being developed that will play video that has been digitized and compressed onto a compact disc, and these devices will probably become more common as the technology becomes more economical.

- Compact Disc Player

  The compact disc player is becoming more important as multimedia applications grow in sophistication and complexity. These players have the ability to store over half a trillion characters of information (over 500 megabytes) that

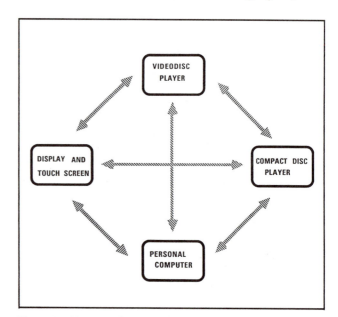

Figure 1-1 Hardware Components

can be used to contain programs, data and high-quality graphics. They can also be used to provide from two to fifteen extra hours of audio, depending upon the quality of sound. As mentioned above, new formats are being developed that will allow them to contain motion video.

• Personal Computer

The wide availability of small, inexpensive personal computers has made them a common component of IVD/multimedia hardware systems. They allow designers to employ sophisticated logic, powerful user interfaces, high-quality computer graphics, and animation. The computer can track user activities and keep training or marketing data. Other computer applications can be integrated with the multimedia presentation to provide even more powerful tools, such as on-line job aids or easy-to-use data entry terminals.

• Display and Touch Screen

New displays are becoming available with touch screens built in. These devices are particularly valuable in public access applications, or for situations where users are not expected to be familiar with computers. Of course, traditional computer interface devices such as mouse, keyboard or light pen work as well, and are preferable in many applications.

Hardware considerations can be complex, and even frustrating as new technology is constantly introduced. You can minimize the confusion, however, by concentrating on the media components that you will need to support your applications. Do you need motion? What level of quality do your graphics have to be? Do you need high-fidelity audio? What kind of user interface device is appropriate? How large will your files be? As you consider these questions, you can match your needs against your available funding, and select the system components that will serve your purpose within your budget. As time goes on, the technology will provide greater quality at less cost, and you'll be ready to take advantage of it as it comes along.

Software Components

As sophisticated as the hardware is, it cannot do the job alone. Software is needed. The general functions of the software are to create and combine the media, define touch areas, build sequences of events, present the application to the user, and interpret any interactions. To accomplish these multiple goals requires multiple software components. They fall into several categories as shown in Figure 1-2.

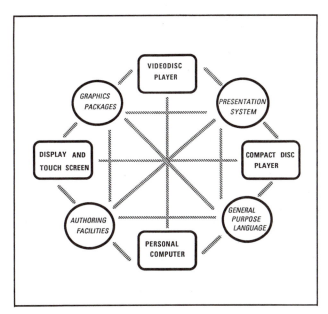

Figure 1-2 Software Components

• Graphics Packages

These enable you to create, save, display, modify, and animate multi-colored images. The images can then be stored in computer files to be used in the presentation.

• Authoring Facilities

These provide tools, templates, and techniques to construct your application. Most projects use a high-level facility which allows authoring without need for programming skills.

• General Purpose Languages

These provide support for unique operations or combinations that high level authoring facilities cannot handle: access to special routines, access to databases, or record keeping tasks.

• Presentation Systems

These are used on the systems at the delivery sites to present the multimedia images, recognize user interactions, and respond "intelligently," all according to the authors' coded sequences.

The different IVD hardware components create one level of complexity; adding multiple software facilities increases that complexity. As project manager for the application, you must evaluate options and allocate resources in this complex environment. What resolution and color set is needed by your graphics? Do you need animation? What functions do your authors need to handle the presentation logic and hardware features? How powerful does your presentation system need to be?

Our models, tools, and methods have been designed to help you manage this growing complexity and put the pieces into proper perspective.

Chapter 9, "Authoring the Presentation," explains the software alternatives and their characteristics.

Contributing Disciplines

Another factor contributing to the complexity of these applications is the variety of disciplines required to produce the finished product. It's not simply their number; each different discipline comes with its own set of terminologies, procedures, and techniques; each one views the application from its own point of view. Some examples of the disciplines you will need on the project team have been added to our diagram in Figure 1-3. They include:

- Writers ... to develop and document treatments, themes and audio scripts.

- Production Specialists ... to translate paper documents into finished media.

- Artists ... to create and capture visual renditions for the graphic and/or video images.

- Authors ... to assemble and test all the application sequences and events using the authoring facility.

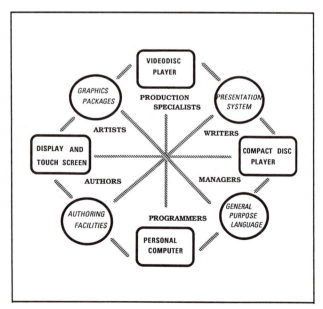

Figure 1-3 Contributing Disciplines

- Programmers ... to code and test special routines for the application using general-purpose languages.

- Managers ... to coordinate the efforts of the project team members and production staffs.

All these disciplines may or may not be under your direct control. Nevertheless, as the project manager, you must:

- recruit and coordinate the right skill mix,

- build the different disciplines into a single team,

- maintain the team's focus on the goals and objectives by communicating a shared vision of the application.

Chapter 3, "Building the Project Team," discusses this management aspect of your job in more detail.

The Application Message

Although the hardware components, software facilities, and different disciplines make these projects complex, they also make sophisticated messages possible. Their capabilities enable variety, richness, and reality. Applications can now be interesting, inviting, and intriguing for the user.

However, creating sophisticated messages is not an easy task. To achieve the polished, professional presentations for the user, every fine detail of your message must first be analyzed, designed, documented, integrated, produced, and authored. As shown in Figure 1-4, the message should be the central focus of all your resources. Some aspects of message development include:

- Intent ... based on the broad goals and objectives of the project, the application may focus on training, educating, marketing, or informing to meet the varied needs of one or more audiences. From this initial decision, a series of "how" questions must be answered.

- Approach ... several possible formats or treatments may be developed for the whole application or individual segments. Example approaches could be tutorials, simulations, games, news panels, conversations, or inquiry helpers (and their combinations).

- Strategies ... to accomplish any of the chosen treatments, even more detailed plans must be documented. These design decisions include media selection, amount of user control, methods of interaction, number of paths, record-keeping

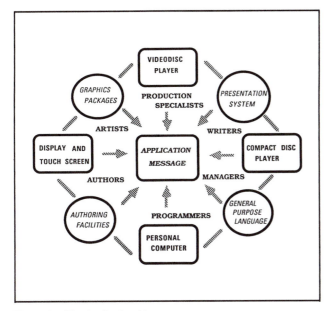

Figure 1-4 The Application Message

and testing, types of assistance, and motivational methods.

- Content ... finally, from all these different strategies the precise content of the message must be developed. The words, pictures, colors, questions, glossaries, graphics, actors, scenes, and props must be interwoven.

The number of factors to consider in just designing your application message can be overwhelming. Hardware, software and different disciplines add to the complexity. By having some mental pictures of pieces and some tools to manage those pieces, the complexity can be contained.

Chapter 6, "Designing the Application," addresses these points.

Components Summary

As we stated at the beginning of this section, the number of different components and their combinations make IVD/multimedia applications interesting, complex and challenging. Each component has its own terminologies, techniques, and tools; merging them further compounds your management tasks. While individual members of your project team may have specific expertise in one or more

areas, you need a more general or conceptual view of these components and their capabilities.

The preceding diagrams and explanations developed this conceptual picture to assist you with the management process: to logically group the different factors and to identify their roles and relationships. Now let's summarize it from your perspective —in reverse order:

- The message ... should be the central focus of all activities and resources. It represents the goals of the sponsor and objectives of the application. Always ask "how does this contribute to the message?"

- Disciplines ... interpret and translate the message; they bring it to life. Individually, team members design, develop, produce, or author segments of the application; collectively, they create your product.

- Software ... provides the artistic tools to build, test, and refine the application during development; it drives the hardware during day-to-day operations.

- Hardware ... delivers the multimedia messages to the user so smoothly that all the complexity is out-of-sight.

As project manager, your task is to turn resources and media components into a completed application —one that meets the original goals of the sponsor. A conceptual picture of these resources can help keep the pieces in perspective.

A Last Word

Many factors contribute to the complexity of interactive videodisc projects. The number of components is only one. You also need to allocate resources, manage schedules, and evaluate phase-to-phase results. Getting the big picture can help, but there are several big pictures we need to develop.

With the components in mind as guidelines, let's look at the next big picture: the phase-by-phase activities required to produce an application. We'll continue to reduce the complexity by breaking these activities into logical, manageable steps and by visualizing the entire process as a model.

Chapter Two

Understanding the Development Model

Preview of Development Activities

To develop an interactive video/multimedia application successfully, you must be able to manage a mass of detail. This detail will be recorded in documentation that is voluminous, varied and vital. If this documentation is not carefully controlled, the project can become mired in its own paperwork. Recognizing the critical role that documentation plays, we've designed a model in which our primary emphasis **is** on documentation. Who produces it? When is it needed? What does it look like? How do you know it's complete? This model traces the project from its original objectives to the finished application. It is your illustrated master plan to guide and manage the team activities. By embracing and employing this model, you can see and control the flow of documentation; you can put all the details into perspective.

In this chapter, we'll introduce the model and how it evolved. You'll see the general relationship of documentation to the project's phases, the deliverables, and your responsibilities. In subsequent chapters, we'll reference and expand on this model with detailed roadmaps, specific activities, and sample forms.

Looking Over the Territory

What We're Trying to Accomplish

A valuable skill in any creative endeavor is the ability to pre-visualize: to see a completed event in the mind's eye, and thereby guide its own development. As a project manager, you need to pre-visualize the entire application (all the events and activities) so you can guide, direct, and evaluate the team's efforts. This way, you can see where all the pieces fit. That's where our model comes in.

How Do We Get There?

In this chapter, we'll construct a model for the development process of creating an interactive mul-

timedia application. Once you understand the working parts of the model, you'll be prepared to look at each part in detail in later chapters, and to learn how to manage the part without losing sight of the whole process. In an IVD/multimedia application, the number and variety of activities increase the challenge of your management task. Indeed, the number of factors to be integrated is just what makes these projects unique. This variety is compounded by the diverse disciplines needed to create and develop the application: graphic artists, video producers, designers, script writers, and media authors — all using their own special languages, symbols, and forms. Remember, each video presentation, touch area, graphic menu, or animation must have been produced by a media specialist. Prior to production, these different media events must have been designed and captured on paper. Your responsibility is to guide the project (and the team) from design ideas, to documentation, to media production, to the finished product. A successful project depends on successful management of the paperwork. A visible model of that documentation process can help.

So What's New?

As you look at our model from a high level, it looks very similar to those used in most other kinds of project management. This is true. The basic tenets of project management do not change, and all of the skill you have used in working with other kinds of projects will certainly apply here. What's new in interactive video is in the unique combination of activities, and in the myriad of details that this combination stirs up. As we proceed to develop the model, we'll try to point out where these differences can have a significant effect on managing the project.

Developing the Model

A Mass of Documentation

Think for a moment about a recent interactive multimedia application you experienced. How many different media events do you recall? Now as a project manager, think about the documentation that must have been necessary to produce that application:

*   written scripts for every audio presentation,

*   storyboards for each video sequence,

*   artist's renditions for every graphic,

*   logic flows for every possible user option and path,

*   treatment descriptions for storyline continuity,

*   coordinates for pictorial overlays and touch points,

*   programming logic for user control,

… and some master document that integrates all of the above!

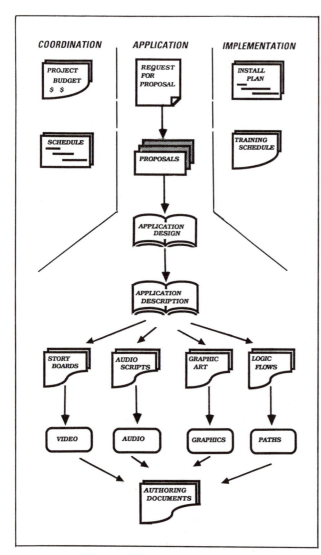

Figure 2-1 IVD/Multimedia Documentation Overview

The documentation that you must control is not limited to the application events. You must also monitor and manage people, time, and money. Additional paperwork for these activities include:

*   budgets for all project resources

*   schedules for construction, production, and implementation

*   legal and administrative forms

*   analysis meetings and documentation

*   vendor proposals

It is this mass of documentation that needs to be systemized. When it's under control, you're in control. Once the paperwork is organized into a logical progression, you can begin to "see" the entire application — before it's complete. The model is our attempt to help you see your application.

Organizing the Documentation

Figure 2-1 represents our first look at the variety and volume of development documentation, laid out in a simplified, symbolic flow diagram. While you may be working with many of these documents simultaneously, let's temporarily separate them (for discussion purposes) into three broad groups:

*   Coordination documents—like the project budget and the schedule. They will be covered in Chapter 12.

*   Implementation documents—like an installation plan and personnel training. They will be explained in Chapter 11.

*   Application documentation—like scripts and storyboards. They will be organized into a model in this chapter, then each phase of that model will be expanded in Chapters 5 through 10.

APPLICATION DOCUMENTS

Let's begin by previewing the application documents—in the order you'll probably encounter them. We'll revisit each one in more detail as the model unfolds.

*   The Request For Proposal (RFP) initiates the development process. (Even if you plan to develop in-house, the RFP format is an excellent way to begin describing the project.) It defines

the application goals, conditions, constraints, and scope of work: WHAT we want to do.

- Proposals are the responses to the RFP. They describe at a gross level HOW the application's goals could be met.

- With one of those proposals as a guide, an Application Description further defines all the critical factors.

- The Detail Design Document organizes all those factors into a logical plan. It becomes your master blueprint.

- From that Detail Design Document, every individual application event must be documented—in enough detail that media specialists can produce them (video, audio, graphics).

- Once the media is produced, Authoring Documentation is required to integrate those events into the application.

THE APPLICATION DEVELOPMENT ACTIVITIES

With these application documents as your end products or deliverables, the next part of our model focuses on the activities needed to produce them. Refer to Figure 2-2. The project team or vendors perform these activities; you monitor and manage the process.

- Analysis ... a preliminary study of the opportunity or problem determines the requirements for the RFP; vendors analyze those requirements to develop their proposals. A more comprehensive analysis studies and documents the application's audience, tasks, environment, and content.

- Design ... organizes the analysis data into a master plan. High-Level design activities include sequencing the major application segments and defining their treatment; Detail design specifies the motivation, media, interaction, and evaluation strategies.

- Development ... takes the design specifications to a more precise level of detail: capturing each individual event, touch area, menu choice, and message on special forms. We've coined the term "producible documentation" for the end product of this development activity.

- Production ... transforms the producible documentation into its corresponding medium: video sequences, audio, graphics, or text. These

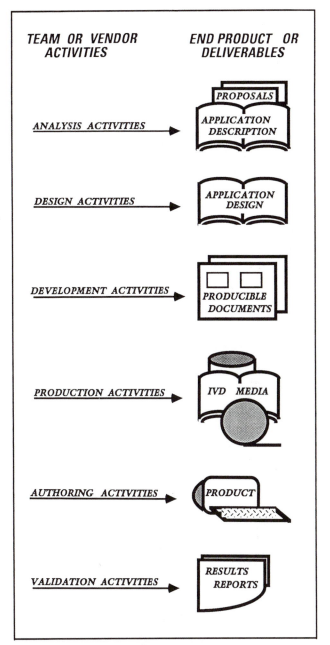

Figure 2-2 IVD Development Activities

activities may be performed by different people —each with specialized skills.

- Authoring ... integrates the individual media elements into a seamless, interactive presentation. Additional authoring activities include transitions, timing, control logic, and recording statistical data (depending on the requirements).

- Validation ... evaluates the finished product against its original objectives. This validation activity could also include refinements of the application and assessment of its contribution to the sponsor's goals.

THE PHASE PROCESS

Given the deliverables and the procedures needed to create them, we can now arrange our model into phases with an Input-Process-Output scheme. In this format, it becomes your visual, step-by-step guide to the application's development. For each major phase, you can ask: what inputs are needed? What activities must be performed? When? What deliverables should I expect? This revised version of the model is pictured in Figure 2-3. Let's summarize it from your perspective:

• With the problem objectives and RFP as input, the project team or vendors must thoroughly analyze all requirements. Preliminary output is

in the form of a proposal; the final product is a complete Application Description Document.

• Given a comprehensive application description, the design team devises application treatments, logical flows, and specific strategies. The results of this work must be consolidated in the Application Design Document.

• Using that Design Document as a master blueprint, each detail (of each event) must be developed on paper. The outcome you should expect is "producible documentation" for the video, audio, graphics, and print.

• With "producible documentation" as input, the media vendors can transform those paper events onto diskettes, videotape, and eventually to videodiscs and compact discs.

• Once the author(s) have individual media segments as input, they can assemble and integrate the pieces with the other application elements. The end product is the first version of the application — ready for testing.

• Using this initial version of the application, validation activities can measure how closely you've met the goals.

EVALUATING THE PHASES

We've stepped through this model one phase at a time, assuming that everything was right the first time. Naturally, you may need to revisit a phase and revise selected activities. Most importantly from a management perspective is the decision of when to proceed and when to return. Our model needs one more component. Unfortunately with multimedia projects, you cannot wait until the application is complete to know if it's right; you have to be right at each phase. These projects are too costly and time consuming. It's your responsibility to know when the deliverables are right, that is, when it's time to move on. So, the final version of our model as shown in Figure 2-4 has added an evaluation step. Evaluation is one of your key project management activities. Now let's put the final model and project responsibilities into perspective. For each phase of the application:

• your primary focus should be on the deliverables;

• vendors perform the analysis, design, and development activities to produce those deliverables; you monitor, manage and measure their efforts;

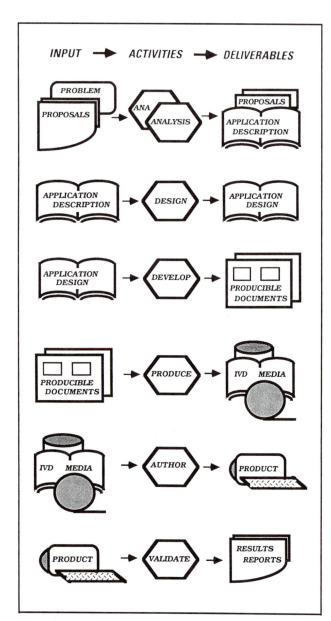

Figure 2-3 IVD Development Phases

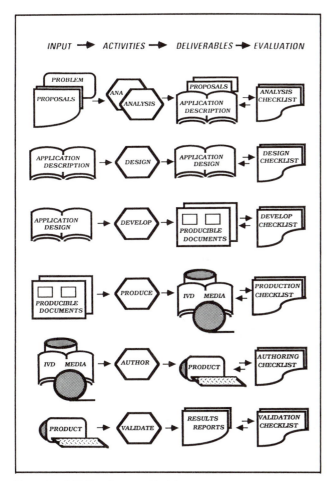

INPUT → ACTIVITIES → DELIVERABLES → EVALUATION

Figure 2-4 IVD Development Model

- when the deliverables are complete, you evaluate them and decide if they're ready for the next project phase.

We've organized this book accordingly. There's a separate chapter for each phase; each chapter expands on our Input, Activities, Deliverables, and Evaluation scheme. Chapters provide goals, detailed roadmaps, sample documentation, and evaluation checklists. This model is your overall plan for the project; the chapters contain the tips, techniques, and tools.

However, don't restrict the model to just your management roles. Make it part of your planning sessions to insure a common understanding of terms, phases, and responsibilities. Make it a prerequisite for your vendors to assure a common understanding of the deliverables. Make it work.

A Word of Caution

Now that we've developed the model that we'll use throughout this book, you may want to know who uses it. The answer is, probably no one. This model

is a composite of methodologies used by many successful developers of IVD/multimedia projects, and each of them has their own version of how it should be done. There are, however, many common components. As we said at the beginning of this chapter, the basic tenets of project management do not change in interactive media, and the progression of activities will be much the same. The differences from one developer to the next lie in the details of how the phases are divided, and what the various documents are called. You should not expect to find a particular vendor using these precise phase definitions, nor using the same terminology that we use in this book. On the other hand, you should expect that the project goes through the same steps in the same order that we describe. The vendor may call his documents by different names, but the **functions** of the documents remain the same. If you understand these functions, you'll have no difficulty understanding the phase process and names of documents used by any developer.

This model has been defined after observing the development of over a hundred IVD projects. Many of them experienced problems. Often these problems occurred because of failure to maintain control of the documentation or to evaluate the phases properly before continuing on in a wrong direction. On the other hand, projects undertaken by successful, professional developers shared certain characteristics. The projects were organized into well defined steps, the documentation was complete, and the progress was checked carefully at every stage. By incorporating the successful strategies and avoiding the problem-causing omissions, we have developed this composite model that should insure your success if fully applied.

A Last Word

As we continue with the book, our model will also serve as the organizing framework. Each chapter elaborates on one of its phases. Before starting the next chapter, you may want to know more about how those specifics fit into the general model.

At this point, you may want to skim Chapters 5-10, read their "previews," and look through the checklists in Appendix A. You can also preview the sample RFP in Appendix E, noting how the documents are listed as deliverables in each phase.

Once you're comfortable with the model and how it works—in the book and in your projects—start the next chapter. We'll describe the team members, their responsibilities, and where they fit into the model.

Chapter Three

Building the Project Team

Preview of Team Building

In the previous chapters we identified some of the factors that make interactive multimedia projects unique: the converging technologies, the different disciplines, and the amount of documentation. Our model was developed to help you see and manage this process. Next, we want to look at another dimension of the project: the number of different people involved. This chapter will shift from the activities to the players; from "what needs to be done" to "who's going to do it." If it's not already evident, these projects demand a team effort. As the project manager, you'll be coordinating, controlling, and communicating with several different groups—each with its own agenda. Beyond the obvious production vendors, you must also consult with sponsors and users. This chapter will focus on the people part of multimedia development:

- identifying the different players,

- building your project teams,

- introducing some new job descriptions,

- defining roles, responsibilities, and relationships.

After you've met these different groups, we'll return to our IVD Application Model to see where everyone fits.

Looking Over the Territory

What We're Trying to Accomplish

Managing the people part of an IVD project can be just as challenging as the paperwork and the procedures. One way to reduce this complexity is to graphically picture team members in groups, so you can "see" their relationships. Before we explain the individual players and their roles, let's look at these relationships from four different points of view. The groups are illustrated in Figure 3-1.

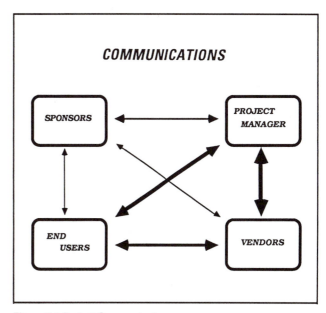

Figure 3-1 Project Communications

- Project Manager ... (That's you.) You monitor and manage the vendor's work effort, analyze and represent the users, and allocate resources to attain the sponsor's goals and business objectives.

- Sponsor ... The source of the project's goals and funding within the organization. You keep the sponsor involved with the application and the vendor's progress through checkpoints and reports.

- Vendors (in-house or out-of-house) ... Perform the actual design, development, and production work. They study the sponsor's objectives and the users' needs to create the deliverables (documentation, media, and materials) for you to evaluate.

- End-users ... The customers, employees, or members of the public who interact with the final application. They may also be involved in the development phases to provide examples, feedback, and data that help shape the final product.

As the diagram indicates, most of the project communication will be between you and the vendors.

However, all lines of communication should be open to collect information, verify priorities, or test ideas.

How Do We Get There?

This book isn't about managing in a team environment per se, but it addresses the subject in many ways. That's because your success as a project manager will depend on your ability to manage and motivate your team. If you're working with a vendor, your actions should also be supportive of the team members who work for the vendor.

In order to build an effective team, you'll need to know who the players are, how to communicate with them, and how to make sure they are communicating effectively with each other. In this chapter, we'll look at who they are, and what they do. In later chapters, we'll provide the knowledge you'll need to speak their language and understand and direct their activities.

So What's New?

Most large projects in any discipline require a team and a good manager of that team. In those projects, however, the team members come from a single discipline or background, and share a common language. In an IVD/multimedia project, the team members come from different backgrounds, and communications can be a problem. In a video production, the entire staff understands what the "program" is; likewise, in a data processing application, everyone knows what a "program" is. When you mix these two disciplines, you get a lot of confusion on this word and many others.

Another new aspect is that multimedia itself is a different medium than any of its components, and without IVD or other multimedia experience, the team members will have to learn what it is and how to develop for it. Moreover, they will have to learn the important differences between the way they have used their own medium in previous projects, and the way it is used in a multimedia project.

The challenge for the project manager of an inexperienced team is that you should not expect or allow the members to just "do their thing," while you manage the schedule and budget. You'll need to monitor everyone on the team carefully, and make sure they understand their own tasks, and that they are interfacing effectively with the other team members. Let's begin, then, by getting an introduction to the team, and finding out a little about their backgrounds.

Roles of the Project Team

The Major Groups

Let's begin by taking a very high level look at the project and the major groups who will be involved.

THE PROJECT SPONSOR

Interactive multimedia projects are expensive. They're justified by realizing important organizational goals: solving business problems, uncovering new opportunities. The project's sponsor is the executive who secures and commits organizational resources in order to achieve those goals. The resources include funding, personnel, and administrative support. As the application develops, the sponsor's primary concern is the investment. Your responsibility is to make it pay off.

The sponsor has little direct contact with the users or the vendors. Any involvement with the applications is primarily through you and your periodic reports. However, the sponsor is ever-present in the form of the original objectives that justified the project:

- improving business operations,

- increasing sales,

- reducing administrative costs,

- reaching new markets,

- improving customer relations,

- providing more cost-effective training.

Before the project can even begin, you must secure approval of the sponsor to commit the required resources. That agreement entails a detailed proposal about how you plan to accomplish the business objectives. (Chapter 4 provides the agenda and backup support you'll need for such a proposal.)

During the project's phases, those business objectives are necessarily translated into specific application events such as:

- presentations to the user,

- problems to solve,

- glossaries and help displays,

- scenes, situations, and storylines.

When you evaluate the deliverables at the end of each phase, you must make a connection between those different kinds of objectives. How does an application activity achieve one or more of the business objectives? As a reminder of this key step, we've built a sponsor signoff into each phase of our model. It keeps the project honest. So, while not an active member of the development team, the sponsor is still involved in the application.

THE END USERS

It's dangerous to continue classifying the users as one big group. Their demographics, needs, and preferences dictate the content, look, and feel of the application. During the analysis phase, we'll introduce a method to identify and prioritize the application's possible audiences and those critical characteristics. Right now let's focus on the users' role during the development process—as members of your project team.

One thing to keep in mind is that this kind of material is very rich; it can be recombined or restructured to serve users beyond the primary audience. For example, if the application was designed to market a new product line, your users could be:

- Customers who want to buy or learn about the product.(Naturally, they have varying backgrounds and needs.)

- Salespersons who setup, assist, or demonstrate the application for the customers.

- Employees who need to learn about the product and how it should be marketed.

- Administrative personnel for operational support.

- Host managers who integrate this product into the local environment.

All these users will contribute to the eventual success of the application. But you cannot wait until the product is finished to see how they like it. These users must be involved in the development process; they should shape the application. You need their multiple perspectives during analysis, their reality testing during design, and their reactions during validation. Make them part of the team. Listen to them.

THE PROJECT VENDORS

Vendors supply the specialized IVD skills needed to design, develop, produce, author, and implement your application. Vendor services may be under contract with an outside firm or under commitment from other departments within your organization. For the rest of this book, we'll use the general term "vendor" to represent the providers of these media services—whether they are internal or external.

These vendor services include development work as well as implementation activities. As shown in Figure 3-2, the total project encompasses building the application and its physical environment. The two efforts complement and influence one another. They will probably be accomplished simultaneously with two project teams. We'll describe the site planning, building facilities, and training activities in the Implementation Section. The rest of this chapter concentrates on the development team.

THE PROJECT MANAGER

As the project manager, you have overall responsibility for the project — its development, implementation, and day-to-day operations. You must insure that the application achieves the sponsor's business goals. But, depending on the skills and services available within your organization, you may not have direct control over all the necessary media resources. If the specialized skills must be contracted, the personnel will report to another manager. We've assigned the title Project Director to the manager who controls this vendor team and its efforts. If all the resources are under your control, you are both Project Manager and Project Director.

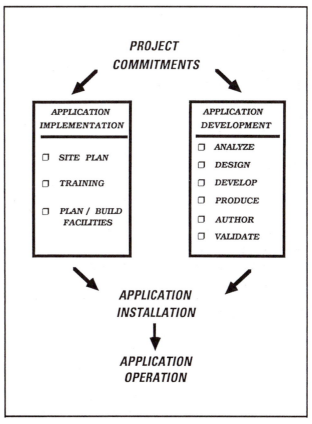

Figure 3-2 IVD Project Activities

Throughout the book we describe the activities and general roles of the team specialists. Our purpose is to give you some insight into their work and how it can contribute to the application to help you manage and monitor the process. However, if you contract for these services, any control and contact with the media specialists will be done indirectly through a Project Director. This is an important management distinction that you should keep in mind later as we discuss the roles of specialists in detail.

The Development Team

The development team is comprised of several specialists who perform the design, development, production, and authoring work. They create the application. As you build this team, maintain a "skills" perspective. You probably won't need a person for every specialty since some individuals may have multiple skills. However, it's unrealistic to expect any one member to possess all the sophisticated skills required to develop an IVD application. Securing personnel with the right skills and building them into a team can be just as challenging as creating the application itself.

While you (and the Project Director) have responsibility for the overall project, the leadership during development may shift to individual team members. From phase to phase, a different specialist may direct the work. Let's meet the development team members and see when they're in charge.

THE PRIMARY ROLES
- Application Designer.
  - Responsible for creating content to meet the objectives.
  - Directs the effort to discover, design and document the most effective sequences, storylines, and strategies for this application.
  - Background should include strong communications and consulting skills, visual creativity, experience designing interactive formats, and the ability to quickly size and synthesize the subject matter.

Note: If the application is for training or education, his or her title may be "Instructional Designer."

- Managing Producer.
  - Responsible for producing the video portion of the application.

- Selects the studio facilities and resources.
  - Coordinates video specialists, and manages their activities during production.
  - Experience includes knowledge of the entire video production effort (from pre-production preparation to post-production wrapup), the capabilities of personnel and equipment, and budget-sensitive scheduling of these resources.

- Art Director.
  - Responsible for the total visual look of the application.
  - Directs the artistic effort for color selection, screen layouts, and menu formats.
  - Knows the capabilities and limitations of the production tools and must set realistic, yet inventive guidelines.
  - Requires both managerial and technical skills to coordinate and control the creative contributions from the artists. These activities are not limited just to graphics; they include visual coordination of video, graphics, and text overlays on the storyboards and in the finished product.

- Video Director.
  - Responsible for translating your paper storyboards and scripts into motion video, still frames and audio.
  - Involved in the project at three different times:
    - prior to production — planning the studio sequences,
    - during production — directing the actors and action,
    - after production — merging the individual segments.
  - Talents should include experience with multiple video formats, visualizing skills to see links between graphics and video segments, and creativity to extract the most powerful message within your budget constraints.

THE SUPPORTING ROLES
In addition to these "assistant managers," several other specialists perform the actual design, development, or production work. They may be involved throughout the project or only in selected phases.

They include:

- Writers.
  - Create and document the video scripts, storylines, and interactive strategies from the design specifications.
  - Talents include strong dialogue writing skills, ability to describe visual material, and identification with the application's audiences.
- Graphic Artists.
  - Design and develop graphic renditions for video or computer graphics.
  - Integrate computer graphics with video presentations, using overlay techniques if the system permits it.
  - Understand both the capability and limitations of the selected authoring facility and graphic tools.
  - Skills include both artistic talent and the ability to use computer based tools productively.
- Developers.
  - Translate design ideas into special storyboards sequences—producible by other vendors.
  - Skills include a precise knowledge of all forms of documentation used by project personnel, and the ability to create it clearly for their use.

  Note: The Developer's role is often combined with that of the designers, writers or artists. The key distinction is the ability to create standard project documentation, control it, and manage changes without losing important details.

- Audio/Video Production Personnel.
  - Create and merge the video, audio, sound effects, video graphics, and any special video effects.
  - Talents include necessary technical skills, preferably augmented with prior experience with similar projects.
- Authors.
  - Integrate the video, graphics, and text presentations into organized sequences with the aid of a computer based authoring facility.
  - Skills should include knowledge of the selected authoring facility, familiarity with

IVD and CBT design techniques, use of graphic development tools, and ability to create smooth transitions between media elements to create a pleasing presentation.

- Programmers.
  - Code special routines in a general-purpose language to support or extend the application.
  - Experience should include an in-depth knowledge of the language, skill in device-specific coding, and ability to link external routines to authoring languages.
- Subject Matter Experts (SME).
  - Consult with the designer, directors, and other team specialists on the accuracy of the application's objectives and content.
  - Provide a continuing review of scripts, storyboards, and exercises to insure the critical objectives are met.
  - Background should include in-depth knowledge of the content, the audience, and their different environments.

  Note: You must recruit qualified SMEs, make them part of the team, and gain their firm time commitment to the project.

- Administrators.
  - Coordinate schedules, maintain a master set of documentation, and assist management during all phases of the project.
  - Skills include exceptional organizational talent, and the ability to manage large amounts of detail.

  Note: All of these specialists may not report directly to you, but for the duration of the project, they are doing your work, and will need your direction and support.

Phase Responsibilities

If we return to the project development phases for a moment, you can begin to appreciate the need for a coordinated team effort and overlapping leadership. While everyone's main concern is the final application, there is a complex set of interwoven factors to be managed: personnel, resources, schedules, budgets, documentation, and ideas. At any one time, the Project Director, the Application Designer, and you may be managing different dimensions of the project.

Using the phases of our model shown in Figure 3-3, here's a possible scenario:

• Analysis.

In this start-up phase, you or the Project Director manages the analysis activity. Market research firms, users, writers, designers, and artists may all participate or provide input to the process.

• Design.

The Application Designer leads the writers, graphic artists, and authors as they

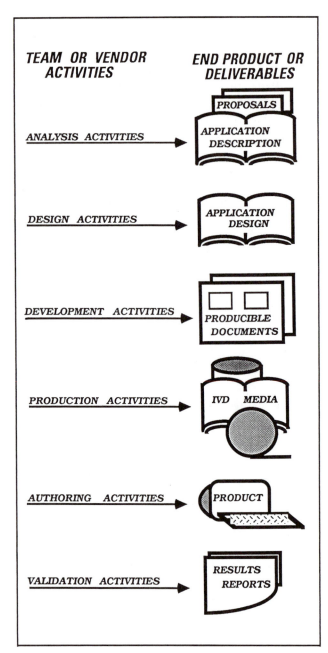

TEAM OR VENDOR ACTIVITIES

END PRODUCT OR DELIVERABLES

ANALYSIS ACTIVITIES → PROPOSALS / APPLICATION DESCRIPTION

DESIGN ACTIVITIES → APPLICATION DESIGN

DEVELOPMENT ACTIVITIES → PRODUCIBLE DOCUMENTS

PRODUCTION ACTIVITIES → IVD MEDIA

AUTHORING ACTIVITIES → PRODUCT

VALIDATION ACTIVITIES → RESULTS REPORTS

Figure 3-3 IVD Development Activities

generate, select, and apply design ideas that can carry the message.

• Development.

The Application Designer monitors the transition of the design to producible documentation. The Art Director leads the development team's artistic efforts.

• Production.

The Managing Producer coordinates the studio's resources, the Video Director "directs" both talent and special effects, you (or Project Director) watch the clock.

• Authoring.

Depending on the number of authors, the Project Director or a chief author manages the authors and programmers. The Art Director settles any visual disputes. The Application Designer insures continuity.

• Validation.

The Application Designer conducts the tests and verifies that all objectives have been met.

Roles of the Project Manager

With all these specialists doing the work and different leaders directing their efforts, what's left for you to do? Quite a bit.

Using our Input-Process-Deliverable-Evaluation sequence in Figure 3-4 as a guide, you'll play a key role in each step—for every development phase. Sometimes your role is more active than others, but nonetheless important to the success of the project. Let's review your involvement with the development team and some of your assignments:

• Securing and distributing the required input documentation from the previous stage.

• Allocating new resources for this phase: funding, personnel.

• Monitoring the vendor processes (directly or indirectly).

• Evaluating the end products, assessing the quality, deciding on revisions and reallocating resources (if required).

• Maintaining control over the project documentation.

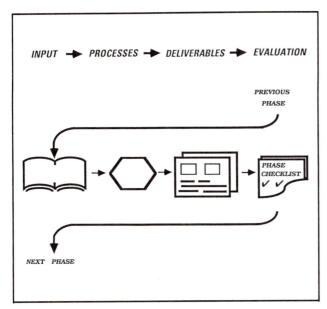

INPUT → PROCESSES → DELIVERABLES → EVALUATION

PREVIOUS PHASE

PHASE CHECKLIST ✓ ✓

NEXT PHASE

Figure 3-4 IVD Development Cycle

- Updating the sponsor and obtaining necessary signoffs.

- Adjusting/refining the schedule based on new data.

- Monitoring/reconciling the budget.

- Conducting status meetings with vendors or Project Directors.

- Preparing input for the next phase.

Enough?

A Last Word

Your challenge as the Project Manager is to manage the people, paperwork, and processes to produce a viable product to meet the sponsor's objectives. Our model can help you see those processes and control the paperwork, but the people have to do the work. Now that you have a general picture of their roles, we'll be ready to describe their specific tasks in subsequent chapters.

As you recruit and build this team, it's important to realize that just as one person cannot do all the work, one person cannot manage all the activities. You should recognize and capitalize on the shared leadership concept. Delegate. Your most valuable personal asset will be a total picture of all the project activities. The most valuable asset you can supply your team is a shared vision of the application.

PART TWO

Preparation

The orientation chapters provided a management perspective of multimedia technology, terminology, a development model, and the team's skills. You should have a big picture of all the pieces, but may still be wondering: "where do I begin?"

Beginning a project requires two preparation activities: project planning and application analysis. These two steps will get you started in the right direction and provide the necessary foundation for the application. During planning you consider all the project factors (vendors, schedules, goals, resources, cost estimates) and organize them into a formal proposal. During analysis, you study and document the application in more detail, looking at its end users, content, environment, and interactions.

This section is divided into two chapters, one for each of these preparation activities.

Chapter 4 ... outlines a working agenda to help you prepare a project plan, present that plan to a sponsor, and secure a commitment of resources to carry out the plan.

Chapter 5 ... describes the basic components and methods of analysis, prescribes a formal approach for content analysis, and introduces a new audience/topic tool.

Once the project team is recruited, the plan is approved, and the application factors are analyzed (and documented), you can move to the actual design and development work.

Chapter Four

Planning the Project

Preview of Planning

The previous orientation section provided several key perspectives for interactive videodisc/multimedia projects: application components, the different disciplines, and our model for developing the application. Now we want to bring those perspectives together into a specific plan for your project. That plan naturally includes goals, budgets, securing and allocating resources, and scheduling each phase of the model.

But before you begin the first phase, you must formulate the overall project plan and get that plan approved by the sponsor. This activity is the first formal checkpoint in the project where you are seeking general agreement on the extent of the application, the commitment of resources, and your management approach. It's the critical first gate.

This chapter prepares you for a checkpoint meeting by developing a working agenda and discussing the considerations and issues that bear on each item.

Looking Over the Territory

What We're Trying to Accomplish

We have three general objectives for this planning stage:

- to force consideration and visualization of the major project activities before development starts,

- to organize those activities into a logical outline that can be presented to sponsoring executives (and guide your subsequent management activities),

- to gain approval of your plan and a commitment of the resources needed to complete the project successfully.

This planning function can be divided into two segments: the preparation of a project plan and its presentation. The plan includes: project goals, potential vendors, key roles and responsibilities, and schedules. A sample planning agenda is outlined in Figure 4-1.

The intent of planning is to map out a strategy for the entire project including its people, schedules, vendors, phases, and approval. Then detailed analysis can follow.

Note. These planning sessions are not designed as a forum for proposing or discussing the specific content of the application. That comes later, during the analysis phase. However, good ideas may surface during your planning sessions. They should be recorded for future use. While these ideas are important and should not be lost, they should not be encouraged now. Keep the application discussion limited to relevant examples that support the project's goals.

SAMPLE PLANNING AGENDA

1 INTRODUCTION TO THE PROJECT

2. IDENTIFICATION OF THE GOALS

3 POTENTIAL APPLICATION AREAS

4 PRELIMINARY SCHEDULE OF MAJOR PHASES

5 KEY ROLES AND RESPONSIBILITIES

6 PRELIMINARY TRAINING REQUIREMENTS

7 DETERMINE NEED FOR FORMAL ANALYSIS

8 IDENTIFY POTENTIAL VENDORS

9 IDENTIFY VENDOR SUPPORT REQUIREMENTS

10 ESTIMATE PROJECT COSTS

11 SECURE AN AGREEMENT TO COMMIT RESOURCES

12 AGREE ON THE NEXT PROJECT ACTIVITY

Figure 4-1 The Planning Agenda

How Do We Get There?

Our approach to this two-stage planning process is to use the agenda (shown in Figure 4-1) as a working checklist. Prior to the proposal, each agenda item is researched, reviewed, and refined by key project members. They develop the detailed examples, rationale, and backup support for the project. Once this preparation is complete, the same agenda serves as your presentation outline.

While the presentation may only take a couple of hours, the preparation may take many people and several days. As the different agenda items are considered, it's obvious that all attendees must be ready to contribute. Many of these items will take extensive thought and deliberation before they can be incorporated into your proposal. A reasonable approach would be to schedule a two or three day informal preparation session as shown in Figure 4-2. Prior to that meeting, a preliminary package with objectives, resources, and questions can help focus everyone's attention on the project.

The rest of the chapter elaborates on these agenda items.

So What's New?

Any new project requires planning. You need to have some idea of where you're going and how you're going to get there. With IVD/multimedia projects, planning is a required activity. The previous chapters have described the complexity resulting from the number of factors, phases, disciplines, and documentation. Larger budgets, more resources, and longer development times make these multimedia projects less forgiving. There's little room for error; there's no room for scrap.

You're about to request a significant commitment of time and resources. That request demands justification and a comprehensive plan. It demands that you anticipate and document your steps ahead of time. Just as critical, you must effectively communicate your plan to gain early participation, concurrence, and support for the project.

Planning Activities

Preparing the Plan

The goals of your preparation meetings are to anticipate project resources, routes, and rocks in the road, then to formulate an action plan. Who's attending and assisting you at these sessions? Invite managers representing the application users, Subject Matter Experts, administrative assistants, committed staff members, and inside or outside consultants who are familiar with the requirements for implementing an IVD/multimedia application. As the session leader, you must insure that all participants understand:

- the organization's goals for the project,
- media technology and terminology,
- the development and implementation process,
- your initial approach to project management.

This itself is a complex undertaking and a critical first step, but it can be done. Some techniques that can help assure a common mind-set and shared vision are:

- visual diagrams of the development steps (our model),
- examples of documentation requirements,
- representative demonstrations,
- an organized information package for each participant,
- using the agenda as a working guide.

Figure 4-2 Preparing for a Planning Session

Presenting the Plan

When your plan is well prepared, you are ready to present it to your sponsoring executive. In the following sections, we'll go through the suggested agenda point by point.

1. INTRODUCTION TO THE PROJECT

On the surface, your introduction simply reviews the rationale for the presentation and its agenda items. Underneath the surface, your goals are to convince the sponsors that you have considered all possible factors, constructed a plan for success, and secured everyone's commitment to that plan.

You'll have similar goals during the preparation sessions, convincing team members, considering many factors, and gaining commitment. The key difference now is that your plan is under construction. You'll have to strike a balance of leadership during these meetings, providing the overall direction while accepting both critical and creative contributions.

Introducing the agenda as a general outline or shell of the major project considerations (to be completed by the team) can help you develop the project plan, build the project team, and create a cooperative atmosphere.

2. IDENTIFICATION OF GOALS

The project goals are the reasons for the application from the sponsor's or organization's perspective. These goals should be fully researched, presented early, and described in your sponsor's terms. During the preparation for this agenda item, your team should take the sponsor's view of organizational problems and opportunities. Where and how can this application contribute? Here are some statements representing typical application goals:

Training Application Goals

- reduce training expense and time
- improve quality
- establish consistent standards
- provide refresher training on demand
- reduce danger (through simulations)

Marketing Application Goals

- increase direct sales
- assist sales personnel
- reach new markets

- provide realistic demonstrations

Information Application Goals

- provide a service
- enhance your image
- focus advertising
- broaden your coverage and presence

Quantifying Goals

While these goals can be described in words, they must also be quantified. Part of your planning task is to translate the goals into real savings or benefits —ones that can offset the project's budget. Invest enough time and study here to be sure that your application is economically justified.

> **Note.** Another valuable activity during this part of the planning is to create a project theme such as a motto, logo, or visual, one that captures the essence of the application and its goals. It becomes the visible (common) banner that everyone can rally around; it becomes the symbolic reminder of what the application is about, and why we're doing it.

3. POTENTIAL APPLICATION AREAS

Once the project goals are developed and documented, they must be translated into potential IVD applications. The general question to ask is: "How can we achieve these goals through an interactive videodisc application?"

More specifically, during the preparation meetings turn each goal into a question, then discuss and debate its potential. How can we reduce expenses? How can we reach new markets? How can we enhance our image? The answers should help you identify worthwhile applications. For example:

- Point of Sale-Customer Information.
- Point of Sale-Salesperson Information.
- Point of Sale-Customer Motivation.
- Salesperson Training (on site).
- Technical Training (on demand).
- Employee Communications.
- Catalog Displays and Demonstrations.

After the team has made these preliminary application decisions, they can be documented for your presentation. Make the link between goals and applications explicit.

4. PRELIMINARY SCHEDULE OF MAJOR PHASES

From the application decisions, the next logical step is to plan the phase-by-phase schedule of activities. You already have an effective method to discuss and present this agenda item: the diagrams of our model. Begin with a general flow of the phases as shown in Figure 4-3. Recall that some of these development and implementation activities may happen concurrently.

From this general flow, expand on each individual phase with its requirements, processes, and its deliverables. Our models provide a visual; the remainder of the book provides the supporting detail. During preparation meetings, this phase preview gives you an opportunity to share a total project map, define technical terms, and establish directions for the team. For the sponsor presentation, the phase review communicates that you have considered and planned the major project activities.

5. KEY ROLES AND RESPONSIBILITIES

As you plan each phase and its requirements, a natural follow-up question is: "Who is going to do that part?"

Don't forget, the activities in each phase include more than just creating a product. Responsibilities for the documentation, coordination, evaluation, and signoff must also be considered. During the preparation meetings, you can use our model to organize and tentatively assign these key responsibilities by phase. For example, you might develop a worksheet as shown in Figure 4-4.

This worksheet can help you identify available skills, and those to be developed or recruited. Reference the material in Chapter 3 for details on the team members, their roles, and their backgrounds. For the final presentation to the sponsor, you can then align each phase with the appropriate resources needed to complete that phase. You can answer the "roles and responsibilities" question before it is posed.

PROJECT ASSIGNMENT WORKSHEET			
PHASE	ACTIVITY	INTERNAL RESOURCE	EXTERNAL RESOURCE
ANALYSIS	AUDIENCE		MARKET RESEARCH
ANALYSIS	CONTENT	PROJECT TEAM	
ANALYSIS	EVALUATION	PROJECT MANAGER	

Figure 4-4 Project Assignment Worksheet

6. PRELIMINARY TRAINING REQUIREMENTS

From your review of the phases and key responsibilities you can determine where critical skills are missing or weak. You have two broad alternatives: train or buy. This decision will be a function of project time lines, available personnel, and the potential for future projects that may require internal resources.

Some training areas include:

* Project orientation for all vendors and support personnel. This planning agenda can be brought into service again.

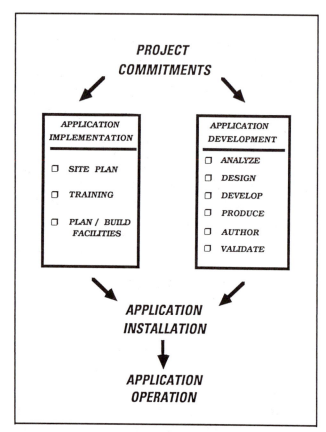

PROJECT COMMITMENTS

APPLICATION IMPLEMENTATION

☐ SITE PLAN

☐ TRAINING

☐ PLAN / BUILD FACILITIES

APPLICATION DEVELOPMENT

☐ ANALYZE

☐ DESIGN

☐ DEVELOP

☐ PRODUCE

☐ AUTHOR

☐ VALIDATE

APPLICATION INSTALLATION

APPLICATION OPERATION

Figure 4-3 Project Activities

- Subject matter research.

- IVD/multimedia design, development, and production.

- Documentation methods and standards. (See Appendix D in the Resource Section.)

- Authoring systems and/or languages.

Training methods may be formal classes, seminars, and textbooks from outside sources. Informal on-the-job experiences and planning sessions like this one are also possible.

During the preparation meeting, you will be planning for these different training needs. The presentation seeks approval of your training plan.

Note. If you anticipate future media projects, you may want to consider an apprenticeship training program. Selected team members serve as assistant project managers, so they will be ready and experienced for subsequent applications.

---

7. DETERMINE NEED FOR FORMAL ANALYSIS

About mid-way through the preparation meetings, you'll start to develop an intuitive feel for the application and its direction. How much do we know? How much more do we need to know? Do we have enough detail? Do we have the capability (and time) to dig out the rest? For example, how well do we know our audience(s) and their characteristics? How critical is it that we have a comprehensive profile?

If there is a degree of discomfort about the quality or depth of the data (and the time or capability to gather more), you should consider a formal analysis step. This process scientifically studies the application factors through surveys, questionnaires, or focus group meetings then statistically reports its findings. The advantages are: securing more comprehensive analysis data, uncovering other (hidden) applications, and avoiding misconceptions from superficial assessments. The drawbacks, naturally, are the time and costs to conduct this detailed study.

If you opt for a formal analysis, the next decision is who should conduct it. Do you have qualified resources within the organization? Should you contract with a professional market research firm? You should think about this formal analysis as a three-step process:

- During the preparation meeting, you are assessing the need for this type of study, evaluating its importance, and selecting the potential resources.

- During the presentation, you will be proposing, justifying, and seeking agreement for the study.

- Once approved, the market research department or vendor conducts the formal study and complements your other analysis activities.

8. IDENTIFY POTENTIAL VENDORS

For those project requirements that are not available internally and not part of the training plan, you must contract with a vendor. The skills may include market research, development functions like design, production, and authoring, or the implementation activities such as construction and installation of the kiosks.

Some general criteria for vendor selection include:

- previous experience with IVD and multimedia development,

- history of project timeliness,

- depth of resources and support personnel,

- working relationships with clients,

- availability (for project duration).

More specifically, identification of potential vendors should be balanced against your internal strengths. Complement what you already have. Most vendors have expertise in one or more critical areas: media, design, production, subject matter, or authoring. Assess your available skills, then evaluate the vendors' strengths. Recruit or contract accordingly.

In effective multimedia applications, the media, methods, and message must be interwoven into a seamless presentation for the audience. One element should not be obvious or overshadow the others. Choose vendors to ensure that your team has these diverse skills equally represented. Sources to help with this decision include colleagues, organization profiles, demonstration packages or sample work, references from other clients and consultants familiar with the field.

During the preparation meeting, weigh the alternatives; during the presentation, make your recommendations.

9. IDENTIFY HARDWARE AND SOFTWARE REQUIREMENTS

In addition to the vendors for implementation and development activities, you must also consider the hardware and software vendors. Their support will be critical to the ongoing success of the application. Assess your project requirements and internal resources against the vendors' short-term and long-term support options.

Some factors include:

- Hardware Support (displays, players, and computers)

    – installation and set-up services,

    – maintenance contracts (options and costs),

    – on-site service / mail program / replacements,

    – upgrade support.

- Software Support (authoring and presentation code)

    – license options (single, site, fixed number),

    – maintenance and upgrade support,

    – education, training, ongoing assistance,

    – supporting documentation,

    – special features libraries.

- Software Support (application code)

    – testing and validation support,

    – modification options,

    – future enhancements,

    – helpline alternatives.

10. ESTIMATE PROJECT COSTS

Since each IVD project is unique, there are no hard and fast rules for determining cost at this stage. Cost will be a function of the number of resource people, level of video quality, application size, number of vendors and the amounts they charge. However, we can define the line items to be considered and provide some reasonable guidelines. You can then gather the appropriate data and complete your project estimates. In Chapter 12, after we have discussed all of the components of project costs, we will cover budgeting. We'll suggest that there are three times during a project that a budget should be prepared, each one a more exact refinement of cost estimates. The first time you must estimate a budget is right at this point in the planning process. You're going to have to make a reasonable estimate of cost to justify the project, and your management is going to want to see those costs.

You'll have a better handle on how costs are determined after you have gone through the book and read Chapter 12. For now, however, we'll present some simple worksheets that will allow you to put together

a reasonable planning budget. If you would like a more detailed explanation, you can take a look at Chapter 12 before continuing. The project costs (and our worksheets) can be divided into two major segments: development estimates and implementation estimates.

Development Costs

The development costs can be divided into five categories:

- direct labor . . . . . . both internal and external
- supplies . . . . diskettes, office, paper
- travel expenses . . local, studio, location
- materials . . . . references, models, etc.
- contract service . . . consultants, video production

During the planning sessions, you need to estimate these costs as part of your presentation. We suggest building a worksheet of the five categories for each project phase. A sample is illustrated on the next page. This method lets you visualize the distribution of your resources and quantify them more precisely.

> **Note.** When you present these cost estimates, be prepared to balance them against the original project goals and the savings or benefits you previously developed.

Figure 4-5 shows a completed worksheet for constructing a planning budget for a large project. There is a blank form for you to copy and use in Appendix C of the Resource Section, "Forms and Worksheets." The top portion is used to estimate costs for developing the application; the lower items list the implementation costs, and we'll discuss them in a moment.

Let's look at the development costs in the top section. The five cost categories we just outlined appear as column headings, and the rows correspond to the development phases. The shaded figures provide a **starting point** for estimating the percentage cost breakdown of a project. The figures entered are a first cut using those percentages, based on a total estimated cost to develop the project of $200,000.

The best place to start a planning budget is with an estimated total cost. In Chapter 12, we'll discuss how to make reasonable preliminary estimates. The cost shown would represent a major custom project for two hours of training, or perhaps a point-of-sale

IVD COST ESTIMATE WORKSHEET

DEVELOPMENT ESTIMATES

PHASE	DIRECT LABOR	SUPPLIES	TRAVEL	MATERIAL	SERVICES	TOTALS
ANALYSIS	10,000 / 5		4,000 / 2		2,000 / 1	16,000 / 8
DESIGN	20,000 / 10	2,000 / 1	4,000 / 2	2,000 / 1	2,000 / 1	30,000 / 15
DEVELOPMENT	20,000 / 10	2,000 / 1	4,000 / 2	2,000 / 1	2,000 / 1	30,000 / 15
PRODUCTION	10,000 / 5				80,000 / 40	90,000 / 45
AUTHORING	24,000 / 12					24,000 / 12
VALIDATION	6,000 / 3			4,000 / 2		10,000 / 5
TOTALS $ / %	90,000 / 45	4,000 / 2	12,000 / 6	8,000 / 4	86,000 / 43	200,000 / 100%

IMPLEMENTATION ESTIMATES

	FIRST YEAR	SECOND YEAR	THIRD YEAR	FOURTH YEAR	FIFTH YEAR
DEVELOPMENT SYSTEM	30,000				
DELIVERY SYSTEM	100,000	250,000	1,000,000		
REPLICATION DISTRIBUTION	30,000	20,000			
CONSTRUCTION SITE PREPARATION	150,000	500,000	2,500,000		
INSTALLATION AND TRAINING	20,000	50,000	200,000	30,000	30,000
OPERATIONS MAINTENANCE	3,000	50,000	300,000	300,000	300,000

Figure 4-5 Planning Budget Worksheet

application for a national chain of retail stores. At this point, just note that the shaded percentage numbers have been used with the estimated total cost to fill in the amounts in the form.

Using these numbers as a starting point, you now would apply information that you know about your actual project to modify them. The shaded percentages are based on assumptions that may not be so. For example, they assume no market research will be incurred as a service cost during analysis; they assume that video production will be done locally and no travel costs will be needed for a location shoot; they assume that no major revisions will be needed after validation. If you expect different circumstances in these or other items, the budget should be adjusted accordingly.

Implementation Costs

The lower part of the Planning Budget Worksheet lists the major components of implementation costs. These will vary widely from project to project. If you are starting from scratch, you will probably have to deal with all of them. The numbers will have to be worked out individually for every case. The numbers shown in Figure 4-5 might be typical for an installa-

tion in 300 retail stores over a five year period. They could be used to establish the cost, and compare them to the payback. In this case, the figures show a cost of about six million dollars. If the point-of-sale applications result in an increase of 1.5% in new or switched sales, it would result in an increase of eighteen million dollars in gross sales over the period (less the development costs of the applications). Numbers like these (kept on the conservative side) can get the attention of management quickly.

11. SECURE AGREEMENT TO COMMIT RESOURCES

Quite simply: ask for the order. You've identified organization goals and presented a comprehensive plan to achieve them. If there has been general agreement on all the preceding items, you're now ready for the sponsor's backing and signature. The best preparation for this agenda item is a dress rehearsal. Role play the entire presentation; look for open issues, discomfort, weak justification, missing backup data, and possible objections. Modify as needed.

12. AGREE ON THE NEXT PROJECT ACTIVITY

Based on the degree of commitment and any suggestions during the presentation, you can decide on the next project activities. These may include:

- contracting with vendors,
- enrolling in training sessions,
- beginning the Analysis Phase,
- returning for additional planning.

You can plan for this step by developing alternative scenarios (what ifs?) during the preparation sessions. Explicitly state your direction and seek the agreement of all attendees. Whatever decision is made, identify and schedule your next checkpoint with the sponsor before the meeting ends.

A Last Word

We placed this planning chapter early in the book for a couple of reasons. Before any large-scale multimedia project can begin, there must be a full and firm commitment of resources: people, time, money, and visible support. It's your first gate. In addition, this planning agenda serves as a personal checklist of your management activities. It alerts you to the number and variety of project factors that must be coordinated. It provides a framework for organizing our remaining advice and material.

Before you actually conduct any preparation meetings or present a plan to the sponsors, you'll have studied the entire book. It will provide much more of the detailed factors and supportive backup you need for each agenda item. You can then revisit this chapter as a guide for preparing the planning session.

Chapter Five

Analyzing the Application

Preview of Analysis

"Well begun is half done."

From the illustration in Figure 5-1, the Analysis Phase looks innocent enough: analyze the problem and document your findings. Looks can be deceiving. Analysis of the application involves a variety of activities by you and several different members of the project team.

You have three broad objectives during the analysis phase:

- **Discover the right problem or opportunity.** Uncover the true purpose of the application and its contribution to the organization.

- **Understand that problem or opportunity thoroughly.** Get beyond the surface facts into the environment, the users, and their specific needs.

- **Document the application.** Provide enough detail for the team or vendors to begin the design activity with confidence.

As the project manager, your tasks include:

- securing and allocating the resources for the Analysis Phase,

- guiding and monitoring the individual steps,

- evaluating the end products,

- obtaining team agreement and sponsor signoff.

The purpose of this chapter is to guide you through these tasks.

To complete their analysis work, your team members must study the problem from several different perspectives. They are looking for answers to who? What? When? Where? Why? Understanding the answer to these questions may require input from resources beyond the immediate team, including market research, outside vendors, host site representatives and end users. You should expect multiple (and sometimes conflicting) viewpoints.

Analysis activities are varied. They can range from observations, surveys and interviews to brainstorming sessions, informal meetings and

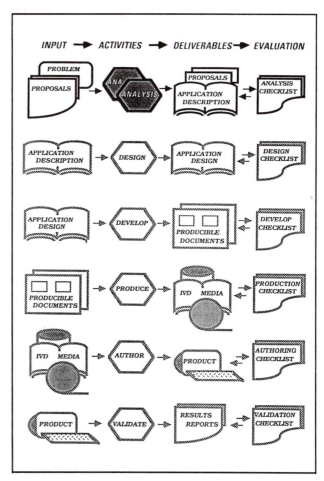

Figure 5-1 Project Development Phases

structured planning sessions. Along the way, you'll be monitoring the process, reviewing the progress, and evaluating the results. By investing resources early in the Analysis Phase, you'll get the project off to a solid start, and save much time and effort later on.

Looking Over the Territory

What We're Trying to Accomplish

The purpose of the Analysis Phase is to provide a clear set of guidelines for future project development that are clearly understood by the sponsors and the team members.

These guidelines will be your most important tool in evaluating the deliverable items in subsequent phases. Each time a plan is brought to you to add a new section, a new expenditure, or a new person, your first thought should be, "Is this addition in keeping with the original project objectives?" If the idea passes this test, you can pass on to evaluating the idea itself.

The output of the Analysis Phase should be a single document called an "Application Description Document." Let's look at a list of its contents.

The Application Description Document

- A statement of the sponsor's application goals.

- A narrative of the general approach or treatment.

- A statement of end user objectives and/or benefits.

- A description of the audience(s) to be addressed.

- A task or needs analysis for the target audience(s).

- A description of the delivery system environment.

- A prioritized list of the application content topics.

When you've completed the Analysis Phase, you should have a clear idea of what you plan to include in the application, and why you're including it. It's not a bad idea to document this information in an Application Description Document. Insofar as possible, this document should become the hymn book that (hopefully) everyone is singing from.

How Do We Get There?

When you're beginning the Analysis Phase, there are a lot of things to look out for. For example:

- It's likely that everyone involved in a project (probably including you) will "understand" what it's about and have a pretty good idea of how it should be done.

- It's likely that a good bit of analysis has been done while the project was being planned, and it looks pretty complete.

- "Time's a wastin'!" and everyone is impatient to get started with "real work."

Occasionally, some of these items may be accurate. More often it is the case that everyone's ideas are all over the map, the prior analysis is inadequate for fulfilling its crucial role, and rushing into design with a loose foundation will waste more time in the long run than you'll save now. It's probably going to be to your advantage to require a formal Analysis Phase to start the project. A further advantage of this phase will be its contribution to team building. If you've got a group that hasn't worked together before, a formal analysis will provide a good short range target for an early milestone in the project. It is relevant, goal directed activity that will help establish positive working relationships between the team members and you, and among each other.

The overall responsibility of the Project Manager in the Analysis Phase is to insure that the analysis performed is adequate for guiding the subsequent design and development activity. The actual activities in the phase can vary, depending on several factors. If the project goal is purely instructional, and your design staff is experienced in the technology of Instructional Systems Design, analysis can proceed in its natural course. Trained instructional designers should understand the role and methodology of analysis better than anyone else. Some of the ideas presented in this chapter, however, may not be familiar to the designers, and you may want to review them with the team to see if the approach makes sense for your current project.

Alternatively, you may be in the position of working with an outside agency to develop the application, either another part of your organization or a professional firm—we'll use the term "vendor" to apply to both. In this case, your role will vary depending upon whether you have a choice of vendors and prefer to bid the job, or if you have already selected a single vendor (or have no choice). Here are two approaches:

Sole Vendor Method

In the Sole Vendor method, the Project Manager and the selected vendor work together to research and document the analysis data. The Request for Proposal (RFP) or other document of understanding is limited to defining the scope of effort which defines the working relationship and the end product(s).

- Select or identify the vendor.

- Develop a Scope of Effort defining the vendor services to be provided and the end product(s).

- With vendor participation, perform a preliminary analysis.

- Determine if formal market research is required. If so, contract with an organization to conduct it.

- Conduct an Application Design Session with the vendor attending.

- Complete the Application Description Document and obtain signoff from the Sponsor.

Bid Method

In the Bid Method, the Project Manager completes the preliminary analysis and uses it as the basis for an RFP. The vendor selected from the submitted proposals then participates in completing the analysis.

- Working with your in-house staff, perform a preliminary analysis.

- Document the analysis data along with the administrative sections of the RFP and have it approved internally.

- Distribute the RFP to selected vendors.

- Evaluate the vendor proposals submitted, and select the one that best meets the goals and objectives stated in the preliminary analysis.

- Determine if formal market research is required. If so, contract with an organization to conduct it.

- Work with the selected vendor to complete the final Application Description Document. If appropriate, conduct an Application Design Session with the vendor attending.

Appendix E in the Resource Section contains the outline of an RFP that you may find useful as a starting point if you plan to bid the project. Naturally, you would review the document with your own legal counsel and define the terms and conditions to fit your specific situation.

So, armed with a determination that you are going to insist on formal analysis, you need to survey your resources and decide how to do it. Here's a reasonable approach:

- Determine what analysis skills exist within your team, and identify the areas that will need outside help.

- Look over the existing analysis documentation from the planning stage, and see what can be used without further research.

- If appropriate to your project, consider separately the idea of professional market research, whether needed and whether you could pay for it.

- Complete a preliminary analysis document that addresses Problem, Audience, Task/Needs and Environment analyses.

- Conduct a formal Application Design Session with your team and other relevant participants.

- Publish an Application Description Document that states the preliminary analysis conclusions and the results of the Content Analysis.

- Apply the checklist criteria to the Application Description Document.

- Obtain sponsor signoff on the Application Description Document.

We've diagrammed those activities as a road map in Figure 5-2. In the next section, we'll consider each of these steps in more detail.

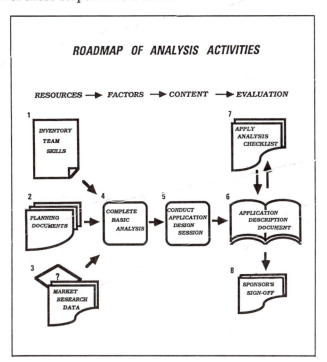

Figure 5-2 Analysis Road Map

So What's New?

You've probably already recognized that most of the analysis activity described here is standard procedure. Every project starts with analysis, whether it's an instructional course, a data processing application, a business activity, a video program and so on. The component parts of the analysis are standard too.

There are, however, a few differences to consider:

- There's more at stake.

As we'll see, IVD and other multimedia projects are more complex and expensive than other kinds of projects to which analysis is usually applied. It's more difficult to correct design flaws or change directions later in the project. Moreover, later changes have far reaching effects on other parts of the project, and getting all the documentation back into shape takes a great effort. To the extent that analysis can avoid these problems, it has a greater value to IVD than other kinds of projects.

- Environment analysis is new.

In most projects, the delivery environment is fixed and well understood. Not so with multimedia. Factors such as kiosk or carrel design, ambient light and noise, or availability of technical or administrative assistance can affect design decisions early in the development process.

- Content analysis is more selective.

In other kinds of projects, content analysis can be obvious, and performed along with the other types of analysis. In IVD/multimedia projects, system resources are limited and expensive. It's common for a design team to dream up much more valuable content than the system or the project resources can support. That's the reason we're suggesting performing all other analysis first, so that if content has to be limited, it can be properly prioritized and selected.

So, if we're of a mind to agree that yes, we will spend the time and effort on analysis to start the team off right and to lay a firm foundation for the design and development to follow, let's look at the activities in more detail.

Managing the Analysis Activities

Let's take the list we suggested earlier and look at each item in more detail.

1

Inventory Available Skills

- Determine what analysis skills exist within your team, and identify the areas that will need outside help.

A full analysis is going to require input from many areas. Let's go over the list. Then it will be up to you to decide who can best provide the information.

- Application Objectives

Someone must be able to address the application objectives in three critical areas:

- The *Sponsor* (the one who's paying for the application).

- The *User* (the audience that the application is intended for).

- The *Host* (the one who must install, administer and maintain the application).

Sometimes, application development gets off to the wrong start by limiting the objectives consideration to only one or two of these. The eventual success of the application will depend on defining objectives that will satisfy all three.

- Subject Matter Expertise

Clearly, you need someone around who knows the subject and how to prioritize the topics. If that person isn't assigned to your staff or available from the vendor, then one of your major tasks is to obtain a firm commitment that the subject matter expert will be available when needed. These experts usually have great demands on their time, so start early.

- Technical Expertise

As plans for content evolve, questions are likely to pop up on the capabilities of the system or software to handle proposed approaches. It will be helpful to get immediate answers if possible.

- Design Expertise

If at all possible, the designers should participate in the Analysis Phase. For one thing, their expertise should include knowledge of the methodology of formal analysis. More importantly, however, they should be privy to the discussions and ideas that pertain to the objectives, the audience, and other key items that will guide their work in the Design Phase.

At this point, you should have the people identified who will provide these skills. They may be members of your own staff, the vendor's staff, or committed resources from elsewhere in your organization.

Now, let's find an appropriate starting point.

2

Evaluate Existing Analysis

*   **Look over the existing analysis documentation from your planning activities to see what can be used without further research.**

To have reached this point in the project, there has already been a great deal of effort expended, and hopefully a fair amount of attention given to justifying the project. This analysis will be useful. In some cases, it may be adequate. For example, instructional projects that involve conversion of a course to interactive multimedia may well have had experienced instructional designers involved in the initial analysis.

It's often the case, however, that the existing analysis was not performed by trained designers, and is based on preconceived notions that are not well enough documented to allow the designers to create what the sponsor had in mind. If the differences in concepts aren't ironed out at this point, you're almost sure to encounter trouble and rework later.

3

Conduct Market Research

*   **If appropriate to your project, consider separately the idea of professional market research, whether it's needed and whether you could pay for it. (This may have been determined earlier in your Planning Meeting.)**

In some projects, professional market research can make the difference between success and failure. It would be a disaster to spend a lot of money on a high quality, technically accurate application that failed to be accepted by the end users. In most applications, the user is free to walk away if they aren't perceiving value, and the job of market research is to identify value perception before product development.

Market research is generally applied to information and marketing applications, not instructional applications. However, many of the techniques used are relevant to instruction as well. It's worthwhile to ponder the question of whether to use market research for any kind of application.

Often, market research can be provided from within your own organization, say from the Marketing Department of a company or as a project in the School of Business. There are also professional firms who will do the research for a fee. The techniques of market research include questionnaires, surveys, interviews and focus groups. If you elect to use professional research, it will cost you some resources. The major considerations are:

*   Time ...

    It will take time to prepare, gather information and summarize and present the results. Plan on three or four weeks at least, and more if you're looking for extensive information.

*   People ...

    The researchers will need access to people who understand the objectives of the application in order to prepare their research tools and questionnaires.

*   Money ...

    Good research costs money, and the more certain you want to be of the results, the more it costs. Typically, the cost for a professional firm may range between $10,000 and $50,000, or even more for an extensive investigation.

Despite the cost of these resources, market research may be the key to insuring the eventual acceptance of your application. If you are looking at a major project with development costs in the six figure range, good research during the analysis phase can be insurance that is well worth the time and cost to obtain.

4

Perform Preliminary Analysis

*   **Complete a preliminary analysis document that addresses Problem, Audience, Task/Needs and Environment analyses.**

You should begin by focusing on four areas of **preliminary** analysis:

- Problem Analysis — **Why** are we doing this?

- Audience Analysis — **Who** are we serving?

- Task/Needs Analysis — **What** are they doing?

- Environment Analysis — **Where** is all this taking place?

These four analyses will define the objectives and requirements of the application sufficiently well to keep you out of trouble. They will also provide the basis for the fifth type of analysis that will have the greatest effect on future project activities: Content Analysis.

If you or a member of your staff has experience in Instructional Systems Design, the content and methodology of these kinds of analyses will be familiar. (If not, you should make every effort to involve a vendor with these skills at this point in the project.) In particular, Problem, Audience and Task/Needs analysis should be done with standard approaches.

Environment analysis, however, is an activity that is not usually included in the standard approach. It is needed in IVD/multimedia projects because the characteristics of the delivery system environment will have significant effects on the design requirements of the application. The environment analysis should include:

- Hardware and installation description,

- Location description,

  - Ambient sound and light,

  - Nearby permanent workers,

  - Distractions, etc.,

- Support personnel availability and description,

- Auxiliary materials (such as workbooks, brochures),

- Existing systems that will be affected by the IVD system.

It might be useful to differentiate the terms "goals" and "objectives" when engaging in these preliminary analysis activities. "Goals" refers to the purpose of the application as seen by the sponsor; "Objectives" refers to the purpose as seen by the end users. Looked at in this way, they are two sides of the same (application) coin. It should be clear from the beginning that if the end users receive the value described by the objectives, then the sponsor's goals will be satisfied. If this is not clear, something is wrong that must be fixed before proceeding.

Now let's take a deeper look at the preliminary analysis step. Having broadly defined what it consists of, let's consider who does it and why.

The answer to the question "Who does it?" will vary from one project to another. It may be you or people working directly on the project. It may be done by other areas of your organization, such as a marketing department or a psychology department if you have access to such a service. It may be done by professional market researchers or specified as a task for your vendor. You'll need to look over your resources to determine the best approach to completing the analysis to serve your purpose.

But what is your purpose? Certainly you'll need to base the goals and objectives of the application on the analysis data, but there is even more to it than this. The analysis will provide you with a tool to prepare for all of the future phases and to determine directions for your team that will help guide their activities throughout the project. The analysis should provide a complete database of factors that affect the application. You need to review this database and determine its **implications** on the project.

Let's consider an example. Suppose your problem analysis for a corporate training application reveals that there are significant differences in procedures used in various regions of the country. By considering the implications at this stage, you can probably save a good deal of effort later. Several solutions might present themselves as you consider them.

- You could seek agreement among regions to revise the procedures to a common standard.

- You could design the application program to take different logical branches to cover the differences based on the user's specific region.

- You could tailor different presentations and release separate versions to each region.

Any area of preliminary analysis may bring up similar kinds of implications for the project. Audience analysis may indicate that more than one level of video scripting is needed to cover the requirement, and this would result in planning more than one version during video production. Environment analysis might uncover the need for special acoustical or lighting requirements that should be included in the original design of the delivery installation. By considering these implications before you get started, you can avoid costly rework later.

This completes the description of the preliminary analysis items. If you intend to send out one or more bids for design and development work to be done by an outside vendor, this information should accompany the Request For Proposal (RFP). The more information you give the prospective vendors, the better job they can do in estimating the cost, and proposing a treatment to meet the goals and objectives.

Conduct an Application Design Session

Notice that in all of the activity of preliminary analysis, you never asked your team to consider what topical content should be included in the application, or how it should be presented. Chances are, both you and your team had some initial thoughts about this, and came up with several new ideas as analysis progressed. Now the time has come to capitalize on these ideas, and identify the content of the application. Most likely, you'll also have to make some tough decisions on topics and approaches you won't be able to include due to limitations of resource. An excellent approach to this final analysis stage is to hold a formal meeting called an Application Design Session.

- **Conduct a formal Application Design Session with your team and other relevant participants.**

The Application Design Session should be one of the most exciting events in the entire project. Its purpose is to consolidate the analysis information, determine the content of the application, and begin to formulate an approach to high level design. If successful, it is a period of concentrated creativity that will provide the spark for the long task of design and development that follows.

As illustrated in Figure 5-3, this meeting forms a bridge between analysis activity and design. The analysis work leading up to it is rather quantitative and methodical. Once the basic approach to the application has been decided, the design work that follows is also an orderly process of making successively more detailed refinements to the documentation until the application can be produced. The "moment of creation" that occurs between these two phases is hard to observe, and is usually not addressed in standard instructional design models. It is just assumed to have happened after analysis based on some vague criteria such as "appropriate media to match the desired level of learner outcome." The Application Design Session replaces this with directed group activity based on accepted goals and

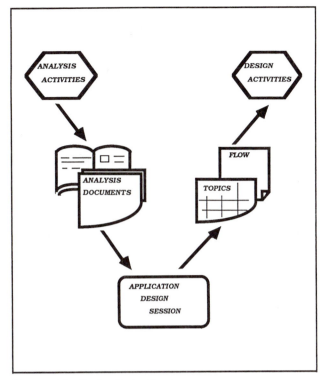

Figure 5-3 Application Design Session

objectives. Before we go into the mechanics of the session, however, let's consider a couple of reasonable alternatives. It sometimes happens in the analysis process that a short-circuit occurs — someone comes up with an idea that obviously meets the goals and objectives in an exciting way, everyone who hears it accepts it enthusiastically, and the design almost builds itself before your eyes. If this happens and your sponsor and development team are signed up, waste no time or resource on a formal Application Design Session. Charge right into the design phase and begin documenting the idea.

Another possibility is that you have gone out for competitive bids, received proposals back, and one among them is so well done and on the mark that you have accepted the vendor and the proposed treatment. The proposal has in effect **become** the high level design document, and if it meets your evaluation criteria for high level design (discussed in the next chapter), accept it and go. If, however, there is no general agreement as to the approach that should be taken, or even what should and should not be included in the final application, an Application Design Session can be a valuable activity. It should serve to flush out the existing ideas, generate new ones, insure that the approach chosen is responsive to the goals, and perhaps most importantly, get the whole team to sign up and take ownership of the application approach.

THE MEETING FORMAT

There are many possible approaches to an Application Design Session; we're going to suggest a formally structured approach that has worked well, and is especially suited to multimedia projects. It is a form of brainstorming session led by a Facilitator, a leader whose job it is to extract and record the ideas and consensus of the group. You may want to appoint a Facilitator from your staff, or even assume the role yourself. Or, you may prefer to obtain the services of a trained facilitator. In either case, here's our recommended approach. See Figure 5-4.

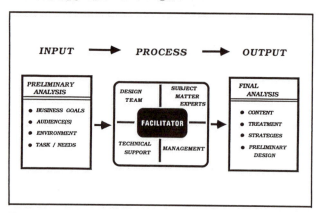

Figure 5-4 The Process of an Application Design Session

First, let's discuss who should attend. Select representatives from four key groups:

- Subject experts — to recommend/verify content,

- Technical experts — to verify feasibility,

- Sponsor representative — to insure goals are met,

- Design team — to understand goals and objectives.

The purpose of this group is first to complete Content Analysis, determining what topics are to be included in the application (and those that will be left out). Secondly, some preliminary ideas about how the topics will be approached are almost certain to evolve, and this statement of "treatment" will be documented.

The first order of business is to get the team working together in an atmosphere where ideas can flow freely. If some of the attendees are not familiar with interactive media technology, a demonstration by the technical experts may be a good starting point. Then, the group should review the work that has been done to this point in analysis. If market research was done, the results should be presented. The group should restate, and possibly expand upon the goals and objectives as seen by the Sponsor, the Host and the End User.

Here is a key point that demands your utmost attention. It is absolutely essential that the application you are about to implement will **satisfy all three parties** — the Sponsor, the Host and the End User. In a retail application, the Sponsor may want to sell more product, the End User may want comparative price information and the Host (store manager) may want to reduce sales staff. In a training application, the Sponsor may want to off-load expensive instructors, the End User (student) may want more individualized instruction, and the Host (training manager) may want to increase the student-day measurement. Some of these viewpoints may conflict. The first order of business in the Application Design Session is to insure that the stated goals and objectives fall in the area where all three viewpoints are satisfied.

IDENTIFYING THE AUDIENCE

One important result of this discussion is to identify all potential audiences represented in the End Users. The preliminary audience analysis may not have captured the full spectrum. For example, in training the audiences may include new students, reviewing students, researchers, instructors, etc. In marketing the audiences may include new customers, repeat customers, sales persons, managers, trainees, and so on. The list should be prioritized from the standpoint of each audience's value to the sponsor's goals. This prioritized list of possible audiences will be used later when we prioritize the content.

IDENTIFYING THE CONTENT

When the group has hashed out the basic goals and objectives, they should be getting to know each other pretty well. It's now time to move into a freewheeling kind of activity, identifying **possible** content. This is a brainstorming session where the group proposes **any** topics they can think of that would be relevant to supporting the goals and objectives. No practical considerations of complexity or system capacity need be applied. The result should be an unordered list of potential topics that **could** be included in the final application.

The next step is to "test" the topics for applicability to the project. Each topic proposed is discussed for a short, fixed amount of time. The topic is to be approached as if it were the **only** topic on the videodisc with no "practical" constraints at all. How could the topic be presented? What kind of user interactions would be designed? The purpose of this activity is to find out which of the topics seem to have rich possibilities, and which seem to be difficult to visualize and implement. This general "feel" for the topics will be used as input to the prioritization process, and quite often there will be some surprises. Topics that appeared dull on the surface may yield exciting approaches, while those that seemed promising may die on the vine.

Now the focus of the group needs to be changed from visual/creative activities to logical analysis. The list of topics now needs to be put in order of priority. Having discussed each topic, the group should have a better idea of how well each topic fits the goals and objectives, and whether it is appropriate to the media. The topic list can be broken down into four categories:

- Those that **must** be done,

- Those that would be done if resources permit,

- Those better done in another medium,

- Those better not done at all.

IDENTIFYING THE PRESENTATIONS

At this point, we have the information we need to select the topics that will actually be included in the application. We previously prepared a prioritized list of audiences. This list and the prioritized list of topics are used to construct a matrix as shown in Figure 5-5. Each cell of the matrix represents a potential presentation tailored for a specific audience. The cells in the upper left corner represent presentations for the highest priority topics for the most valuable audience segments. The cells in the lower right corner are the least valuable topics and audiences. Presentations in the other two quadrants are in the middle, and can be prioritized by emphasizing the audience addressed or the topical content.

By working from the upper left to lower right, the group can identify a set of presentations that are prioritized according to the goals, objectives and audience types previously agreed upon. The matrix may also suggest certain approaches that will save resources. For example, it may be noted that a certain presentation would serve both reviewers and researchers, or that a customer presentation could be converted to a sales trainee presentation with only a few additions.

Now the prioritized list of topic presentations can be examined to see how much of it can be practically included within the system and development resources. If you plan to use videodisc, each side holds less than 30 minutes of motion video, and this material costs from hundreds to thousands of dollars per

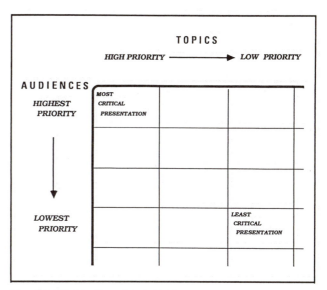

Figure 5-5 The Audience/Topic Matrix

minute to produce, depending on the quality of production. You may be able to include more topics by using less expensive media, such as video still frames, second track audio or graphics and audio stored on CD-ROM. Nevertheless, it is likely that it won't **all** fit, and you'll have to draw a line somewhere on the list. When you've done this, Content Analysis is complete.

It's typical of an Application Design Session that a lot of enthusiasm and momentum are built up. Therefore, it is often a good idea to follow through with a first cut at the preliminary design. This will probably be a high level flowchart showing the basic structure of a hierarchical design, or the general sequence of a linear/branching program, etc. It will provide a good starting point for the design team to proceed with more detailed design in the next phase.

In summary, you have gone through an exercise in the Application Design Session that has produced Content Analysis in the form of a prioritized list of presentation topics. Hopefully, this has been a team effort where all have been able to see the list develop, and why it is the way it is. The prioritization will be of tremendous value in subsequent phases as decisions are made to concentrate resource and expense on individual parts of the application. You have now achieved the firm foundation for design that you sought when you began the Analysis Phase.

TREATMENT IDEAS

When we began the discussion of the Application Design Session, we mentioned that one of its purposes was to develop some ideas about possible "treatments" of the content.

If you have a background in video, the term is probably familiar. Basically, a treatment is a general narrative of the approach to be taken to the topic. It would cover such items as the visual content, the characters, the story line, the themes and sub-themes to be developed. For example, one treatment of an application whose objective is to explain the workings of the stock market might propose the use of stock footage of American industry and the Stock Exchange interspersed with scenes of a new customer in a broker's office. Another designer might suggest using the metaphor of starting up a lemonade stand in the style of an "Our Gang" comedy as a treatment for the same subject.

Selection of treatment is often the first step in design. It comes up here because it is characteristic of the discussions during an Application Design Session to spend a lot of time on possible treatments of the topics. As the participants become more familiar with each other, the creative synergy builds, and it's not uncommon to see the major treatment approach develop out of such a session. The Facilitator should be poised to encourage these discussions when they occur, and should have a special board or flipchart ready to record these "useful tangents" to the main business of Content Analysis. The ideas suggested may spark the design team and provide the treatment that will knit together the whole application.

As we'll see later in the design phase, the treatment concept applies at each level of the application. As the general design is broken down into specific activities, the designer must select an approach, or **"micro-treatment,"** for each activity. Therefore, any treatment idea is welcome during the Application Design Session. Even if it is not adapted as the major theme of the application, the idea or a variation of it may serve to make a particular presentation come alive.

When we began this section we started by saying that the Application Design Session formed a bridge between analysis and design. Note that we started by conducting a formal Content Analysis, and we have ended by focusing on design issues of treatment and structure. We know **what** we're going to do, **why** we're doing it, and have some good general ideas about **how** we're going to do it. If you have accomplished all of this, you have gotten maximum mileage out of the Analysis Phase, and you can be sure that your project has started out well.

Publish an Application Description Document

- **Publish an Application Description Document that states the preliminary analysis conclusions and the results of the Content Analysis.**

At this point, you should have all the information to complete documentation for the Analysis Phase. The Application Description Document should present all the preliminary analysis including additions and modifications made during the Application Design Session. Content Analysis is added as well.

The deliverable item for the Analysis Phase is:

The Application Description Document

1. A statement of the Sponsor's application goals.

2. A narrative of the general approach or treatment.

3. A statement of End User objectives and/or benefits.

4. A description of the audience(s) to be addressed.

5. A task or needs analysis for the target audience(s).

6. A description of the delivery system environment.

7. A prioritized list of the application content topics.

The Application Description Document will play a prominent role during the rest of the development activity. A major theme in this book is that the Project Manager must maintain a two-way view whenever a decision relating to the application is required. This perspective is illustrated in Figure 5-6.

- Look backward to insure that the decision is in accord with the application goals and objectives.

- Look ahead to insure that the decision will be easy to implement in all subsequent phases.

The Application Description Document will provide the basis for all project activity from here on out.

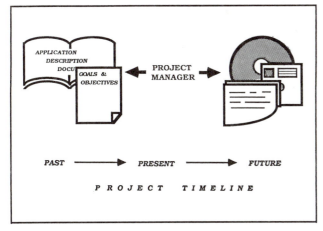

Figure 5-6 The Two-Way Perspective of the Project Manager

Evaluate the Analysis Phase Work Products

• **Apply the checklist criteria to the Application Description Document to evaluate the Analysis Phase**

Now is the time to go off by yourself and review the progress of the team up to this point. We've provided the checklists as a tool to help. As Project Manager, the buck stops with you, and it is your responsibility to make the decision to proceed into the design phase. We've made every effort to keep the checklists as brief and simple as possible. No matter what your training or background, phase approval should be based on your own common sense. There is no way for your team to have covered every element of analysis, or to have answered every question that might arise, but your job is to determine to your satisfaction that the major bases are covered, and you have provided a solid foundation for the design work to come.

The checklists are contained in Appendix A in the Resource Section. This is a good time to take a look at the checklist for the Analysis Phase. You may want to apply them now to a project you're working on, or one you have in mind.

An effective way to use the checklist is to check off those items about which you can make a positive response. Otherwise, use the comment section to document your thoughts on why the item doesn't apply, or why you feel you can proceed without checking off the item. If you have detected a problem, follow the general procedure found at the bottom of each checklist.

Obtain Sponsor Signoff

• **Obtain sponsor signoff on the Application Description Document**

As a final step in this phase, and in the phases to follow, check with your sponsor and obtain a signoff on the analysis documentation. If the sponsor had a representative who participated in the Application Design Session, this task should be easier. At any rate, make sure the sponsor knows where you're going, and agrees that if you accomplish what you say, his or her goals will be met.

This completes the activities in the Analysis Phase. Order in a nice cream cake for the team, and congratulate yourselves on a job well done.

A Last Word

In the real world, the analysis phase is usually performed in a cursory manner. Almost everyone will give lip service to its value and necessity, but rarely will they actually spend the time and effort that it deserves. The key reasons for this are that everyone is impatient, and everyone assumes they have the same understanding as to what is to be accomplished. As a Project Manager, you will be subject to the same pressure and assumptions. However, it's your responsibility to determine how much of the project's time and resources will be spent in analysis. If the results of the project must satisfy people other than yourself, or if the scope of the project is so large that many individuals must work on it as a team, then time spent in analysis will pay for itself many times over.

There is, however, another side to the coin. It's quite possible to spend **too much** time analyzing the problem. There is always more information that can be gathered about tasks and audiences, but the time will come when enough is a feast. As Project Manager, you should be on the lookout for a reluctance to leave the analysis process and get on with the project. When this happens, the probable cause is indecision about how to proceed with design. A common symptom is to find the team creating "flow-charts" that are really organizing the information content instead of specifying how the user will interact with the application.

If you see your project stalled in analysis, the remedy is to force the team into the design activities that we will discuss in the next chapter. Even if the first efforts are not satisfactory, it is easier to modify an existing design than it is to create it in the first place.

In summary, make the Analysis Phase the foundation of your project. Make sure you and your team have a clear picture of what you are going to accomplish. When the picture is clear enough, then move on to the Design Phase with confidence that your project is on the right track.

PART THREE

Construction

After securing the sponsor's commitment and analyzing the multiple requirements, you're ready for the next level of detail, constructing the application. This multi-stage process includes:

- designing the treatment, flows, and strategies,

- developing the detailed documentation,

- producing the audio, video, text, and graphics,

- authoring and integrating these media elements, and

- validating the finished product.

This section is divided into five chapters, one for each of these major construction activities:

We'll elaborate and guide you through each of these phases using our project development model. During each phase, we'll provide examples and explanations of the team activities, end products, the evaluation process, and phase checklists. As you successfully complete the deliverables for each step, they become input to the next phase; when you successfully complete all these phases, the application will be ready for implementation.

Chapter Six

Designing the Application

Preview of the Design Phase

Although each phase contributes to the overall success of the project, design plays the critical role. Design activities result in the most significant changes during the project. At the start of this phase, you have a description of the application; at the end, you have a blueprint for the rest of the work. Design moves you from **what** needs to be done to **how** it should be done. Design decisions determine the final "look and feel" of the application.

During this phase you'll find the vendor activities exciting and different. Their responsibilities include structuring all the individual presentation events into logical schemes, experimenting with alternative treatment ideas, choosing the appropriate media for each segment, and planning interactive strategies. Expect several iterations and a few friendly disagreements until everyone finally agrees on the "look" and then documents it.

Your management responsibilities will also be interesting and challenging. You have to decide if the "blueprint" meets the original objectives and can be accomplished within the budget and schedule. To assist you in this effort, we've provided two evaluation instruments: (1) a comprehensive checklist to insure all components of the design document are in place, (2) a series of design assessment matrices to verify that the emphasis is in the right place. These management tools will help you decide when the design is ready for development.

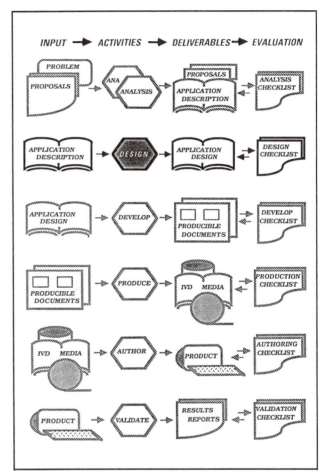

Figure 6-1 IVD Development Phases

Looking Over the Territory

What We're Trying to Accomplish

The primary purpose of all design activity is to transform the descriptive factors from analysis into a structured, unified plan for development. During analysis the project team has collected the necessary data, but it's unorganized. It's ready to be designed. The process is usually divided into two sub-stages: high-level design and detail design.

If you think about all the analysis data as captured on index cards (actually, not a bad idea), then high-level design's task is to arrange the index cards into logical groupings. Detail design tasks would then specify the treatment, media, or interactions for an individual card (event). Of course, there's a little more to design than arranging index cards. We've outlined the design deliverables in Figure 6-2. Study them for a moment.

As you can see from the outline, the completed Application Design Document represents a comprehensive, critical, and centralized reference for the rest of the project. Although the summarized analysis data may already be documented, it must be reviewed by new design team members. Those factors establish the criteria for all design decisions. High-level design provides the overall context; detail

53

design describes the strategies for each major application event.

When this documentation is collected, it represents the first complete view of the entire application—its look, its feel, its options. You need to secure agreement and commitment to this design plan from the sponsor, the vendors, and project team members. This design document also represents a significant investment in time and creativity. Changes to the design can be costly, but better now than later!

Now, let's walk through the steps of the design process.

Deliverables from the Design Phase

The end product of the varied design activities is a Design Document. It's a consolidation of the Analysis Description, High Level Design, and Detail Design. While your documentation may not be assembled into these three distinct sections, you should insure that all the elements shown in Figure 6-2 are present or considered.

So What's New?

Design is different.

On the surface, Design is just one more phase in the project. As our model shows, it's the bridge be-

tween Analysis and Development, that is, the process to move from a description of the application to its documentation. However, once you begin this phase, you'll realize that design is different. Where analysis asks: who? what? when? where? and why?, design asks: how? Where analysis is scientific, design is artistic. Where analysis takes things apart, design puts them back together into a structured set of specifications. To build this description-to-documentation bridge, your team may need new members with varied backgrounds: visual artists, writers, users, and subject matter experts. They'll have tools, terms, and techniques unique to their discipline. As a team, however, they must generate and consolidate the right plan for this project. In the process, you should anticipate floods of wild ideas and droughts of treatments. You should expect and foster their multiple viewpoints; they can enhance the application's final design.

The differences extend beyond processes and people. Interactive multimedia itself has its own distinctions. When compared to traditional development projects, you must now consider different design approaches:

- beyond a single medium to multiple (concurrent) media;

- beyond a single treatment to multi-layered strategies;

- beyond a single designer/developer to a team effort;

- beyond passive presentations to active user involvement;

- beyond single linear paths to multi-option sequences.

The design phase is where you'll feel most removed, most unproductive, and most out of control. It's the phase where you must stay completely involved.

Design is different; design makes the difference.

How Do We Get There?

In true design terms, "how" do you manage this phase? The road map in Figure 6-3 is our design for Design.

- Assess the design skills of the current project team and identify where additional expertise may be required. Recruit or contract for these design services.

SUMMARIZED ANALYSIS DATA

1. A complete statement of the problem or opportunity

2. Application goals and objectives (sponsor's and end user's)

3. Design parameters and constraints

4. Content analysis documentation

HIGH - LEVEL DESIGN DOCUMENTATION (FOR THE APPLICATION)

1. Content outline of the major topics

2. High-level logic flow for the application

3. General approach or treatments for the application

4. Authoring Facility -- selection , capabilities , limitations

DETAIL DESIGN DOCUMENTATION (FOR EACH PRESENTATION)

1. Expanded content outlines for topics and sub-topics

2. Logic flows connecting each specific presentation event

3. Detail description of micro-treatments , characters , and content

4. Strategy statements for media , motivation , sequence , interaction , adult learning , and evaluation

5. Preliminary estimates for :
   > user time on system
   > disc layout by time and topic
   > media allocation

Figure 6-2 The Application Design Document

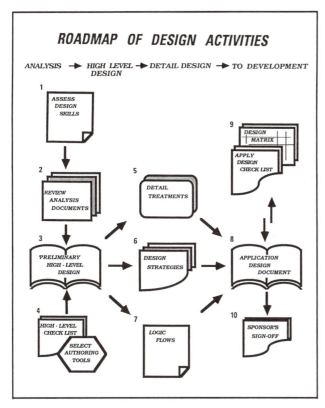

ROADMAP OF DESIGN ACTIVITIES

ANALYSIS → HIGH LEVEL → DETAIL DESIGN → TO DEVELOPMENT
DESIGN

1 ASSESS DESIGN SKILLS

2 REVIEW ANALYSIS DOCUMENTS

3 PRELIMINARY HIGH-LEVEL DESIGN

4 HIGH-LEVEL CHECK LIST / SELECT AUTHORING TOOLS

5 DETAIL TREATMENTS

6 DESIGN STRATEGIES

7 LOGIC FLOWS

8 APPLICATION DESIGN DOCUMENT

9 DESIGN MATRIX / APPLY DESIGN CHECK LIST

10 SPONSOR'S SIGN-OFF

Figure 6-3 Roadmap of Design Activities

- Assemble the newly formed design team to restate the project's objectives and review the Application Description Document, including any design ideas from previous brainstorming sessions. Secure agreement on the goals, objectives, and directions.

- Complete the High-Level (preliminary) Design Documentation. It contains general approaches, directions, and guidelines for the detail design work. Select the Authoring Facility.

- Apply the High-Level Design Checklist against this "design." Using this preliminary documentation as a guide, the design team develops detailed treatments, strategies, and logic.

- Create and document the design treatments for the application. These include the themes and activities that carry the content.

- For each major episode, consider and document the application strategies: media, interaction, motivation, sequence, adult learning, and evaluation.

- Arrange the individual segments into a logic flow for the user. Walk through all the possible options.

- Consolidate the treatments, strategies, and logic flows into the Application Design Document.

- Apply the design matrices and the design checklists to evaluate the application for completeness, allocation of resources, and alignment with the original objectives. (Recognize that you may need to execute steps 4 through 8 multiple times.) Secure the agreement and commitment of the project team members.

- Obtain sponsor signoff on the Application Design Document.

The remainder of this chapter elaborates on these ten steps.

Managing the High-Level Design Process

The first three activities in the process make up High-Level Design. Its purpose is to set the gross boundaries of the application and develop a general plan for the detail work. Although the plan is general, it has specific requirements. For this reason we've built in a mid-phase evaluation and a High-Level Design Checklist.

As we describe these various design activities, be aware of the different roles and responsibilities. Vendors or team members do the actual design work; you monitor, manage, and encourage. Once the design is documented, you take a more active role in the evaluation of their end products.

Assess Design Skills

Your first management task is to evaluate the capabilities of the current project team. The vendors or team members who conducted and documented the analysis may not have the right skill mix for design. They performed the analytical who, what, when, where, and why; they may not be prepared for the visionary "how."

The critical criterion for design is visual imagination. It is the ability to take the facts from analysis and translate them into visual scenes, stories, sequences, and strategies. Without this capability, the application suffers. If your team doesn't possess these skills, buy them. It will make the difference. These new team members may have some familiar names. Their roles and responsibilities during the design phase are:

- Writers ... to suggest story lines and scripts,

- Authors ... to introduce system capabilities,

- Artists ... to visually paint graphics and scenes,

- Designers ... to logically arrange instructional patterns and informational sequences.

Once you've assessed the current team's capabilities and recruited the missing design skills, you can reconvene the group. Before they begin designing, conduct a review of the sponsor's goals, the application's objectives, and the project's constraints. You may also want to summarize the minutes of prior planning sessions and share the phases/deliverables of our IVD Model. After you provide copies of the analysis documentation, the leadership of the group shifts to the application designer.

2

Review Analysis Documents

This is a preparation step for the shift to visual imagination mode. Through group discussions and individual study of the analysis documents, the design team agrees on the intent, directions, and boundaries of the application. In addition, you want to insure shared mindsets and terminology. Once this common background is established, design can begin.

Some design ideas and treatments may already be available from previous content analysis sessions. New ideas will occur during this analysis review. These are valuable and they should be reviewed and recorded. However, the guideline at this point is to

> **Note.** Timing of this analysis review may vary depending on a sole-source versus bid method approach to the application development. Recall with a sole-source approach, the vendor has been actively involved in all the analysis steps (including the Application Design Session). In the bid method, however, vendors have not shared in all the fine points. The selected vendor and any new design members must revisit this analysis data in greater detail. In either case, you must assure a common understanding among all team members prior to the documentation of the High-Level Design.

remain fluid. Suspend judgment. Don't commit to a detailed plan too early.

You will note that parts of our High-Level Design checklist reference both design content and proposal administration.

3

Create the High-Level Design Work Products

Once the analysis review is done, the newly-formed team can begin the High-Level Design. Let's look at this step from three perspectives: the deliverables, design activities, and your evaluation process.

DELIVERABLES

The end product for this stage includes:

- A more refined statement of the business and/or instructional goals, the analysis data, and general application objectives.

- A Preliminary Design Plan. This plan presents the vendor's initial concept or approach to the project. Although the presentation form may vary from vendor to vendor, you should look for three key items:

  - The Structure of the Application. This depicts the paths, options, sequences, and how the end-user will access the content. Often the structure is illustrated with flowcharts or diagrams of the application's major topics.

  - The Application Treatment. It describes the "look" and types of activities presented to the end-user including themes, story lines, characters, settings, and menus. These may be illustrated with sample scripts, storyboards, and artistic renderings.

  - Application Strategies. They describe the vendor's approach to critical aspects of the content. These areas include motivation techniques, media usage, user interactivity, and evaluation methods.

- A Description of all Delivery System Configurations.

- A Description of Administrative Requirements. These include preliminary estimates of budgets, schedules, personnel resources, and authoring facilities.

DESIGN ACTIVITIES — Making the Creative Leap

Just as the documentation can vary from vendor to vendor, their design activities usually take different routes. Team members bring their own unique methods, skills and discipline to the design effort for this application. The creative process is difficult to predict; it's even more difficult to direct. From your perspective, here are a few guidelines:

- Time invested in design pays dividends in later phases. Allocate time accordingly.

- The team must generate, select, and apply design ideas for the treatments, strategies, and content structure. Activities will include: brainstorming, role playing, sketching, borrowing and combining ideas from other sources. Encourage and foster this creativity.

- Some design possibilities, priorities and the primary audience came out of the earlier content analysis sessions. Make them available to the design group.

- IVD/multimedia applications need themes or connections that are powerful enough to carry the entire application with all of its different presentation possibilities. Be looking for that continuity.

- Finally, be aware of the wrong turns and side tracks that can misdirect the design (and the application):

  - Considering too few alternatives or viewpoints. Keep ideas (visual and verbal) on separate index cards or computer outline processors that can be easily moved around to try new combinations. Don't document the design too soon.

  - Forgetting the end-user, application environment, or the original objectives. This analysis data is documented and available, but it can get lost during the design process.

  - Proposing treatments beyond reasonable time frames or budgetary constraints.

  - Failing to capitalize on the integration of media. Depending on team member skills, a single medium can dominate the application design.

Evaluation of the High-Level Design

During the design process, your primary responsibility was encouragement. Now it shifts to evaluation. As with most phases, you must strike a balance between business goals and creative directions. Remember, you are representing the sponsor, the end-user, and the site/location managers.

The main purpose of this mid-phase checkpoint is to ensure a solid foundation and framework for the detail work that follows. You have a series of evaluation steps and tools for this activity. It may be helpful to think about a current project during this section. We'll walk through the process by posing several questions that you should be asking.

- "Does this design meet our original objectives?"

The analysis data describes the environment, audiences, tasks, and objectives. Does the design plan consider all these factors? Evaluate the proposals from three perspectives: sponsor, end-user, and administrator. Put yourself in their positions as you weigh the ideas. The High-Level Design should restate the business goals and **how** it plans to meet them.

- "Does this design match our application priorities?"

The content analysis identified the primary audience and the critical presentations for them. Our matrix showed the application's emphasis and direction. Now you must evaluate the design plan against that criteria. You're looking for the degree of alignment with the previously documented content priority and selection.

- "Is this design plan complete and ready for detail work?"

In addition to its administrative components, the design proposal must document the structure, story line, and strategies for the application. Each of these must be complete enough to guide the detail design activities. Structure should organize the major topics; story line should carry the major themes; strategies should show implementation of media, motivation, and interaction.

Require flow diagrams, sample illustrations, visual walkthroughs, and prototypes from the vendors to assist you with this part of the evaluation.

• "Can this design be accomplished with our resources?"

One measure of the structure, story line, and strategies is the resources required to implement them. If the high-level design is complete, your vendors should be able to estimate the time, costs, and personnel needed to make it happen. You can then match these estimates to your schedule, budget, and staff.

Naturally, if any of the preceding checkpoint items are incomplete, apply the "what's wrong" procedure on the bottom of each checklist:

• specify the missing or inaccurate item;

• identify the sources of misunderstanding;

• allocate the resources required to fix the situation.

Keep a log of this re-design activity, and make sure you keep your team informed of your interest. If this project is under a bid method, you may be evaluating several high-level design proposals (and vendor presentations).

Note. Checklists for evaluating the high-level design activity are located in the Resource Section, Appendix A. Turn to them now, and look them over. Imagine yourself at this point in a forthcoming project, alone and asking these questions. Your common sense should lead you to make a sound evaluation. When you're done, return here.

Selecting the Authoring Facility

Another important High-Level Design activity is choosing the authoring facility. Your options include general purpose languages, IVD authoring languages or systems, timeline processors, application shells, and hypermedia generators. The capabilities of these different facilities are described in Chapter 9, "Authoring." It will help you with this decision. But, why make the choice now? First of all, there may not be much of a decision to make. Your organization may already be committed to a particular authoring facility for other applications. The vendor may prefer a certain facility based upon the skill level and experience of their personnel. In any case, you must know the strengths and weaknesses of the authoring facility **before** detail design work begins. You cannot

afford to invest valuable time and effort into design ideas that are difficult or impossible to implement.

We are not suggesting that the authoring facility should dictate the application's treatment. Rather, you should recognize these facilities as resources with capabilities and restrictions. Just as you don't have an unlimited budget or unlimited time, a "do-it-all" authoring facility does not exist. By knowing the strengths and weaknesses now, designers can create alternate strategies around the limitations and capitalize on any unique strengths.

Part of our High-Level Design Checklist covers the selection of the application's authoring facility. If you are already familiar with these different facilities, take a look at these checklist items now; otherwise, you may want to wait until you've studied Chapter 9.

Managing the Detail Design Process

Once you have team agreement and sponsor sign-offs for the high-level plan, the detail design work can begin. Your role now shifts from evaluating back to encouraging. The design team will again be employing creative techniques to generate specific strategies, story lines, and sequences. The major difference in this process is tighter boundaries. Any new design ideas must fit within the high-level master plan, the selected treatment, and the authoring facility's capabilities.

On the design road map we've shown these detail activities as three serial steps: detail treatments, design strategies, and logic flows. This is for explanation purposes only. During design, these activities may happen simultaneously, randomly, or iteratively. Depending on the division of labor, design assignments, or personal preferences, the group process will vary each time. Your concern should be with the end product: the Application Design Document. During detail design, the vendors generate specific ideas, incorporate them into the plan, and create a development blueprint. Let's observe this design process from your management perspective: activities performed, terminology used, and the deliverables. Your critical question during this phase should be: "how does this detail contribute to the larger application design?"

5

Detail Design—Treatments

SUPPORTING THE MAIN THEME

We've initially defined a treatment as the "look and feel" of the application. During high-level design, your vendors documented a major theme or story to carry the application's message; during detail design, that theme must be completely developed. Each separate module and event in the application should contribute to the major theme, like the chapters of a book or the acts in a play.

However, detail documentation of the treatment extends beyond the main theme. It also includes the elements of the application that support, reinforce, and complement that treatment: role models, scenes, choice of language, menu options, and props. For each application segment, these factors must be considered, integrated, and documented. In short, they must be designed.

For example:

- Role models and characters should match the audiences that your previous analysis identified.

- Scenes and settings should support locations that your specific audiences will recognize or find familiar.

- Choice of language and conversations should be scripted differently for each audience type.

- Menu options should be meaningful to every potential user (customers, trainees, or sales).

INTERACTIVE FORMATS

Our method of extending high-level treatments down to the detail level is to break them into specific structures we call **interactive formats** to accomplish a specific application objective. For instance, one aspect of an application might be carried out through a demonstration, while another might be better done via a metaphor.

Think of an "interactive format" as a method or language that a multimedia designer employs to converse with the application users. Sometimes the system is in charge of the conversation, presenting information to the user in a mostly one-way exchange. Other times, the user is in control, requesting information and manipulating the system according to his or her own wishes. In either case, however, interactive formats add power to the designer's ability to carry a message. They work better than words or pictures alone. They are the designer's technique of putting the content into an appropriate context to deliver a specific message.

Formats can vary from the simple to the complex. Simple formats are primarily system controlled. They are straightforward to design and easy to produce. They are basically designed to present information in an effective way. Their drawback is that, unless the presentation is especially memorable, the user may not reach a level of understanding of the message that leads to long term retention. More complex formats tend to place the system at the service of the user, and the user in control of the "conversation." Such formats demand more of the designer, require more programming and logic in the system, and are probably more expensive to produce. Their advantage lies in the increase of user involvement and the higher likelihood of understanding and remembering the message.

Here is a list of interactive formats, loosely organized in an ascending hierarchy of complexity:

- Exposition …

  presenting the content through words or media with minimal intervention from the user.

- Tutorial …

  a structured series of presentations, questions, feedback and remediation.

- Drill/Practice …

  an organized set of activities or exercises that users can try, test and review until satisfied.

- Demonstration/Example …

  showing real-world artifacts, situations, operations and procedures that serve as models or incentives for the viewer.

- Metaphor …

  representation of concepts that can't be demonstrated or are especially complex with more simple, familiar and often, more entertaining illustrations or dramatizations.

- Inquiry …

  user initiated searches into glossaries, visual or information data bases, and other application materials.

- Case Study …

  a multi-faceted problem situation that builds on previous decisions, actions and materials.

- Games ...

  user participation in realistic or metaphorical situations, in a competitive environment with attainable rewards.

- Interviews ...

  users engage in a more or less free form conversation with one or more experts.

- Simulation ...

  users manipulate an environment provided by the system that responds close to the same way that the real-world environment would to the user actions.

Naturally, each episode in the application may employ a different format or a mix of formats, as long as they complement the overall treatment and achieve that presentation's objective. It's up to the designer to select the format for each presentation. It's up to you to be sure that you are comfortable with the approach. The message must be communicated, but the cost must be reasonable. Simple formats often carry effective messages. Not every presentation requires complex interactivity. On the other hand, a slow paced "page turner" may not be worth the money to produce it at all. Here is a place where you must rely on your own common sense to review the designer's work and make sure the project is on track.

6

Detail Design—Strategies

In addition to a treatment elaboration into interactive formats, detail design work includes documenting the IVD/multimedia strategies. These are the specific techniques to achieve the "look" and "feel" of the application—the methods to bring each treatment to life. If you focus on a single episode for a moment, its format is the detailed treatment to carry the message; its strategies are designed to support that treatment.

We have identified six key strategies for interactive multimedia applications:

- Media selection,

- Motivation,

- Interaction,

- Sequence or structure,

- Adult learning,

- Evaluation.

Although your vendors may not separate and document these six specific strategies, you need to insure that each factor is considered.

In explaining these six strategies, our intent is not to make you a designer, but rather to make you aware of the critical components that make a difference. They are the key factors that will help you evaluate the product that your designers have produced. We'll introduce these six strategies now and provide some new assessment tools for you at the end of the chapter. Again, we've separated them for discussion and evaluation purposes; in the final product, they are interwoven into a seamless series of presentations.

MEDIA SELECTION

Media is the most obvious detail strategy to be designed. The hardware offers such a rich set of alternatives and combinations (video, audio, graphics, text, and sound) that a media allocation plan must be established. Every presentation can not be, and indeed should not be, full motion video with stereo sound. Conversely, everything should not be a screen full of words to read. Depending on the selected formats, you'll probably have a mix of media for each presentation.

A media selection strategy must allocate resources to each of the application's presentations. Some choices include:

- Broadcast quality motion video,

- Industrial quality motion video,

- High quality computer graphics (possibly animated),

- Audio Segments (CD or videodisc second track, usually to be used with computer graphics),

- Video Still Frames (photographs, artwork, video graphics),

- Graphics digitized from video input,

- Computer text screens.

Part of this decision hinges on presentation value, part hinges on resource constraints. We'll have some tools at the end of the chapter to help you evaluate these media decisions. There are some additional budgetary considerations in Chapter 12.

MOTIVATION STRATEGIES

Motivation is the detail strategy designed to capture and hold the user's attention. How do you keep customers or learners interested and involved in the content? How do you maintain their desire to continue with an application to its logically designed end points? They don't have to stay; motivation strategies make them want to stay.

Motivation is a subtle quality. If the users are highly motivated, the application will probably succeed with any technique; if they are not, the most innovative design will likely be insufficient. Motivation comes in two flavors. The first has to do with the needs that come from the users themselves, "intrinsic motivation." For example: job advancement, desire for a product, or natural interest in the subject matter. The second type is outside the user, "extrinsic motivation." This is the kind of motivation that must be designed into the presentations.

Similar to the media alternatives and combinations, many techniques are available to accomplish your motivational strategy. Some are more costly than others, and some are more effective than others. The choices will depend upon the resources available and the presentation's requirements. You should not expect every segment to employ a unique motivational technique, but the designers should plan and document how they will motivate the user. They should consider, and you should look for, these approaches:

*   Fantasy ...

    creating a vicarious experience in which the user can participate.

*   Role models ...

    depicting a desired behavior in a way that the user is encouraged to emulate.

*   Reward ...

    providing an interesting, entertaining, or satisfying activity after the user has achieved the desired result.

*   Challenge ...

    creating a game-like situation in which the user competes with the system. (This challenge may or may not be directly related to the subject matter.)

*   Curiosity ...

    causing discontinuity by presenting some unfamiliar, surprising, or puzzling (but not confusing) event that encourages further pursuit of the topic.

It's also possible to increase user motivation by using media techniques that have high entertainment or interest value. These approaches may be necessary in a marketing environment, for example, if the application is contending for attention with surrounding distractions. Some motivational media techniques include:

*   High video production value ...

    using exciting video effects like those seen on commercial television.

*   Location shooting ...

    setting the presentations in real or simulated attractive environments.

*   Face-recognition talent ...

    employing well-recognized personalities to endorse the application's message.

*   Animation...

    using one of several automated and artist-created techniques that are available (and that cost from $6000 to $40,000 per finished minute).

*   Puppetry and "claymation" ...

    gaining attention and delivering a message with humor and high interest.

INTERACTIVITY

Interactive strategies are the techniques designed to encourage active participation and involvement with the application. A useful analogy is a two-way conversation where either party may question, answer, explain, react, or interrupt. During any part of the application, users may want help, directions, clarification, or simply a review. The system's recognition and responses to these user-initiated requests make up an interactive strategy. Interactivity can complement your motivation strategies by providing a more varied experience for the users. While you should avoid interactions for interaction's sake and the mindless "touch to continue" approach, do capitalize on the system's capabilities and the power of IVD to actively involve the user, both physically and mentally.

The selection and mix of interactive techniques can affect the quality and appearance of the final product, but there are cost considerations. The more sophisticated techniques require more complex logic, therefore more programming, and in general, more media events to support them. This list of interactive strategies is in descending order of sophistication:

- Simulation ...

  designing the application to react to user input exactly as a real-world system would.

- Direction ...

  adapting user activities, options, and paths based on previous performance or selections.

- Input/Feedback ...

  accepting varied user inputs, analyzing them, and presenting intelligent responses.

- Selection ...

  allowing user choice of topics, presentation format, or input method through menu options.

- Pacing...

  providing mechanisms or information that give users control over the presentation's pace.

- Interruption...

  allowing users to interrupt, redirect, repeat, or resume presentations at any time. Usually this capability is provided by the Authoring Facility's Presentation System.

SEQUENCE/STRUCTURE

This strategy maps out how users will travel through the application—its paths, options, and signposts. The actual geography is documented in the logic flowchart, but the philosophy is established here. Some of the general structuring decisions include:

- Branching ...

  number of alternate, remedial, or enrichment options.

- Mobility ...

  amount of freedom to move around the application.

- Modularity...

  how many segments and how big.

- Hierarchical structure...

  number of levels from the top to the bottom.

- Orientation ...

method of providing a sense of location in the overall structure.

The complexity of multimedia designs and the need for the user to stay in control demand a structuring strategy. These are some of the designs that your vendors may be discussing. The list is arranged in approximate order of logical complexity — which can affect programming costs as well as the number and type of media events.

- Simulation...

  application logic follows the structure of the simulated system. This often requires an authoring or general-purpose language to accommodate its complexity.

- Network ...

  allows users to access other information related to the present display by following author-provided links. Each display is linked to several others, and the user may browse through the entire set without following author-prescribed paths. (This approach is often called "hypermedia structure.")

- Criterion-referenced ...

  requires an evaluation strategy to determine if the user has achieved a level of competence before continuing with more advanced segments.

- Advance organizers ...

  precede major topics by short introductory presentations that provide a structure or an overview for the ensuing information. They require extra development and production, but the material can be reused in the body of the presentation.

- Linear/branching ...

  structures are basically linear, with side branches based on user input, usually designed for elaboration, remediation, or user-selected presentations.

- Open hierarchy ...

  allows users to directly access other paths wherever they are in the presentation logic.

- Closed hierarchy ...

  requires users to choose other paths by retracing the current path until they reach a choice frame or menu that offers the new path.

ADULT LEARNING STRATEGIES

If your application is planned for adult audiences, your design should take into account the research findings that have identified the approaches to learning that adults prefer. These findings conclude that adults:

- are psychologically ready to control their activities,

- are problem focused (rather than subject centered),

- have experiences to build upon or reference,

- can diagnose and pace their own progress.

Application designers should be aware of these factors and create their activities accordingly. Some related design strategies are listed below. Once again, you must balance their value against the time and cost to develop them.

- Alternate media ...

  present the same information in different media to help different people learn better or process information better. This strategy suggests giving users their choice of a delivery medium. The cost is multiple development of the topics.

- Progress validation ...

  allows a sense of accomplishments that is important to adult learning. One strategy is to provide voluntary quizzes or checkpoints so they can assess their progress without a feeling of being tested by "the system." (Naturally, if the application is criterion-referenced or for certification, these checks may be required.)

- Positioning ...

  provides a mechanism for users to establish where they are, what's already completed, and how much remains.

- Experience recognition ...

  takes account of user's background by including prerequisite tests to assess appropriate starting points and presentation treatments for each audience.

- Free user controls ...

  provide mechanisms for controlling the presentation that most adults prefer. Choices are always available to review, scan, repeat, interrupt, or access optional material. The "side trips" are easy to execute and return to the main presentation.

EVALUATION STRATEGIES

These assessment strategies complement your interaction techniques, but more from the system's perspective. How do you recognize, assess, and respond to a user's input—planned or unplanned? Designers should answer three general questions about the evaluation process:

- Is the evaluation voluntary or required?

- How much user activity is being assessed?

- What type of feedback is provided?

- The Voluntary/Required Question

  Voluntary (self) assessment, as previously noted, is a sound strategy for adults. Required evaluation is when the user must select prescribed activities, in a specific order, and may not bypass them. This evaluation is generally reserved for certification purposes. An additional certification requirement is the ability to keep administrative records for each user.

- The How Much Question

  - Single items ... usually voluntary, to verify understanding of single concepts.

  - Grouped items ... a test on a logical unit of material, often used for criterion-referenced structures.

  - Multiple groups ... a final test, which may be used as the basis for certification.

- The Feedback Question

  - Informative feedback ... confirms if the response is right or wrong with no further elaboration.

  - Reinforcing feedback ... may be positive congratulations or negative criticism. (This technique should be used sparingly or not at all.)

  - Diagnostic feedback ... using the analysis of the response as a guide, offers relevant comments or suggests reviews.

7

Detail Design—The Production Flowchart

In High-Level Design, the logic flow was a series of blocks that identified the major segments of the application. They set the general boundaries for the detail activities we've been describing. Now in Detail Design, each of those blocks must be exploded into its component parts: its individual presentations, interactions, and connections. But this logic flow is more than just a detailed diagram. It's the document where your design decisions are synthesized. It's a vehicle to identify and assemble the topics, strategies, treatments, and options into an organized plan, the Production Flowchart.

At this point, you should be familiar with the mechanics and symbols required to construct this production flowchart. Now let's summarize the process of capturing these detail design ideas. Here's a possible scenario for the design team:

- Pick one of the major high-level topics to work on; divide (and diagram) that topic into its logical sub-topics.

- Pick one of those sub-topics for detail design work.

- Simulate (out loud and on paper) what happens both on the display and to the user. A general set of questions can help stimulate the process:

  – What's on the screen now?

  – What does it look like?

  – What media is being used?

  – How does the user continue? Stop? Go back?

  – If the user selects **XXX**, what happens?

  – Now what's on the screen?

> **Note.** The Production Flowchart is a key document in detail design. If you haven't done so yet, you should go to the Resource Section, Appendix D, and look over the material pertaining to flowcharts in "Components of Multimedia Documentation." Even if you are familiar with flowcharts used for data processing applications, you'll find that flowcharts for interactive video applications are somewhat different.
> When you are familiar with the form and purpose of the Production Flowchart, return here.

- Record these detail design decisions on paper with notes, media symbols and arrows. Revisit each idea and elaborate or refine according to the needs of the application: scenes, characters, menu options, graphics, user guidance, etc.

- Repeat this process for each of the sub-topics; revise other sections as conflicts or gaps become apparent.

- Consolidate these sub-topics into a complete production flowchart using the appropriate symbols and notations.

The complete production flowchart represents a significant part of the detail design document. It depicts the topics and their connections, user options and interactions, media and their combinations, and (depending on annotations) some design strategies. Since it shows so many aspects of the whole application, it can become a centralized reference for the rest of the design and development documentation.

A more comprehensive production flowchart means fewer misunderstandings in later phases. If everyone understands the conventions and symbols used, it can substantially decrease the number of narrative descriptions. However, except in very short or simple applications, it cannot represent all the design strategies and decisions. Other forms of detail documentation are required. As we have said before, you should recognize that most vendors will have their own conventions for design documentation. Some may use other template shapes, or create their flowcharts using a computer. The form is not important. The existence of a detailed Production Flowchart that everyone understands is crucial.

A note of caution: The route from a high-level logic flow to the production flowchart is not well marked. Beware of dead ends, detours, and false starts. The trip may take several iterations and lots of paper. Capturing and organizing these random design thoughts on paper is difficult. Expect some inertia at the outset; provide some provoking questions.

8

Documenting the Detail Design

We've described the Application Design Document as the master blueprint to capture all the design decisions on paper. It will enable you to "see" and evaluate each of the topics, their connections, their treatments, and the design strategies. Certainly the production flowchart is a significant step toward that goal, especially with its annotated design ideas. But it's not enough.

This document must also consolidate any revised analysis data, the high-level design documentation, and the detail design descriptions that the flowchart could not capture. Although many of these individual pieces may have been documented during the design process, they have not been integrated into a single, centralized resource. Why take the extra time to consolidate this design paperwork? From a project management perspective, you need to evaluate the total design, not isolated or unorganized pieces. From a development perspective, the vendors need a comprehensive, reliable reference for their work.

Let's recap the contents of the Application Design Document to see what's already available and then look at some options for what's left.

- Analysis activities provided the problem statement, application objectives, design parameters and constraints, and the content analysis decisions. This same data, with any changes or additions, should be incorporated.

- High-Level Design activities produced a content outline of the major topics, a flow diagram, a general treatment philosophy, and the authoring facility's capabilities. These documents should represent a major section of the design notebook.

- Detail Design activities refined the treatments, strategies and logic flow. The amount and format of this documentation may vary quite a bit. Here's what you should expect:

  - Expanded content outlines and logic flows in the form of detailed production flowcharts.

  - Detailed descriptions of the treatment, interactive formats and visual content. While some of these may be annotated on the production flowchart, more detail is required. Acceptable formats include narrative to describe treatments and their implementation; prototypes to demonstrate visual content, color, and characters; and sample storyboards to depict representative menus, graphics, and overlays.

  - Strategy statements for the media, motivation, sequence, interaction, adult learning, and evaluation. Some of these may be captured on the flowchart (media, sequence, and interaction). The others may be documented through narratives, sample storyboards, or prototypes. Remember, these six strategies may not be documented separately, and you'll have to review the documentation to determine for yourself if the strategies are well formed and effective.

- Preliminary estimates for the user-time-on-system, disc layout by time and topic, and media allocations. While these are rough estimates, vendors should be able to provide them—if their design is complete.

The sum of all these design decisions on their various forms equals the Application Design Document. It's now ready for your evaluation.

> **Note.** Most detail designs include written documentation accompanied by a verbal presentation. During the presentation, missing documentation may be casually deferred to the development phase: "We'll document that on the storyboards." Get it all on paper now, so you can evaluate it now!

9

Evaluating the Design Documentation

With the completion of detail design, you again take a more active role and shift into evaluation mode. Given this set of flowcharts, narratives, and illustrations, your task is to assess the quality of the design. Will it do the job? Is it complete? Clear? Appropriate? Similar to the evaluation of High-Level Design, you'll apply a series of questions and checklists to the documentation. But, since the detail design is so critical, we've added another evaluation tool to assist you, the design matrix.

In the evaluation process, you work with the design team and their deliverables. Your task is to ask the right questions. Two general questions you want to keep in the background are:

- Does this design still meet our original objectives? And,

- Can this design be completed within our schedule and budget?

More specifically, you need to ask:

- "Is this detail design complete?"

  Earlier in this chapter, we outlined the contents of an Application Design Document. You need to verify that all those components are present: flowcharts, treatments, and strategies. To assist you in this effort, our checklists for design have been organized into sections, one for each major design component. Using the questions within each section, you can check for completeness.

- "Is this detail design clear?"

  Can you read the documentation and "see the design" without someone giving you a lengthy explanation? More importantly, can the developers read the documentation and prepare their scripts, graphics, menus, or storyboards without help? Ask your writers, artists, and programmers to assist with this evaluation question.

- "Is this detail design comprehensive?"

  All the design elements can be present and clearly stated, but still be inadequate for development. As you review each presentation topic, look for detailed descriptions beyond a superficial identification: characters, setting, media, user controls, and options. Again, involve your development specialists in this assessment.

- "Is the documentation consistent?"

  We have harped on the fact that IVD/multimedia documentation requires many different forms of documentation, all interrelated. The volume of documents is growing fast, and will grow faster in the next phase. Now is the time to check to make sure that all of the documents are in agreement with each other.

- "Is this detail design appropriate to our needs?"

  Here is where you need to take a backward look to revisit the application's objectives and match the detail design specifications to those original goals, environments, audiences, and tasks. Are we still on target?

If you're satisfied with the answers to these general questions about the overall design, you're ready to ask some more detailed questions about the effectiveness of the strategies that the designers have proposed. You need to make a judgment as to how well the available resources have been used to achieve the application's goals while containing the cost. You need to ask further questions like:

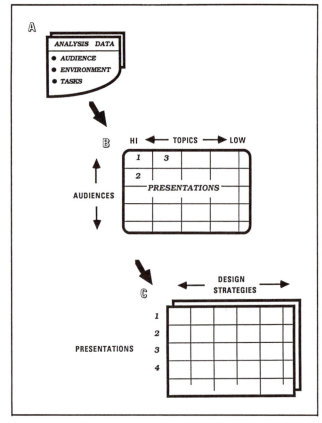

Figure 6-4 Documentation Sequence

- "Have the media resources been allocated appropriately to our primary and secondary audiences?"

- "Have the most sophisticated (and costly) design strategies been assigned to our high priority topics?"

- "Are we employing a variety of interaction techniques? Are they being used effectively?"

These are critical aspects of the design, but difficult to assess. Part of the problem is the number of factors, part is their abstract nature. To make this dimension of the evaluation more manageable (and more tangible), we've developed a series of Design Matrices, one for each of the key IVD strategies. These tools can help you visualize where you're spending your resources. Let's see how they work.

The Application Design Matrices

Before we explain how to use these new evaluation tools, let's review where they fit with some previous analysis work. Figure 6-4 shows the progression from analysis to these design matrices.

A. During preliminary analysis, your vendors identified and documented primary (and secondary) audiences along with their characteristics. Further analysis into the application's goals and objectives uncovered several activities or tasks for these different users. This was valuable data, but unorganized.

B. In the content analysis or Application Design Session, more specific topics were discussed and documented. These topics were then aligned with their appropriate audiences into a table or matrix. By assigning a priority scheme to the topics and audiences, the most critical presentations were identified and numbered. The next step was to design each presentation.

C. The design of those presentations included decisions on what treatments and interactive formats were used, what sequence, media, and interaction—our six IVD strategies. With this design documentation complete, you must now evaluate it. How and where will your resources be spent? That's the purpose of these strategy matrices.

As an evaluation tool, the design matrix lets you focus on one strategy at a time. Each matrix plots a series of its techniques across the top, from most

> **Note.** All matrices are located in the Resource Section, Appendix C, for your future projects. Review them for a moment, then we'll describe some in more detail.

PRESENTATION ID (*format type*)	HIGH-PRODUCTION MOTION VIDEO	INDUSTRIAL QUALITY MOTION VIDEO	HIGH-QUALITY COMPUTER GRAPHICS	SECOND TRACK AUDIO SEGMENTS	VIDEO STILL FRAMES	COMPUTER TEXT SCREENS	BUDGET ESTIMATES ($ 000)
1 A (simulation)	5 minutes		20				21.0 k
2 A (game)	5		20				21.0
1 B	2		8				8.4
2 B	2		8				8.4
3 A	2		8				8.4
5 A	3		30				13.5
4 B	:30 sec.		25				3.3
6 B	:30		25				3.3
7 B	:30		25				3.3
8 A	:30		25	6 minutes	25		6.3
8 B	:30		20	6	20		6.0
1 C (tutorial)		1 minute		3		20	2.0
2 C		1 minute		3		20	2.0
9 A	:30		15	3	15		4.5
10 B	:30		20	4	20		5.5
	22: 30	2 min.	250	25 min.	80	40	120,000

MEDIA STRATEGIES

Figure 6-5 Media Selection Matrix

sophisticated to least. (These techniques were presented earlier in the chapter.) The vertical axis lists each presentation in its priority with its annotated interactive format. Entries recorded at the intersections will help you see and evaluate allocation patterns before development begins. For example, are greater costs being applied to the higher priority presentations? How many graphics will be needed?

MEDIA SELECTION

The most useful of all the matrices is the one dealing with media selection. An example for a typical one-side IVD presentation is shown in Figure 6-5. It not only illustrates the media strategy, it serves as your decision tool for allocating the limited video and graphic storage capacity. For each presentation on this matrix, you fill in the number of video minutes, the number of graphics, second track audio minutes, and the number of computer graphics. The totals give you initial media estimates.

As these media decisions are made, the system's capacity restrictions become obvious. Since this is a one-sided videodisc application, the total motion video minutes cannot exceed 30 minutes per side. Twenty-five is a more realistic figure at this stage, leaving room for overruns and still frames. Second track audio should also be limited to twenty-five minutes. Complex color graphics can occupy 50K or more bytes of disk storage, which can be a major constraint if no CD-ROM storage is available. By working with this matrix, realistic design constraints can be recognized and reconsidered early in the project.

Cost estimates can also be figured from the totals on this matrix. By assigning a cost-per-unit for each type of media, the preliminary production budget can be calculated. Your media vendors can supply their current costs for graphics, motion video, and video still frames. This procedure is discussed in more detail in Chapter 12.

When the strategy matrix indicates that certain media have exceeded their storage capacity (or are inappropriate for a specific presentation) tradeoff decisions must be made. The hardware offers a wide variety of media alternatives. Each medium has different advantages and drawbacks relating to production, presentation, and maintenance. New technologies provide new capabilities and cost considerations. Making wise tradeoff decisions is a demanding part of the design process.

The designer's job is to optimize the available development and capacity resources, insuring that the most costly media are reserved for the highest priority goals and objectives. Your task is to evaluate their allocation. The media strategy matrix can make this easier.

EVALUATING OTHER DESIGN DIMENSIONS

While media decisions are critical and the most obvious place to begin your evaluation, the other design strategies play an equally important part in the application. The matrix tools can help you evaluate these dimensions also. In each case, your activities will be similar:

- Select one of the six design strategies for evaluation.

- Using the entries on the matrix as a guide, review each presentation (and its treatment/format) to see how that strategy will be developed. Remember, your vendors may not explicitly describe or isolate these individual strategies.

- Record the specific techniques used for each presentation on the strategy worksheet.

- Study the completed matrix for distribution patterns, continuity, variety, and obvious omissions. Look for conflicts or inconsistencies with other strategies.

Your entries on these matrices may vary from check marks to numbers to notes, but your objective is the same: does the design allocate the most effective resources to the most important presentations? Visually, the upper left part of the matrix should be more concentrated than the lower right. Other observations and questions include:

- Motivation

  Is there a general motivation strategy? How does each individual approach contribute to that strategy? Are the motivational methods varied? Are they distributed throughout the application (not just at the beginning)? Are the techniques consistent for your audience(s)? Do the methods complement or reinforce the media strategies?

- Interaction

  Do users have more than one way to advance through the application? How do they interrupt, review, or change directions? Where/when do users get "navigation rules?" How realistic are the simulation situations for each audience? How intelligent are the system's responses?

- Sequence

  How many alternate, remedial, or enrichment paths have been designed? How many levels or modules in the application? Is the structure obvious to the user? How much freedom or control is built into the design? Is the structure consistent with our objectives?

- Adult Learning

  Can users take control at any time? How does the design keep users informed of their progress? Of their location? Of their options? Does the design have alternative (parallel) presentations of the material? How does the design recognize the user's experience?

- Evaluation

  Is evaluation voluntary or required? How frequent is the assessment? Are records for certification required? How sophisticated is the analysis of the user's input? What level of feedback is appropriate?

The sum of the matrix entries and these evaluation questions gives you a tangible tool to assess the application's design, identify critical trends, and visualize resource distribution.

> **Note.** This matrix approach looks more scientific than it is. It's really a method that tends to get important issues on the table so they won't be overlooked. The actual evaluations that are made concerning the appropriateness of the selected strategies remain subjective. They still depend on good sense and individual judgment.

Evaluating the Total Design

The matrix worksheets help you focus on individual parts of the design, assess those segments, and make tradeoffs where appropriate. But, you must also evaluate the design as a whole. How does the total application unfold with all its strategies and treatments? Two procedures that emphasize a global assessment are "peer reviews" and "structured walkthroughs." You should plan and promote these techniques as part of the evaluation process.

Figure 6-6 A Peer Review in progress

- Peer Reviews

  Individual designers, responsible for major segments of the application, present their approaches to the team in a risk-free environment. Their treatments, strategies, and methods are discussed, enhanced, refined, and related to other parts of the application. These peer reviews may occur several times during the design phase. You should probably not participate or attend these self-evaluation sessions, but you should get summarized reports or results that describe the design decisions.

- Structured Walkthroughs

  Vendors or the design leader walk(s) through the entire application one step at a time, as if it were complete. This presentation may include verbal descriptions, prototype code, sample storyboards, and role playing. The intent is to visualize the final product and to give everyone a shared mental picture of the characters, scenes, interactions, story lines, conversations, look, feel, and sound of the application.

  This technique may be employed early in the design phase as an idea generator, but its real value comes at the end of design when you're seeking convergence and agreement on the whole plan. You might evaluate one design walkthrough with your checklists and strategy worksheets. After any changes or tradeoffs have been made, a second walkthrough can be scheduled to "see" and "listen" to the total application.

How Can Anything Go Wrong?

Although we've outlined a set of procedures and activities to structure and manage the design process, don't expect an ideal plan the first time around. Design is a complex affair; IVD design, more so. You must consider, assemble, and integrate numerous design components. It's quite easy to overlook some. Indeed, the checklists and the strategy matrices were specifically developed to uncover and correct these easily-missed aspects:

- missing topics,

- incomplete treatments,

- misallocated media,

- exceeded resources,

- inappropriate strategies.

Your evaluation tools and procedures can catch these design flaws and oversights. By invoking a "what's wrong" procedure, you can revisit and repair the problem situations:

- Identify what's missing, incomplete, or inaccurate.

- Using the design road map as a guide, where should the adjustments be made? By whom?

- Determine if additional resources are required.

- Evaluate the impact of any corrections on other parts of the application.

- Update the central design documentation.

- Reschedule evaluations as necessary.

Expect (even promote) several design cycles. You'll get a more comprehensive plan. Better to invest your resources now while the ideas are fresh, than to return for redesign after some costly development or production effort.

10

Obtain Sponsor Signoff on the Design

After several design cycles and evaluation sessions, the Application Design Document should be complete. You and the project team should agree on this design plan and be committed to its development. Your final management task is to obtain the sponsor's signoff. At this point in the project, the sponsor may also want to "see" what's being paid for. Here are some options:

- A well organized Application Design Document as we've outlined. Add executive summaries, budget estimates, and sample scenarios that address business objectives.

- Demonstrations, if some prototype segments have been developed.

- Attendance at one of the final structured walkthroughs (or a subset).

- Your assessment and status report of the project. It should highlight significant changes to the original objectives, budget, schedule, or resources.

A Last Word

Design is a creative process that is difficult to define and manage. Through the activities and techniques presented in this chapter, we've tried to picture that process from your viewpoint — the events, the expectations, the players, and the deliverables. We have not explained design itself. If you need more background or information on that dimension, we have recommended several excellent books in the Resource Section, Appendix F. If you don't have a background in design, however, you should still feel confident about your ability to evaluate the work of the designers. Despite the wealth of theory about instructional systems design that has been developed over the last decades, good design is still a matter of creativity and imagination. Evaluating design is still a matter of common sense.

The Strategy Evaluation Matrices that we have provided here will provide a solid foundation for your opinion. As you consider the proposed design from these six viewpoints, you are not likely to overlook any major flaw that prevents it from accomplishing the original objectives. If you use these worksheets thoughtfully, you should be confident that your project is ready to proceed into the intensive work of the Development Phase.

Chapter Seven

Developing and Documenting the Design

Preview of the Development Phase

Development is capturing all your design decisions on paper. Complexity surfaces not only from the number of these ideas, but from the different specialists involved in the process, their unique (sometimes conflicting) vocabularies, and the different forms of documentation they need. All of these factors must eventually fit together to produce a single set of consistent documentation. More than any other phase, development becomes a paperwork coordination effort. Because your evaluation is an evaluation of the documentation, managing this phase requires understanding both the technical documentation standards as well as the development process. We've structured these two different dimensions of development into two separate parts of the book.

- The technical aspects of documentation:

  The forms, symbols, terminology (and the development sequence) are located in the Resource Section, Appendix D, "Components of Multimedia Documentation." It serves as a stand-alone self-study module for you or other project personnel.

- The development process and evaluation:

  These aspects are discussed in this chapter. It addresses the management considerations for this phase.

  Both dimensions are necessary. They complement one another. Depending on your background or study preferences, you can read them in any order. If you want a recommendation, we'd suggest reading the appendix material first.

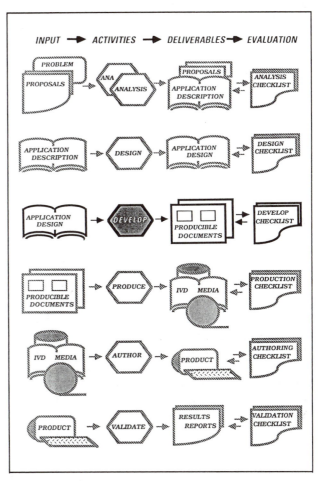

Figure 7-1 IVD Development Process

Looking Over the Territory

What We're Trying to Accomplish

The purpose of the Development Phase is to create **Producible Documentation**. In the last chapter, we covered the design processes. During development, we'll translate the design strategies into a set of documents that are ready for the various producers to create the media elements that make up the application development.

Let's begin by redefining what we mean by development activity, since once again, there is no standard terminology among IVD/multimedia producers. We use the term to mean the writing or sketching of the actual content of the application **as it is to be produced.** It includes:

- the new, consolidating documents called "Super Storyboards" that describe how all the media elements in each presentation event fit with each other,

- developing the traditional storyboards or scripts to be produced by the video producer,

- writing of the words to be said by narrators or actors,

- careful rendering of the computer screens and video graphics,

- planning to insure that the material can be produced within the available monetary budget, and that the system limitations (such as videodisc capacity) will not be exceeded.

Team members tend to work with extreme concentration at their desks or computer terminals when engaged in development activity. The result is paper or computer documentation that will define the requirements for each individual producer in minute detail

The list of producers will depend on the types of media elements that were called for in the design. It could contain a video producer, graphic artists, audio producer, video graphic specialists, photographers or commercial artists. We'll address each of these in turn as if they were individuals. In reality, except for the largest and most expensive projects, these creative production roles may be shared between a few multi-talented individuals. Also, it is unlikely that the design called for **all** of the possible elements, so every form of documentation is not needed on most projects.

Nevertheless, whatever documentation is developed during this phase, it must meet the three principle attributes of Producible Documentation:

- It must be **Clear** — to the team and to the producers.

- It must be **Complete** — no missing details.

- It must be **Consistent** — all documents agree with each other.

Deliverable Items for the Development Phase

Development is concerned with two types of producible documentation. The first is the overall document that describes how all media elements are related to one another at each point of the application. We've called this the "Super Storyboard." The second type is documentation intended to support the production of individual media elements: the audio scripts, graphic renditions and video storyboards.

So What's New?

Previous chapters have stressed that the sheer complexity and volume of documentation is a new factor in IVD/multimedia projects. In addition, there are several other considerations that will concern developers, especially if this is their first experience with these projects.

One critical factor that may catch some developers unaware is the need for communications with other members of the team. Other kinds of projects are typically developed by one person in isolation, such as script writing, picture making or developing computer based training. In these projects, each developer depends on many others to integrate his or her piece of the program with the other parts. At times, the need for intercommunication becomes so great that the project can get grid-locked until all parties come together in a general meeting. Communication is made more difficult because of the different vocabularies used by video producers, artists and computer people. Once again, the Project Manager must insure that the documentation is clear to everyone, and serves to bridge these gaps in a way that all parties understand.

Finally, it is important to realize that developers with experience in one medium may bring along some ideas that do not fit well with IVD applications. A good writer of linear video scripts must learn new techniques when writing for IVD. An experienced author of computer based training programs may have to work to get familiar with the expanded set of media available in IVD. As in many other activities, what you don't know may cause fewer problems than what you think you know that isn't true.

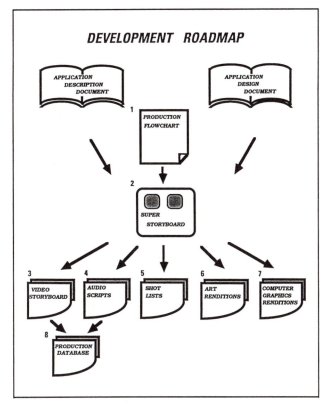

Figure 7-2 Development RoadMap

How Do We Get There?

The road map diagrammed in Figure 7-2 depicts the development steps in a rather orderly sequence. Some of these activities, however, may be happening simultaneously. For example, artists are probably working on art renditions while writers are scripting video. The major development steps are:

1. Reviewing the Application Design Document,

2. Developing the Super Storyboard,

3. Developing the Video Storyboards,

4. Developing the Audio Scripts,

5. Developing the Shot List for still frames,

6. Developing the Art renditions,

7. Developing the Computer Graphic Renditions,

8. Assembling the Production Data Base.

Since multiple individuals are employing multiple forms, a critical management task is the coordination and orchestration of this producible documentation.

A simplistic way to look at the development phase is to complete the Super Storyboard, then provide copies to the developers who will produce the documentation for each of the individual media components. In reality, there is likely to be a great deal of revisiting of the design documentation as the development documents are created. There always seems to be more detail needed at every point than was originally planned. The application always seems to be on the point of bursting its seams. The design document, the detailed objectives and even the basic analysis are gone over again and again. Adjustments are made to add content here, cut it back there. New ideas are born, evaluated and worked in or rejected.

If your responsibility as Project Manager extends to managing the development effort, it will seem like a bewildering task the first time through. This phase is extremely paper intensive, whether in the form of handwritten documents or computer printouts. The decisions made by one individual will depend on information from several others, and communications becomes a problem.

As confusing as all this may seem, it can be managed effectively if a few procedures are in place. First, it is critical to manage the change process. A single master copy of the SSB is the best way to do this. In a large project, a Super Storyboard Coordinator should be assigned to make sure that changes are posted, and that all developers affected by a change are informed.

Second, it is important to keep lists of required elements by category, and monitor the status daily. If there are 28 motion video segments called for in the design, then there must be 28 individual storyboards prepared; they should be filed and checked off as they are completed.

Third, the evaluation of the content must be done on a continuing basis. If the style of the scripting is not acceptable, or the video production techniques are too expensive, the developers should be redirected as early as possible to avoid expensive rework later.

All of this work takes time. The good news is that the time is relatively cheap. A typical project schedule should allocate at least thirty percent of its time to the iterative activity of detailed design and development. Changes and rework are done on paper, and don't require expensive resources.

At the end of the phase, however, the change activity should come to a halt. The completed documents should be clear, complete and consistent, and ready for production. From then on, further changes will be extremely costly, and may severely impact the budget and schedule.

Developing the Documentation Components

Reviewing the Application Design Document

As you begin each new project phase, new members may be joining the group; all members may need an update. A kickoff meeting that reviews existing materials, provides a status report, and defines the current objectives can help insure continuity.

Starting the Development Phase, your review would include a review of present documentation, including the Application Description Document (high-level design) and the Application Design Document (detail design). Pay special attention to the Production Flowchart in the latter document.

This meeting will help ensure that everyone understands the application objectives, how their individual tasks fit in with the whole, and how to interpret the documentation.

Developing the Super Storyboard

The "Super Storyboard" is the central document from which all others will be developed. We use the quotes because the term is by no means universally used by all vendors. It is universal, however, to use a form that describes all elements from the videodisc and/or CD-ROM and computer, and how they relate to each other. The form is usually unique to the vendor, and often is redesigned for each application. The form presented in this text is one we have used with success to develop several applications, but the form used by your vendor may be quite different. The purpose of the document and the information it contains, however, is fairly standard.

The Super Storyboard form developed by the authors is shown in Figure 7-3. Its contents and relationship to the other documentation is covered in Appendix D of the Resource Section, "Components of Multimedia Documentation." Now we'll take a look at how it gets created in the Development Phase.

"Hey, wait a minute!" you may be saying. "As I look at the Super Storyboard form you guys are recommending, I see a lot of creative work going on there at the detail level. Isn't this document really a part of Detail Design?"

This is a valid point.

Much of the information on the Super Storyboard is really the last and most detailed level of design. It is probably created by the Application Designer, and it is almost certainly going to entail many revisits of the design objectives as it unfolds. At the very least, the first entries on the Super Storyboard provide a bridge between Detail Design and Development, much like the Application Design Session was the bridge between Analysis and Design.

When the Designer/Developer picks up the blank Super Storyboard, a critical moment in the project is at hand. Here is the first time that a description of the actual content that will really be eventually recorded on the videodisc or CD and produced for the computer will be committed to paper*. From now on, the various ideas that have been floating around about what we **could** do are going to be consolidated into documentation about what we **will** do. What doesn't get written down won't be done; what is written down will cost real time and money to produce. Now is the time that the firm foundation you have laid in analysis and design will pay off.

Once again, the approach to developing the Super Storyboard will vary from one developer to another. Most developers work first to create the Production Flowchart. As they enter the blocks on the flowchart, a mental picture forms about the video and computer content of the event they are adding. When they have completed the flowchart and begun to create the Super Storyboard, the mental pictures from the blocks return, and they record them on the Composite section of the Super Storyboard. Some describe the content in narrative form, others more artistically inclined will sketch the content. Appropriate notes, comments about objectives, descriptions of the detailed treatment and so on are added. The developer will probably do a quick sketch of the graphics that will come from the computer, so the graphic artist and script writer can keep their own responsibilities straight. Most developers will leave each page here, without going on to the more mechanical tasks of showing the touch areas, or describing the logical branches.

If you look over the shoulder of a developer at this stage of the game, you should ask questions like, "Will the script writer understand enough about our objective at this point to be able to write an effective video storyboard? Will the graphic artist be able to come up with an attractive and effective graphic theme, and create accurate screens from this document?" You should also be able to see the more concrete form of the application beginning to take shape, and make a preliminary evaluation of whether it looks like it will do the job.

---

* It may be that the development documentation will reside in a computer, and only appear on paper in printouts. We'll discuss the documentation in this chapter as if it were being developed on paper forms.

Super Story Board		LAST REVISION		EVENT	SEQ
		DATE/TIME	INIT.		

COMPOSITE

SCENE/SHOT ID: | AUDIO TRACK:

AUDIO/PRODUCTION NOTES:

TIMING/Read: | Cumulative:

GRAPHICS

10			
20			

GRAPHIC ID: | TOOL: | MODE:

INSTRUCTIONS:

CONTROL

10			
20			

REFERENCE/LABEL:

AUTHOR DOCUMENTATION:

NOTES:

VIDEO: | DOCUMENTS UPDATED:

SHOT	DESCRIPTION	STILL	SET/LDC	PROPS	TALENT	ON/VO	DVE	VIDEO GRAPHIC	PC GRAPHIC	OVRLY
1										
2										
3										
4										
5										

MASTER TAPE TIME CODE		RUN TIME		CHECK DISC FRAMES	FINAL DISC FRAMES
IN:	OUT:	ACTUAL:	CUMULATIVE:		

Figure 7-3 A Sample Super Storyboard form

The Super Storyboard is a living document that will gain in detail as the Development Phase continues, and will undergo many revisions as better ideas are formulated, and as later work affects earlier work.

Note. If your project has a Super Storyboard Coordinator assigned, the integrity of the document will probably be improved. Especially in larger projects, the size and complexity of this key document can only be managed properly by one individual who has the specific responsibility.

Media Element Documentation

Depending upon what elements have been called for in the design, any or all of the following documents may be needed:

- Video storyboards

- Audio scripts

- Shot lists for still frames

- Art renditions

- Computer graphic renditions

Let's discuss each one in more detail.

3

Developing the Video Storyboard

When the Super Storyboard has been completed up to the point of describing the content, objectives and treatment of the events that contain motion video segments, it can be passed on to the writers to create the video storyboards. Of all the development activities that will determine the final look, feel and quality of the application, this is the most important.

It will be up to the Managing Producer (the person in charge of audio/video production) to actually create the visual and all-important audio content of the segments, but the input for video production comes from the writer's desk in the Development Phase. It will be up to you to evaluate the quality of this input to prevent the Managing Producer from being put in the position of having to create silk purses from sows' ears.

The mechanics of this process are simple:

1. A list of every required motion video segment should be produced from the design documentation.

2. A label should be assigned to each segment that will be used to track it all the way through the Production and Authoring Phases.

3. Each segment must have a video storyboard written for it. (Some vendors will call this a "video script.")

Although these segments are connected by theme, talent (actors and narrators), sets and locations, and so on, each one of them must be written to stand alone with a discrete beginning and end. At the same time, the writer must consider the thematic transitions from each segment to all of the other segments that the user could possibly select.

There are many rules and techniques for writing good video that apply to any kind of program. There are other techniques that apply especially to interactive video. It may be that the writer on your project is quite familiar with the former, but not the latter. A good linear video writer is used to using many techniques for establishing scenes, developing characters, expounding on content (since the viewer can't choose what is presented) and achieving smooth scene-to-scene transitions. Much of this kind of writing is inappropriate for interactive video.

It is an advisable practice for the Project Manager to review a sample script or two submitted by the writer before giving the go ahead for development of the entire storyboard set. The Checklists for the Development Phase in Appendix A provide important guidelines for reviewing the video storyboards. Let's elaborate on them here.

1. **Each sentence should make a point that responds directly to the selected topic.**

   Interactive video should be much "tighter" than linear video. When the user selects an item on the screen for further information, only information pertaining to that selection should be presented. In merchandising applications, adding "salesy" material to an information segment is not only extraneous, it often actually annoys a user who did not ask for "a commercial."

2. **A visual picture accompanies and amplifies each point.**

   This, after all, is what IVD is all about. Just make sure the visual picture is clearly related to the words.

3. **If words appear, match them to the audio track with the same words in the same order.**

   This principle applies to both linear and interactive video, and it is often violated. If the script calls for the words, "RPM dial," don't put up a visual with the word, "TACHOMETER." It's a sound concept to use both sight and sound to make a point, but they must work together. If they do not, you create "media cross-talk," and users have to sort out the mismatch and make the connection themselves between the spoken word and the visual.

4. **Acknowledge the selected topic by using the topic title from the previous menu in the first sentence, or repeat the title visually, or both.**

   Any time a user interacts with an IVD presentation, there should be immediate feedback that acknowledges the interaction and verifies that the system understands the message. When we discuss authoring techniques, we'll talk about touch acknowledgments that provide an indication that the item pointed at on the screen was indeed selected. Video scripts need to provide another kind of acknowledgment to provide continuity from the screen that offered the choice to the start of the scene that is displayed.

5. **Keep segments as short as possible, responding to the user's selection, then quitting. Allow the user to request further information.**

   There are two reasons for keeping segments short. First, room on the disc is limited; second, the user is looking for a limited amount of information in a given segment, and packing it with unasked-for material is distracting and annoying. Writers who are new to interactive video often have trouble with this technique at first.

6. **Keep audio and visual material as general as possible in order to avoid early obsolescence of the videodisc.**

   Once a disc is pressed, you're stuck with its contents. If you include specific references to items that will probably change in the near future, you're likely to have to re-record video and re-master the disc sooner than would have been necessary if the writer had left them out. These items include dates, prices, model names and so on. Information like this can be put into graphic

screens or printed material without affecting the videodisc. (On the other hand, if the changes are planned for and the master tape is designed to change easily, the disc could be updated for a fairly reasonable cost.)

7. **Check inter-segment transitions for smoothness and continuity— remember these transitions are directed by the user.**

   This item has to be checked with the full set of storyboards. An example of a glaring mistake once appeared in a presentation about visiting Paris. A couple was shown emerging from their hotel in the morning and getting into a taxi. The user got to choose whether they went to the museum or the restaurant. If the expected choice of the museum was made, the couple was shown a few minutes later going into the Louvre. If the user chose the restaurant, however, the couple was shown arriving in the taxi — after dark! The unexpected transition was very distracting.

8. **Read the audio script to make sure it is written for the ear.**

   This is a general principle of good video writing, and it applies to interactive media as well. Some phrases look OK when read silently, but are difficult to say and understand when spoken out loud. The best way to judge this factor is to read the script out loud yourself and see if it is easy to say.

9. **Time the script with pacing and pauses for visual movements and effects to take place.**

Figure 7-4 The Script Writer: a good writer with special knowledge of how to use the medium

The limited space on discs makes time a critical factor. The video storyboards have to be timed to take account of the phrasing and pacing of the narrator, and the time it will take for the visual scene to unfold. Judging this will take some experience, and the ability to run the scene "in the mind's eye."

10. **Minimize use of difficult camera moves and positions to speed production.**

    Another aspect of script review is to keep production costs reasonable. A script that calls for fancy camera work, with low angles, high angles, "truck" or "dolly" shots (where the camera is moved during the recording of tape) are sure to take more time and dollars in production. Make sure if they are called for that the objective of the segment is well served by the extra expense.

11. **Use special effects only where needed for achieving a natural flow of information, such as continuity, pacing, highlighting a point, heightening interest, etc.**

    From the point of view of minimizing production costs, this item is an extension of the last one. Some special effects require expensive equipment, time and skill to produce. A common example is the "DVE" (Digital Video Effect), which requires specialized equipment to be used during the post-editing process to achieve the "squeeze-zooms," "flips" and "fly-ins" that are used so often on broadcast television. Make sure that expensive effects are affordable and used to accomplish the objective of the presentation. Another consideration is to avoid using too many effects just because the high-technology equipment allows them to be created easily. Too much of a good thing can get to be distracting to the user who is looking for information or training, not a display of the latest video tricks.

12. **Be careful when using background music —interactive video segments are often too short to benefit from a music track.**

    Music can add an important dimension to some IVD presentations, but it is not easy, and usually not cheap to achieve these effects. As a project manager, you should take a close look if background music has been called for in the storyboard. If the music has not been composed especially for the production, royalties for each "needle drop" (individual music segment) must be paid for separately. If the music fits the topic, however, and does not result in a choppy presentation, it may be well worth it.

13. **Use humor and references to topical material carefully — or not at all.**

    Humor is the most dangerous treatment that can be used in a script. Unless your main objective is to amuse, it is rare to find a writer that can support serious subject matter with humor. The treatment is almost certain to offend someone (and if that someone is the sponsoring executive, you're in trouble indeed). Topical material, such as catch phrases from current TV programming or commercials, can wear thin quickly and date your presentation way before its time. There can be exceptions, of course, and if your writer has written a script that combines humor with good taste, consider yourself fortunate.

Note. We've spent a lot of time on discussing video scripts, but the time you spend evaluating them will be well worthwhile. The motion video segments will be the heart of your application, and its success (and possibly yours) will be judged largely on the video quality.

4

Developing the Audio Scripts

Well-written audio can create an impression of high quality that rivals the impact of motion video, and it is much less expensive to produce. In a straight IVD application, the audio is used for voice-over commentary for video segments and graphic screens, and is recorded on the audio tracks of the videodisc. The advent of compact disc technologies has provided many new audio formats that can be used with stand-alone CD-ROM applications, or in combination with the videodisc.

This audio is just as important for the quality of your presentation as the audio for the video storyboards. The same principles apply, such as writing for the ear, keeping content general, avoiding phrases that date your presentation and using humor with caution.

Here are some points to consider:

1. **Check the writer's qualifications as carefully as you do the video storyboard writer's ability.**

    An ideal situation is to have both video and audio scripts written by the same talented writer. This will insure the style is the same and the quality is consistent. If you don't have this situation, get a sample script and check out the audio writer the same way you did the video writer.

2. **Don't overrun the system's graphic display ability to keep up with the narration.**

The timing of audio with motion video takes care of itself, but when an audio narration is supported with a series of graphics, the coordination does not occur until the authoring phase. This can lead to trouble in timing. Graphic screens stored in a computer file can be very large if the picture is highly detailed and has many colors. This large file can take time to load into the computer, and the time can vary if several computers with varying basic speeds are used to present the application. The time can also vary depending upon the presentation software you're using. Some rules of thumb are to separate graphic changes by at least five seconds on computers with a fixed disk, or ten seconds if your presentation will reside on older or slower models without fixed disks. CD-ROM drives vary in their access times, and graphic files, especially those captured from video input, can be extremely large. The five-second rule is usually adequate for later model, faster CD-ROM drives. The best course is to test the sequences on the actual hardware before committing to them.

3. **Consider whether to use the video talent to read the audio script.**

The execution of this decision won't come until the Production Phase, but the plan needs to be considered now. The design may be served better by using the same talent, or better by using a different voice. The budget may benefit from using a less expensive voice talent rather than scheduling an expensive video talent for a day in the audio studio. On the other hand, it may be economical to have the video talent read a reasonable number of voice-over segments on the set, and record them on video tape.

4. **Consider using alternate voices.**

If your presentation has a lot of audio, it may benefit from having two narrators to alternate back and forth between major points. Perhaps the application would especially benefit from using a male and a female voice.

Developing the Shot Lists for Still Frames

Each video still frame called for in the detailed design must be separately produced, and (except for those frames produced in conjunction with motion video segments) must appear as an item in a "shot list." If your presentation uses more than one kind of source image, there will be more than one shot list. For example, separate lists might exist for photos to be shot, stock photos, "card art" to be drawn by an artist and video graphic frames to be produced at a video post-production facility.

The reason for having separate lists is, of course, that each type of still frame must be sent to a different type of producer. The types would include photographers, commercial artists, and video graphic artists. Each would need a separate list. There needs to be a master list as well that will keep track of all still frames that will eventually be used in the Production Phase to make sure all of them are recorded on the master tape.

Your interest in this detailed procedure as a Project Manager is to be sure that the system works and that all needed still frame elements are accounted for on the proper lists. It can be costly to discover missing elements during the Production Phase; it can be disastrous to discover them after production.

Developing the Art Renditions

Just as each motion video segment must have a storyboard, each still frame on the shot lists must have some kind of description of what it is supposed to look like. We have used the word "renditions" to mean the documentation from the developer that describes the content of the still frame to the producer.

The storyboard form is a good way to document these renditions. The way the still frames are described depends on the needs of the producer. Sometimes a sketch of the picture is best, other times a word description is more effective.

If you are responsible for the work of developers, you should be sure that the renditions are clear enough for anyone to produce if they had the talent. Many projects have been delayed because the sketches of the developer look like left over spaghetti. If your developer just doesn't have the skill to draw good renditions, get someone who has adequate talent to help him. Many of the considerations for video still frame renditions are the same as those for computer graphic renditions. We'll take up this important subject next in more detail.

7

Developing the Computer Graphic Renditions

Computer graphics play a key role in determining the quality of a presentation. Everybody "knows" what good video looks like, but there are no standards for graphics. A talented graphic artist can make an interactive presentation sparkle with creative screens. If the presentation system supports graphics with many colors and high resolution, the artist can adapt a wide variety of styles to support and improve the visual presentation. On the other hand, if graphics are left in the hands of authors or programmers with little artistic talent, the results can be detrimental to the entire application. Some factors in creating good graphics are considered by the developer, and others by the artist when the graphic is being produced. The kind of specification included in the rendition depends on how the two relate. In one project, the developer may specify every detail, font and color. In another, the developer may provide a brief sketch and the artist will fill in all the details. In large projects where several artists are working on the graphics, there needs to be an Art Director who will oversee the work, make sure the renditions are clear, and provide direction to the artists to insure a consistent and high quality style.

The checklists include several points about evaluating graphics. We have included them all in the Development Phase section to keep them together, although some of them may not be applicable until the artist is actually creating the pictures. With that in mind, let's discuss the checklist items for evaluating graphic renditions, and the final products, the graphic screens themselves.

1. **First things first: check spelling, grammar and technical accuracy.**

    This is an obvious point, but one of the most common sources of trouble. A developer's error that gets through to production is probably an

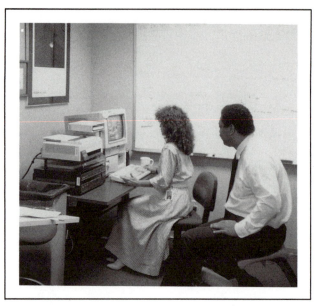

Figure 7-5 The Art Director works with graphic artists to insure a consistent look to the screens

error in spelling of an unfamiliar technical term. Other errors tend to be caught by the artist, but a careless error by the artist may need another eye to catch it.

2. **Format text screens for easy reading to increase retention:**

    - Five or fewer major points,

    - Center text,

    - Break lines at natural pauses or phrases,

    - Separate individual points with space to avoid a crammed appearance,

    - Use tasteful highlighting to emphasize important words and phrases.

    This is a key point. All of these techniques have been subjected to formal research and found to have direct effects on understanding and retention of information.

3. **Keep the style consistent: background colors, art style, fonts, etc.**

    If you're using more than one artist, the best way to keep the style consistent is to have an Art Director. Appoint an artist to this role if you don't have a professional graphics director available.

4. **Use consistent colors to indicate text classifications.**

    Examples of text classifications include:

    - Auxiliary detail information about content,

- Required user action (e.g., "Touch to Continue"),

- User Choice options (e.g., Menu items),

- Information about presentation structure or mechanisms (e.g., Maps or Help screens).

This point extends the last point to include use of colors as visual keys as to the purpose of each graphic element.

5. **Use fonts that are easy to read on the delivery system monitor**

This should be a major concern of the art director, but you may want to check it out as well. If the style of font is too fancy, or the wrong colors are chosen for a two color font, the resulting words can be hard to read and generally distracting. Some of this decision is a matter of taste, but you can make a more objective decision by viewing the screens from the same distance as the user will. Find someone who wears low power reading glasses and have him check the graphics with and without them.

6. **Limit use of different colors — usually four colors are adequate.**

This is also a matter of taste, but it is a good rule of thumb. It especially applies to screens that are mostly text that have a graphic art look (as opposed to an illustration or painted look).

7. **Be sure icons are clear and unambiguous to all users.**

Most developers have adopted the term "icon" to describe the small graphic areas on the screen that the user can touch to exercise individual control over the application. Examples include [Main Menu], [Pause], [Return to Previous Menu], and so on.

Since the advent of iconic street signs, it's been tempting to get clever with pictorial control icons. Unfortunately, the symbols may not be understood by all users. Sometimes the best approach is to spell out the function in words, draw a box around it, and be done with it.

8. **Match the graphic to the accompanying audio script.**

- Use the exact same words in graphic and audio script.

- Graphic words should be placed in same order as they come in the script, from left to right, top to bottom.

- Art or icons should suggest the same words as in the script.

We made this point when discussing video storyboards concerning using video graphics; it applies equally to using computer graphics with an audio script. The two media must work hand in hand. And **never** let a developer try to convince you that he can get twice as much information across by saying one thing and displaying another!

9. **Allow for touch area design considerations.**

- Leave sufficient room to place the touch areas.

- Use "tall" touch areas to reduce parallax errors (that is, misaligned user touches due to the thickness of the glass screen).

- Match shape of touch targets to rectangular shape of touch areas.

- Choose colors that support planned visual touch acknowledgments (that is, touch areas that change color when touched).

Touch screens are becoming more and more common in multimedia applications, especially in public access applications. Developers and graphic artists who design screens to work with them have to allow for these special considerations.

10. **Screens to be used as overlays are matched to video picture, with allowance for small alignment variations between systems.**

If your system allows the combined use of computer graphics "overlayed" on video pictures, your project takes on the added complexity of matching the work of the graphic artist and the video producer. First, the developer must make it clear in the Super Storyboard as to how the total picture will look, and which parts of the picture will be displayed in each medium. Then, the two parts must be matched up. Occasionally, the graphics are produced first, a delivery system taken into the video studio, and the video matched to the graphic. More often, the video is produced first, and a tape or disc is used to match the graphics to the video. In either case, the artist and producer must be aware that on some types of systems, there may be slight differences in registration of the two pictures between different delivery machines, so the graphics should not be drawn to an exact match. Leave a little overlap to allow for the variations. The developer must be aware of this requirement, and not design a screen that would depend on an exact match of images on all systems.

Note. We've looked at a lot of detail concerning graphic development. As Project Manager, you probably won't be involved in day-to-day evaluation of either the development of the graphic renditions or the production of the graphics themselves, even if the people who do this are in your organization. It's wise, however, to get involved for a short time at the point where the first graphics are beginning to be produced. A quick inspection can determine whether the artist is having any trouble following the renditions. You can judge the level of skill of the artist, and see that the style of graphics is acceptable to you. Once you are confident that the graphics development and production tasks are proceeding well, you can follow the progress after that with just an occasional look in.

8

Assembling a Production Data Base

Figure 7-6 shows the bottom part of the Super Storyboard form we showed previously in Figure 7-3.

It is used to record data that can be made into lists of valuable information to aid the production process. Most of the entries pertain to video production items, such as identifying the set or location where the scene will be shot, the props, the talent used for on-camera work or voice-over, and the video graphics needed for production or post-production. We'll discuss these items in detail in the next chapter covering the Production Phase. For now, let's note in passing that the planning for the production activity is done here during development. The information captured in this section of the SSB can be entered into a database program, and become the production database for video. The database program will allow the data to be sorted into sequences that will enable efficient production. For example, rather than shooting scenes in the order they'll appear on the disc, all of the scenes shot on one particular set or location can be shot together. The actors and actresses can be called to shoot their scenes together, possibly avoiding a day's shoot. (They are paid by the day, no matter how little time they work.) Lists of graphics and props can be compiled and checked to make sure the full crew isn't standing around while a critical item

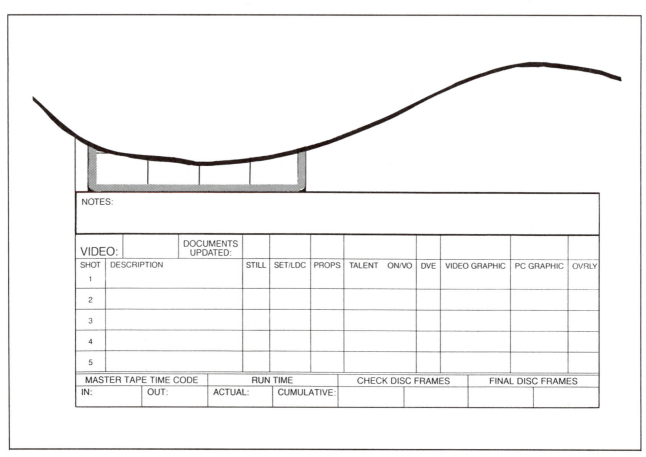

BOTTOM SECTION OF SUPER STORYBOARD

Figure 7-6 Information for a Production Data Base

is being scrounged up at the last minute. In a complex project, conscientious use of a good production database can lead to substantial savings.

Review of the Deliverable Items

Just as a quick review, let's list the documents that we have discussed in this chapter.

- The Super Storyboard
- Video Storyboards
- Audio Scripts
- Shot Lists for Still Frames
- Art Renditions
- Computer Graphic Renditions
- Production Database

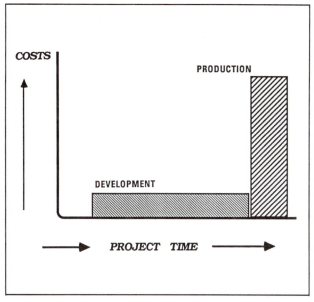

Figure 7-7 Development/Production Relationship

Roles of the Project Manager

Managing the Creative Process

Creativity is achieved most easily by hiring or selecting creative people. Managing creative people can be a challenge. They can be temperamental and sensitive to criticism. They can view the content of the application as their turf, and become very protective when Project Managers begin to question whether their treatment is appropriate to application objectives. Most developers are competent professionals who will work with you as hard as it takes to achieve a quality product. If you do run into the exception of the temperamental artist, however, remember that in the final analysis, you hold the purse strings, and you win the arguments. Having too little creativity on a project can be disastrous, but having too much can be a problem too. Many projects have gone off the track because the script treatment has been too bizarre or esoteric for the objectives. The treatment issues should have been settled way back in high-level design; the task during development is to ensure that the developers are staying on the track.

A key management task is to ensure effective communication among the team members who depend on each other for information about their interrelated documents. In a large project, regular meetings to share information are advisable. In any project, you should make all efforts to keep in touch with the developers and see that meetings are held whenever progress is getting bogged down.

Managing the Business Process

PREPARING FOR PRODUCTION

The main business factor that is affecting the Development Phase is that it's the last chance to get fully prepared for the Production Phase. It's useful to keep the diagram shown in Figure 7-7 in mind when you're in development:

The diagram indicates that dollars are being spent in the Development Phase at a low rate over a long period. Dollars are spent in the Production Phase at a high rate over a short period. It makes good sense to spend more time during development before production schedules are set to concentrate on the following:

- Achieving higher quality and effectiveness in the application.
- Planning less costly production approaches.
- Ensuring that all information and documentation needed to complete production is available.

On the other hand, spending time during the Production Phase on these considerations is extremely costly. It would be naive to assume that you will be able to cover all the bases, and that no deviations from the development plan will occur during production, but that is a worthwhile goal to set for the Development Phase.

Evaluating the Deliverables

Your first evaluation criterion is to re-apply the three development attributes of producible documentation:

- Is it **clear**?

- Is it **complete**?

- Is it **consistent**?

In addition, the media elements that are described by the documentation must meet your standards for quality content. One way to look at this is to ask the question, do these elements meet the design criteria, and the goals and objectives of the application? Another question is, do these elements look like "good" interactive video components? Clearly, there are some very individual and subjective judgments to be made in this area.

A final consideration is to be sure that the elements described can be produced within the application budget. At this stage, the content of the elements and their cost should be able to be gauged with great accuracy. If a developer has called for approaches that will blow the budget, now is the time to catch the problem before production is committed.

Most of this chapter has been spent on evaluation considerations, and now would be a good time to review the checklists. When you do, you'll see that they are very similar to the Design Phase checklists. The reason is clear when you think about it. In Design, your objective was to evaluate whether the proposed design was an effective plan to accomplish the application goals. In Development, your objective is to evaluate whether the plan was captured on paper. In each case, the points to consider are the same—you're just looking at two ends of the same stick.

A Last Word

The Development Phase is the longest, and occasionally, the most tedious part of the project. The creative sparks of the Design Phase have given way to concentrated effort in documenting the design, and make no mistake, this is hard and painstaking work. A significant percentage of the total project time will be spent in development. Progress is slow and results are hard to see. When a lot of people are on the team, their interdependence can lead to frustration and short tempers if information isn't flowing efficiently. In other words, watch out for the Development Phase. It can test your skills in managing people to the utmost.

You need to stay closely involved during this phase to head off problems before they become serious, and to constantly encourage the team. At the same time, you need to be constantly evaluating their efforts. We've tried to provide you with communication terminology and objective criteria. In the final analysis, however, the evaluation will be based on many subjective factors of taste and creativity as well. You should be ready to accept the input of the professionals on your team at all times, but the project that you take to your Sponsoring Executive will be yours, not theirs. Faith in yourself and in your own common sense must ultimately be the foundation of your decisions.

Chapter Eight

Producing the Media

Preview of the Production Phase

The purpose of production is to translate your paper documents from the development phase onto the appropriate media for authoring. That process includes:

- storyboards onto video tape,

- audio scripts onto audio tape,

- graphic renditions onto computer files,

- text and print materials onto camera-ready forms.

From these production media, the application contents will be recorded on distribution media such as videodisc, diskettes and CD-ROM.

The question: "Is this documentation producible?" is about to be answered.

There are, of course, many types of media to be produced. In this chapter, we're going to concentrate on the mainstay of interactive video application, video itself. If you do not plan to use motion video, or are planning to use a generic videodisc, or one that has already been produced, you may wish to skip this chapter. If you are going to produce video, however, and are not already familiar with the process, this chapter will cover the activities of what will unquestionably be the most exciting phase in the project.

Production consumes the shortest part of your schedule, but the largest part of the budget. This phase will be over before you realize it. To maintain your control (and composure) during this critical phase, we've organized the chapter into a tour of the production process, its dangers, and its opportunities. We'll introduce you to the studio, the production specialists, and the key activities, so they'll be familiar when you meet them. Your involvement can be divided into three time periods:

- before production ... planning, rehearsing, and organizing all the materials for an efficient studio experience.

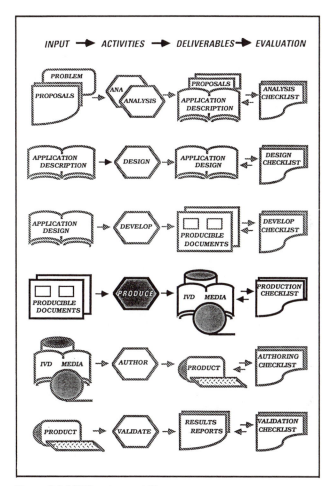

Figure 8-1 IVD Development Phases

- during production ... observing, checking, and deciding if the content is covered, correct, and complete.

- after production ... editing, consolidating, and evaluating the media components against your criteria and the application's objectives.

When the individual application elements are captured on the appropriate media, they are still independent and isolated. The next step is to merge them (author them) into a finished product.

Generic Videodiscs and Repurposing

The high cost of video production makes it prudent to consider using video that has already been created. Some publishers and universities have produced "generic videodiscs" for general use. Several are available in such fields as art and medicine.

It may also make good sense to consider producing your own generic videodisc that would contain all the images needed to support an entire series of IVD applications. This would allow you to replicate and distribute a single videodisc, and deliver the individual presentations on diskette or CD-ROM.

Another way to save production costs is to "repurpose" existing video. The material may consist of linear video tape that can be transcribed to a videodisc. The new program is developed by extracting single frames or video segments, and adding new audio and computer graphics. Sometimes, a previously produced videodisc can be repurposed with a new set of application code and graphics.

Although these approaches are seldom as effective as producing new video, the cost savings are worth their consideration if suitable material is available.

Looking Over the Territory

What We're Trying to Accomplish

After all the weeks of preparation, it's finally time to go into production. At last we're going to see material created that will become part of the actual application. For a brief but exciting time, we'll be spending time on sound stages or shooting locations, and in edit suites where the video elements will be built into final form in front of our eyes. The completion of production will be a major milestone in the project, and if all goes well, your team will deserve a real celebration.

The goal of video production is to record all of the video elements on time and on budget, while achieving the highest possible level of quality. The quality of the video will be the most important factor in determining the quality of the "look and feel" of your application. Making the right balance between controlling cost and achieving quality is the key ingredient in successful production, and as Project Manager, you'll play a key role.

During this phase, you'll work closely with an individual we will call the "Managing Producer." This is the individual who is responsible for video production. As Project Manager, you'll work closely with the Managing Producer, but your tasks will be very different.

Along with the aspects of fun and excitement that accompany the Production Phase, as Project Manager you have major responsibilities. Project funds—your project funds—are being spent at a rapid rate. The video material being recorded on tape is permanent; changing it later will be expensive and maybe impossible. Mistakes are bound to occur, and they must be caught and corrected immediately. Decisions will have to be made whether to incur the cost of shooting a scene again, or whether it is "good enough" as it is. You'll need to be available at all times to work with the Managing Producer to monitor the production and to make decisions relating to cost and quality when they're needed.

There are other items beside the video that must be produced during this phase. Computer graphics are produced in a separate process which is independent of video production except when the graphics are overlayed over video. We discussed the considerations for developing and producing computer graphics in the Development chapter. Your application may also call for printed materials to be produced that must be made ready for publication during this phase. In this chapter, however, we'll concentrate on the process of video production — the largest single item in your budget.

Deliverable Items for the Production Phase

The deliverable items for the Production Phase consist of all of the individual media elements that will be part of the final presentation. These may include:

- the videodisc with all video motion segments, still frames and audio segments,

- audio segments on other media, if any,

- computer graphics recorded on a machine readable medium,

- camera-ready material for print publishing if printed matter will be needed to support the final application.

The video material will exist in several forms. The first deliverable video item is a master videotape that contains all of the video and audio material, and has been edited into a format acceptable for videodisc replication. From this master tape, preliminary copies will be made in formats that can be used by the authors to begin the authoring of video elements. The tape will be sent to the videodisc manufacturer to begin the final replication of the actual application videodiscs. We'll discuss these various items in detail later in this chapter.

If you plan to use CD-ROM, the material may be produced in one of two ways. Computer files are used for graphics, data, and some forms of digital audio. Audio tapes are used for producing various audio formats available on CD-ROM. The process of creating a master compact disc tape is called "publishing." This tape is used by the CD-ROM manufacturer in much the same way that the master video tape is used to replicate videodiscs. The techniques used in CD-ROM publishing vary according to the format being used. The details of the process, and the requirements for the material to be submitted should be obtained from the specific manufacturers.

So What's New?

There are some important differences between production of standard linear video and production slated for an interactive videodisc. In standard production, the video is itself the final product. When the master tape is complete, the program is complete. In IVD, of course, the video is a critical, but partial piece of the total presentation. Often, this is a new idea to the video producers.

The Director who is primarily responsible for creating the original tape has to deal with several new considerations in producing video for IVD.

- He must be aware that he is shooting a series of individual segments, and must treat each of them as a self-contained program.

- He must be aware that his material will be interacting with other kinds of media that may not be present at the time he is shooting.

- He must allow for the fact that the sequence of individual segments will be selected by the end user, and smooth transitions will require planning for all the choices available.

These differences require some considerations on the part of the Managing Producer and you regarding the Director. First, it will be to your advantage if you have a Director who has prior experience with IVD production. If your Director is new, then you and the Managing Producer need to make sure that he is given an in-depth familiarization with IVD applica-

tions and the technology of the videodisc. Second, the Director will have to spend a good deal of time going over the total set of producible documentation, including especially the Super Storyboards. He'll need to make notations on his shooting script when his video is being used in combination with graphics or other system facilities. In short, he must be completely aware of the total presentation content as he creates his part. Another group which must deal with new concepts is the camera crew. They are used to composing their shots for the full screen, with no allowance for other components that may be present in IVD. It is good practice for the Director to keep them informed when he is calling for a shot that may seem unnatural to the camera crew.

An even more important individual who must understand the new aspects of IVD is the Video Editor. First, it is necessary that the master tape be created according to unique specifications required by the videodisc manufacturer. The Editor must be aware of these specifications and comply with them. Second, the Editor needs to understand videodisc technology. More than one master tape has been created with long periods of black frames between video segments to "keep them separate and easy to find." Another common error for a new Editor is to record still frames for 30 seconds or "so the viewer will have time to read it."

In other words, the personnel involved in video production may be familiar only with linear video techniques, and you and the Managing Producer must be on guard to insure that the new requirements of IVD are met.

How Do We Get There?

Video production requires a lot of people with highly specialized skills, and a great deal of expensive equipment. For this reason, video production is often handled by sub-contractors to the prime vendor (although many vendors keep key talents on their own staff such as producers, directors and writers). If you work for a large company or institution, video production may be handled by a department that provides this service. In any event, it is unlikely that as Project Manager, you'll be directly involved in the production. However, it remains your responsibility to monitor the activity.

As Figure 8-2 illustrates, video production is divided into three steps:

1. Pre-production

This step consists of all of the planning activity

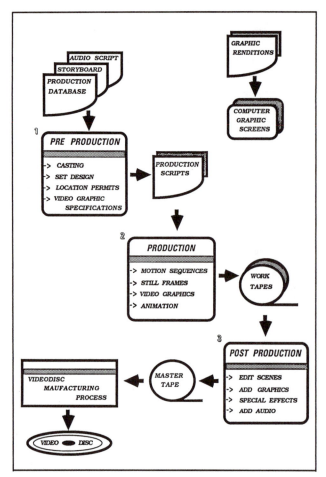

Figure 8-2 The Production Process

that precedes the actual shooting of tape. The Managing Producer and Director will take the video storyboards that were written during the Development Phase and make preparations including casting, set design, location selection and so on. Video graphics or artwork that will be needed during production are designed and made ready. Props are lined up. All in all, pre-production can take weeks to prepare for a large project. The time is well spent, however, since production itself (when really big dollars are being expended) may take only a few days if the preparation was done carefully.

2. Production

Production takes place on location or on a sound stage. In addition to the creative personnel who have worked on the project, you are suddenly joined by a raft of technical experts to handle lighting, sound, video engineering and camera work. If you are using professional actors for "talent," they show up, read their lines, and are quickly gone. When it's over, the Director has a large volume of footage "in the can" that consists of the final images that will go on to the

videodisc, plus a great deal of unusable footage and "out-takes."

3. Post-Production

The work tapes that were shot during production are then taken to post-production where they will be merged with video graphics and edited into the final videodisc master tape. Editing the original high quality tape requires special and expensive equipment, so to minimize cost, the first step in post-production is to carefully plan each editing operation that will be done. This process is called "off-line editing" and is accomplished by making copies of the original tapes, using inexpensive equipment to plan the edits and recording them on an "EDL," or Edit Decision List. When the EDL is ready, the original tapes are taken to a post-production facility for "on-line editing" where the final video master tape is constructed. This tape is then sent to the videodisc manufacturer for replication.

The Video Production Process

Roles in the Production Team

Before we review the various steps of video production in detail, let's review the roles of the team that will perform the tasks. You may not interact with all of them directly, but you should be aware of who is involved, and what part they play in the overall production.

THE MANAGING PRODUCER

In an IVD project, there should be one person who is responsible for delivering the video and audio content of the application. We will call this person the "Managing Producer," although in an actual project, a different title may be used. If you are working with a vendor, the Managing Producer may be on the vendor's staff, or working under a sub-contract. Whatever the case, the Managing Producer will play a key role in controlling the cost, schedule and quality of the video production. You should plan to interface directly with the Managing Producer concerning these issues.

THE DIRECTOR

The Director is in charge of the production team during the shooting of the videotape, and usually plays a key role during pre-production and post-production as well. He or she is the one person most responsible for achieving high quality in the finished product. Often the Director and the Managing

Figure 8-3 The director walks through the scene with the talent to rehearse the scene before rolling tape

Producer are the same person. When the production team is in action, any questions or comments that you have should be made only to the Director.

TALENT

The actors and professional narrators that appear in the video and audio portions are usually referred to as "talent." You'll play a key role in selecting or approving them for the production.

PRE-PRODUCTION PERSONNEL

There are several roles that may be active during pre-production, some of whom you may never meet. They include video graphic artists, set designers, casting agents and so on. The Managing Producer and Director will handle most of the interface with them.

PRODUCTION CREW

A limited video production can be accomplished with as few as two people who share many roles; a large production can involve a large crew. When you watch the "credits" at a movie, you can get an idea of how many roles there are in a full production. Some of the more important roles are:

- In the control room or at the video recording station:

  - Video Engineer — monitors the video recording equipment and insures a high quality, standard signal is recorded.

  - Audio Engineer — monitors the audio recording and insures clean sound at a consistent level.

  - Technical Director — on the Director's commands, handles the switching of cameras, video graphics and special effects.

  - Script Supervisor — keeps careful detailed notes of every scene, shot and "take" recorded on the tape for use later during editing.

- On the stage or shooting location:

  - Floor Director — if the Director prefers to work from the control room, the Floor Director acts as his agent on the stage to direct the crew.

  - Lighting Director — lights the sets and makes necessary adjustments during shooting; helped by assistants called "Grips."

  - Stage Manager — constructs and manipulates sets and props; helped by assistants called "Gaffers."

  - Camera Persons — frame and focus shots and move cameras as instructed by the Director.

If the production is elaborate, this list may be extended further to include many others, such as wardrobe for costumes, make-up, chaperones if children are used as talent and wranglers if the script calls for animals. In a complex production, there may be more people in the studio on shooting days than have been involved in all other phases of the project put together.

In practice, however, most video productions will have a few members on the crew performing multiple roles. An adequate crew for an uncomplicated

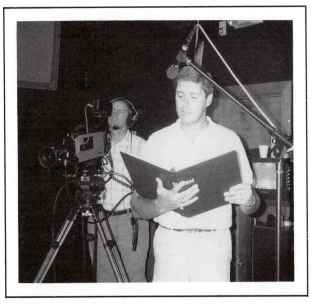

Figure 8-4 Voice-over recordings are often done right in the studio for quick and easy production

production could consist of the Director, Camera Person and Gaffer/Grip on the stage, and a Video/Audio "Tech" (engineer) and Script Supervisor in the booth.

POST-PRODUCTION PERSONNEL

The key person in post-production is the Video Editor. If you are doing your "post" in a professional facility, the Editor will be seated at a console that may look more complex than an airliner cockpit. His job is to work with the Director, using the Script Supervisor's notes, to select and merge the shots from the work tapes into the finished production on the master tape. Most Editors bring a high degree of creativity to the project, achieving special effects that improve the original production, and finding ways to remove or mask errors that occurred on the set.

Behind the scenes there will probably be several people working that you will hardly see. There will be "Video Techs" (engineers) keeping the equipment properly adjusted and solving technical problems, and "Tape Ops" (operators) putting up and pulling down tapes on the big tape recorders that are usually off in another room.

Another job in post-production is the Audio Engineer who mixes the sound recorded in the studio with other sound such as music and sound effects, and "sweetens" the audio track if necessary to achieve the best possible clarity and quality.

Looking over this list of people with specialized skills, and the equipment needed to support them, it's easy to see why production costs are high, and why careful planning in managing the activities in this phase is so important.

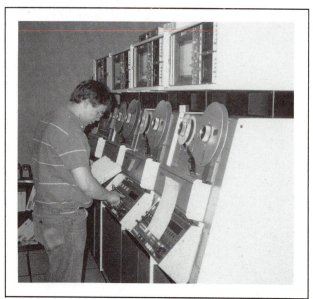

Figure 8-5 In the back room, the tape operator keeps the right tapes mounted for editing

Pre-Production Activities

In a very real sense, pre-production begins as soon as the video treatment is decided on in high level design. Many of the needs for talent, sets, locations, and other special requirements will be identified at this time. For this reason, it makes sense to involve the Managing Producer and/or the Director as early as possible. This will also give you the benefit of their ideas and advice on video content. A good Director should be able to offer many suggestions as to how to achieve objectives with innovative and less expensive techniques. If you're working with a vendor, you should recommend that the Managing Producer and Director get on board in the project as soon as possible.

CASTING

As soon as scripting has progressed far enough to identify the talent that will be required, casting can begin. This can be a time consuming project, and you will need to be involved. One decision involves the degree of professionalism you plan to use. This can range from recruiting in-house talent from around your own organization to hiring nationally recognized personalities. There is danger at both ends of the scale. If you hire talent with "face recognition," you are going to pay a substantial premium, and you run the risk of overwhelming the message you're trying to get across with the personality of your talent. If you use amateur talent, you may never get the portrayal that you're looking for, and if you do, it may require many more takes on the set than a professional talent would have needed.

A middle course is to hire professional actors and actresses from a casting agency who are not well-known, but fit your concept of what the roles should look like. You may begin by working with the Director to select some likely candidates from photographs in a casting book. Then you may request casting tapes, or if your budget allows, have your Director record them at a casting session.

> **Note.** If you chose only one detailed decision in which to involve your Sponsoring Executive, make it this one. Nothing affects the perception of quality in IVD as much as the video, and nothing affects the video as strongly as the look and personality of the talent. Make sure your management buys off on the talent! Most other factors can be fixed if necessary, but if they don't like the people, the whole project could be scuttled.

SCHEDULING

The number of people and facilities involved in production makes scheduling a non-trivial activity. There are often conflicts for the services of good Directors and production personnel and their calendars get booked weeks in advance. Facilities such as editing suites can be booked for large blocks of time, and you may end up having to go farther away or working the graveyard shift. If you are shooting in remote locations, it usually makes sense to schedule local people to minimize travel and living costs. These arrangements need to be made well in advance of the shoot.

Location shooting permits may also be a major concern of the Managing Producer. You can't just set up on the street somewhere and start cameras rolling. Sometimes a police cordon will be needed, or a release from the owner of the property that will be used for background. In some states, these permits can be quite costly.

PRODUCTION APPROVALS

Approvals for all kinds of production elements need to be in place before they are committed. These include sets, locations, costumes (or styles of normal dress), art work, video graphic styles and so on. These decisions aren't as critical as casting, but you will probably still want to be involved with the Managing Producer to make sure that the decisions made are appropriate and will support your objectives.

FINANCIAL MANAGEMENT

The Managing Producer must pay up front for many of the production services, and it is his responsibility to see that payments are made. You should be aware of this responsibility and be sure that your own payments are made on time to avoid cash flow problems that could lead to production delays.

Production Activities

PREPARING TO SHOOT

After all these many weeks of preparation, the day for shooting the video elements of the application has arrived. When you arrive at the shooting location, a lot of activity is already underway. The sets were probably constructed a day or two before, and most of the surprisingly large number of lights have been put in place. The crew is busy in taking care of last minute adjustments and details. Cables are being rerouted on the floor, and grips are up on ladders adjusting the "barn doors" (light shields) on the overhead lights as instructed by the lighting director. (Or, in a smaller production, all of these tasks are

being done by one gaffer.) Your natural inclination will be to find a spot out of the way of all this activity and stay there quietly. Your inclination is good—that's just what you should do.

After a while, things will calm down a little, but there seems to be nothing happening! Everyone is just standing around, except maybe one "tech" fooling with a mike boom (a small crane-like contraption with a microphone at its end) or clipping a small "lavolier" mike to the talent and hiding the cord. What's going on here is the final checkout and adjustments of the recording equipment by the video and audio engineers. Sometimes the systems can get cantankerous and the checkout drags on while everyone gets more impatient. If all goes well, however, the OK will be given reasonably soon in the day, and the Director will begin working with the talent to rehearse and shoot the first scene.

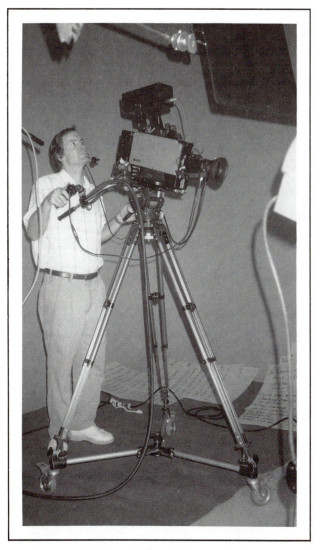

Figure 8-6 A camera operator with a steady hand and a deft touch can give the director just the right shot

Figure 8-7 The critical tasks of video and audio engineering and script supervision take place in the control room

Figure 8-8 Unobtrusive but critical, the line monitor in the studio is the director's best tool for judging quality

Certain members of the crew will be wearing headsets and getting information from the engineers in the booth. A light stand may be appearing in a corner of the picture, or an item on the set may be causing a "hot" reflection into the camera. The crew will correct these problems as they come up.

When a scene is actually going to be recorded, you may hear one of the crew members with a headset say "Tape is rolling . . . Speed!" This means that the camera's images are being recorded, and the Director will signal for a "slate" — a visual and voice identification of the scene to help identify it later when it's being edited. Then the Director will call "Action!" and the scene will be played out by the talent. This process may be repeated several times until the Director, the engineers and you are satisfied with the take.

At times during the shoot, the Director may call for quiet on the set to record "room noise." This is a contingency in case an audio edit has to be made later to correct a scene. The talent can be hired to come in again, but the exact background noise in the room can never be reconstructed again. By mixing the voice with the room noise recording, the later audio edit can be made to sound fairly smooth and unnoticeable.

Another contingency action that an experienced director will take is to record several "cutaway shots." These are just a set of takes of individual talent making various kinds of reactions such as listening and nodding, smiling, chuckling, surprise, and so on. They also will be used later in editing if material needs to be cut out, or if sections of two

scenes need to be knit together into one. The cut would be obvious if the camera remained on the speaking talent. By editing in a cutaway shot, the revision will go unnoticed.

Your tool for following the production is the line monitor. A *line monitor* is a TV set that is showing the same picture that is being recorded on tape. Wherever the Director has chosen to place himself, on the stage or in the booth, there will be a line monitor present. A good director will make his judgment of the acceptability of a take by watching the line monitor live or on playback. You should be close to the monitor and make your evaluation the same way.

YOUR ROLE DURING THE SHOOT

Your evaluation and the role you play in production is critical, but it should be unobtrusive as well. The major questions about the content and treatment should have been decided during pre-production planning. If all goes well, the planning will have been sufficient, and you won't have to intervene in the process at all.

It's likely, however, that all won't go as planned. Problems in production may arise that prevent a scene from being shot the way you and the Director would like it. To get it just right might require significant time and production costs. Or, a new idea may occur to the Director that would result in substantial improvement for "only a little more cost." Is it worth it? The decision will be up to you. Other problems may come up that only you recognize. The talent may have mispronounced an unfamiliar technical term, or for some hard to define reason, the scene may just not look realistic. When this happens, you need to make your concerns known.

In any of these cases, it will be important that you work directly and **only** with the Director. On the set, the Director is the General in charge, and every person expects their instructions to come from him. As the sponsor, your importance is recognized, but you can cause confusion if you give any orders or opinions, no matter how minor, to other members of the crew. A simple comment to the Director, "John, I've got a problem here with that take," will suffice to hold things up until the problem can be fixed, or the scene reshot.

Let's review the major items that you want to be alert for as you evaluate a take:

• Review your objectives; is the production meeting them?

• Is the content accurate?

• Are the visual pictures on the line monitor being presented properly? Are the important parts of the picture clearly visible?

• Are the lines being read with correct pronunciation and natural presentation?

• Is the talent believable in the roles they are portraying?

• Is the set dressed out properly? Does it look like what it's supposed to?

• Have any glitches such as reflections or stage equipment crept into the picture and escaped the notice of the crew?

Even if you can't put your finger on it, however, if you have a feeling that the scene is wrong, call it to the attention of the Director, and see if he can help you define the problem. His job is to satisfy you with the final product, and he and the crew will go to extreme lengths to meet that objective.

Post-Production Activities

When the shooting days in the studio or on location are done, there are likely to be several reels of tape "in the can." It's likely that most of the footage is waste between scenes or "out-takes" that weren't acceptable for one reason or another. Selecting the good takes and combining them onto the final master tape is done during the post-production process.

While this task is going on, several other activities will take place, such as creating special effects, adding video graphics and mixing sound effects and music with the original audio track. All in all, post-production can be just as exciting and creative a process as shooting the original tape.

OFF-LINE EDITING

It will be very costly when the original tape is taken to a post-production facility for final editing, because the process will involve a lot of skilled talent and expensive equipment. To minimize these costs, the edit session is thoroughly planned out in a process called **off-line editing**. "Off-line" is accomplished by making copies of the original set of tapes on inexpensive cassettes that can be viewed with 1/2" or 3/4" VCRs. Time on these machines can be purchased cheaply — in fact, some off-line editing is done with regular video players at home!

Because S.M.P.T.E. time code is used so much in post-production, it will be worth a small digression to explain it here. The code is a standard means of frame identification developed by the Society of Motion Picture and Television Engineers — S.M.P.T.E. It is an eight-digit number of the form:

HH : MM : SS : FF

which stands for "Hours: Minutes: Seconds: Frame." The numbers fall into these ranges:

HH : 00 - 23 (24 hours)
MM : 00 - 59 (60 minutes)
SS : 00 - 59 (60 seconds)
FF : 00 - 29 (30 frames per second)

In broadcast applications, the numbers sometimes are used to correspond to the wall clock time of broadcast. In non-broadcast and videodisc applications, the hour number usually identifies the tape reel. For example, a scene near the beginning of tape 2 that lasts about 40 seconds might have its "in" and "out" points identified as:

IN — 02 : 05 : 10 : 12   OUT — 02 : 05 : 50 : 18

The frame numbers are often ignored when recording time code for locating scenes — they run at thirty frames per second and are almost impossible to read accurately. During the final edit, however, frame numbers are used extensively to time edits down to the exact fraction of a second.

Two factors make it possible to plan the edit session during the off-line edit:

1. The complete set of notes kept by the Script Supervisor during the shoot lists every take on each reel by frame numbers recorded on the tape in "S.M.P.T.E. time code."

2. These time codes are "burnt in" on the cassette copies so they can be seen on the TV screen.

Thus, the final edit session can be planned in detail by selecting the "in" and "out" points (start and finish) of each segment to be recorded on the final master. The time codes are recorded on a form called the "Edit Decision List," or "EDL."

The Edit Decision List may be just a list of time codes written down by hand on a form. On the other hand, there are also special facilities that are set up especially for off-line editing that will keep track of the in- and out-frames on a computer diskette that can be used later to control the equipment during final edit. Some of these facilities will actually play back the scenes as they will appear on the final tape. Naturally, these facilities cost more than just using a standard home tape recorder, but the resulting efficiency in the edit suite can be well worth the investment. Your Director will make the decision as to which is the least expensive route to take.

Unless you have used a sophisticated facility to preview the final result, you probably won't have a clear idea of what the final production will look like after the off-line edit. Most of the work in this step is spent in identifying the takes to keep and what to throw away. The sessions can be long and tedious. Unless your Director specifically requests that you be there, it is probably not necessary for you to attend. By being aware of what goes on in off-line, however, you'll better understand what is happening in the crucial final editing process that takes place in the edit suite.

THE ON-LINE EDIT SESSION

The on-line edit session is undoubtedly one of the high points of the project. The video footage that was shot in a seemingly disorganized fashion during production is constructed, segment by segment, into the final video presentation that will carry the message you originally conceived of so many weeks ago. The construction will take place under the eye of your Director, and a new individual with unique and creative talents—the Video Editor.

Even a simple editing suite can contain an intimidating amount of equipment. If you are editing in a professional broadcast quality post-production

Figure 8-9 Surrounded by banks of equipment, the video editor puts the last creative touch on the production

facility, it can be downright overwhelming. There will always be a board with long rows of lighted keys and switch handles that look like jet airplane throttles. This is called a "switcher/fader" or just "switcher." There will also be television monitor screens that show the original material and special graphics and effects that the editor is constructing. The most important monitor, however, is the one that shows what is being recorded on the master tape as it is being built.

As the client, you will probably get special treatment. You'll be given a special chair, plush, comfortable and out of the way. For most of the session, that's where you should stay. Post-production editing is as technically demanding as it is creative, and a button pushed out of turn can ruin an entire sequence of operations. The wrong button at the wrong time can even destroy original material. It's best not to bother the editor with a stream of questions.

There are, however, legitimate questions to be asked. Most editors are experienced in normal video editing procedures, but they may not be familiar with videodisc requirements. They may not be aware of the videodisc player's capability of displaying a single frame for an indeterminate amount of time, or of the computer's capability to add graphic overlays to the material they are editing. They may not know that tapes intended to be used for videodisc replication have different format requirements than those edited for videocassette distribution. These items are discussed later in this chapter when we discuss the Disc Production Work Order, along with the key checklist items you should review with the editor before the session starts.

Another time to raise a question is if you see something being recorded on the master tape that you don't find acceptable. Sometimes, however, it may be difficult to follow just what is being temporarily put together as a step in the process, and what is actually being included on the master tape. Special effects are built up one operation at a time, and it may take many steps to achieve a final result. While this is going on, pictures are appearing and disappearing on various monitors, tape drives are spinning (if you can see them) and the editor is punching buttons like a mad man.

For example, consider what it takes to create a simple dissolve from one scene to the next. Since during a dissolve, pictures from both scenes are required, they must be recorded on two tape recorders so they can be played back at the same time as input. If both scenes were recorded on the same tape in the studio, the first step will be to record the second scene onto a work tape. Then, the two input tape recorders and the master tape recorder must be exactly positioned so that when the first input tape scene comes up, the master tape recorder is running and exactly positioned to begin recording. Since tape recorders do not start and get to recording speed immediately, this requires that each machine be "back-rolled" a precise amount. Now, when it's almost time to dissolve to the second scene, the other tape recorder must be started so the picture will be there, and the dissolve from scene one to scene two can be accomplished. Now, if we want to add some character graphics to the second scene ... well, you get the picture.

Figure 8-10 Simple text video graphics can be created quickly and added to the program with a character generator

Most of these operations in a modern edit suite are taken care of automatically by the system; the editor controls the process by providing the critical frame numbers to start, stop and perform edit functions from the Edit Decision List. He will often set up an effect and try it out before it is recorded. Even with experience, it can be quite confusing to follow exactly what is going on.

You are there for a purpose, however, and that is to make sure that you are satisfied with the content of the final video elements that are being created. It's perfectly legitimate to ask, "Is that the way you're going to record it?" If it is, and you're not happy with the accuracy, the way the material is presented, or anything else, discuss it at the time. Once the editor has moved on the next scene or segment, it will be extremely expensive to go back.

On the other hand, you should probably resist the temptation to become involved in the creative process. As you become familiar with the capability of the equipment, you'll probably get some new ideas about how a certain point could be presented. By using electronic techniques similar to those we see all the time on broadcast television, almost any idea for presentation can be accomplished. It may require more time and expensive equipment than your budget allows, however, and most of the time it's probably best to stick to the original plan and EDL.

Perhaps the most important reason for you to be present in the edit suite is to make final decisions as to how to handle unforeseen problems. For one reason or another, equipment failure or mix-ups during original production, the editor may not be able to create the presentation exactly as it was planned. An unwanted image or a wrong word may have slipped by unnoticed during the taping. At these times, you'll be called upon to weigh the cost and time of correcting the problem versus accepting what can be done quickly and moving on. In these situations, you'll have to use your common sense to thread a path between reasonable compromises and your own demands for a quality product. On one hand, cost overruns have to be avoided, but on the other hand, you'll be living with the finished video for a long time. Overall, however, most of the time in the edit suite will be an exciting culmination of weeks of preparation. You'll have the experience of seeing what was only imagined before come to life before your eyes, and usually it is a very satisfying moment.

After the video has been recorded on the master tape, there is usually still more work to be done to finish the final audio work. The audio that accompanies the video picture may need some work to be "sweetened" if the acoustics were not perfect on the set. If music and sound needs to be added, there will have to be a "mixing" session where all of the audio sources are balanced and combined with each other into a single track. If your project calls for second track audio, the second track will have to be prepared, then recorded on to track two of the master tape.

When all of the post-production activity is complete, you will have created one video master tape that contains everything put together and probably cost tens of thousands of dollars. Therefore, the final step in video post-production is to "dub" (copy) a protection master. This tape will usually be kept in a temperature and humidity controlled vault at the post-production house in case any disaster should befall the original master. The original master has the highest quality, however, and is generally the one that is sent to the disc manufacturer for replication. We'll discuss the replication process next.

Videodisc Replication Activities

THE REPLICATION PROCESS

Videodisc replication is a highly specialized activity that is done at only a few facilities in the world. The basic steps are:

1. Take the original master tape you have created and add the frame numbers and control signals that the videodisc player will recognize.

2. Create a master videodisc image on a polished glass disc with exact precision in an industrially clean environment.

3. From the glass master, create one or more negative image stamper discs that will be used to form the final videodisc replications.

4. Using the stamper discs in injection molding machines (similar to those used to press LP records), make clear plastic replications of the original glass master.

5. Complete the process by surfacing the discs with a metallic coating, applying a backing (or second disc side), and bonding the disc with a protective clear plastic layer.

6. Apply the label and insert the discs in their slipcases.

These steps are time consuming and expensive. Most manufacturers will offer a fast turnaround service for limited quantities of discs in one day or three days, but these services require a premium price. As Project Manager, you can help control prices by early, accurate scheduling, and avoid costly errors by ordering one-time copies of the disc that are called "check discs," "proof discs" or "DRAW discs."

THE CHECK DISC

Videodisc manufacturers offer a service to their customers called the "check disc." This is a single copy of the disc, usually the first one replicated from the glass master. The check disc is sent to you for inspection to be sure that everything is correct before proceeding to complete the replication process. If you find a problem that the manufacturer caused, they will remaster the tape. If you find a problem that was on the tape, you have saved the cost of replication of a run of defective discs.

You may also give the check disc to your authors to begin final authoring before the rest of the discs are delivered.

Another term you may hear is "proof disc." This term is applied to the first copy of videodiscs that have a control program recorded on them that will allow them to operate with a standalone videodisc player. (This type of videodisc is called a "Level Two" application, as opposed to "Level One" applications that are manually controlled, and "Level Three" applications that are controlled by a computer.) The proof disc contains the program as well as the video material, and is used to test the complete application before going on with replication. If your delivery system will control the videodisc player with a computer (a Level Three application) then you won't be concerned with Level Two discs or proof discs.

THE DRAW DISC

Another kind of disc used to preview the application and to get a head start on authoring is called a "DRAW disc." "DRAW" stands for "Direct Read After Write." A DRAW disc is a "one-off" copy of the master tape recorded directly on a disc medium that can be immediately put into a videodisc player and played back. They are recorded in real time, just like making a tape copy. Therefore, they can be created in just a few hours. Some post production houses have the ability to create DRAW discs themselves immediately after the final master tape has been edited. The DRAW disc itself, however, cannot be replicated; if you need a second copy, you merely repeat the DRAW process from the beginning.

DRAW discs provide the ability to view the presentation in its interactive form soon after production is complete. They are good for reviewing the video material, authoring the presentation, and seeing the visual combinations of video and graphic elements.

There is more than one DRAW format, and they vary in cost, quality and turnaround time. Some early formats were inexpensive, but required modifications to the player to avoid risk of damaging the disc and player. Some formats will only play back on machines similar to those that they were created on. Some formats are very fragile and require special handling. Some formats are durable and exactly similar to replicated discs, but cost more time and money to produce than other DRAW formats.

This technology is developing rapidly, and you should check with your disc manufacturer or post production facility to get their advice on which format is best for your requirements, or if the check disc itself is adequate to meet your need to check content and begin authoring.

The cost for obtaining DRAW and check discs can sometimes cause confusion. As this is written, typical costs for DRAW discs are:

- About $300 for a locally produced, more fragile DRAW disc.

- About $750 for a DRAW on a medium similar to replicated discs.

A check disc typically cost about $750, and it is essentially identical to the replicated disc. However, you can't **just** order a check disc — you must pay the entire mastering costs of about $1800 **plus** the $750 for the check disc. Most Project Managers authorize both DRAW and check discs. The DRAW disc allows review and authoring to go forward without delay. The check disc provides insurance that the disc is correct before committing to the entire replication run.

THE DISC PRODUCTION WORK ORDER

When the master tape is sent to the videodisc manufacturer, it is accompanied by a form called the Disc Production Work Order. Each manufacturer has a form for this purpose, but they all contain similar information. A typical form is shown in Figure 8-11. As Project Manager, you need to satisfy yourself that the form is completed by a knowledgeable individual who is aware of the technical details required in videodisc replication.

You probably won't be involved with all of these technical details, but you should make sure that **someone** on the project is looking after them. If your post production facility is not experienced in editing for videodisc replication, they may not be aware of certain requirements that are not important in linear productions. In particular, you should be sure

that the following items are covered before the final editing session begins:

1. Layout to Manufacturer's Specifications

Your disc manufacturer will provide a description of the layout of the master tape that the video editor must comply with. This specification will consist of:

- A period of color bars and audio tone used to set up the recording machine.

- A period of black frames with no audio used to record the "lead-in" signal on the disc.

- The "active program" consisting of the video and audio program elements with specific frames identified as the first frame or "S.A.P." (Start of Active Program) and last frame or "E.A.P." (End of Active Program).

- A period of black frames with no audio used to record the "lead-out" signal on the disc.

2. Non-Drop S.M.P.T.E. Time Code

Color video frames are actually a bit longer than 1/30 of a second, and broadcast facilities use "Drop-frame" time code which drops an occasional frame to keep the S.M.P.T.E minutes and seconds synchronized with the wall clock. Videodisc mastering equipment requires **no** missing frames; this form is called "Non-Drop Time Code." You should insure at the beginning of the session that the master tape will be encoded with Non-Drop S.M.P.T.E. time code.

3. Consistent Field Editing

A video frame consists of two "fields" which scan the complete picture on alternate, interlaced lines in 1/60 of a second each. The editing equipment can be set to edit either on field 1 or field 2. In linear video, it makes little difference because the edits go by so quickly, they are never seen. The single frame capability of videodisc, however, makes it critical that each edit be done on the same field. (Which field is unimportant unless you are using material edited previously on one field or the other—although field 2 is becoming a more general standard.) You should be sure that the editor is aware of this requirement, and will be able to tell you which field was used so it can be specified on the Disc Production Work Order.

4. Dual Independent Audio

If you are planning to use audio track 2 of the disc for some other purpose than a stereo track for video, the editor should be aware of this, and be sure that

Managing Interactive Video / Multimedia Projects

ORDER FORM

Technidisc, Inc.
2250 Meijer Drive • Troy, Michigan 48084
(313) 435-7430

No. 15547

COMPANY NAME: _Excellent Bicycle Inc._   TECHNICAL CONTACT: _Diana Kent_

ADDRESS: _6000 BlackWater Park_   PHONE: _(404) 555-5876_

Building 195   MASTER TAPE NO.: _1290_

Atlanta, GA 30095   PURCHASE ORDER NO.: _61542_

BILL TO: _-SAME-_   SHIP TO: _-SAME-_

DRAW DISC ORDERS (Please check if there is a proof disc or check for replication order.)

TITLE: _____

☐ DRAW DISC   ☐ PROOF DISC   ☐ CHECK DISC   ☐ EDITDISC*   ☐ CHECK CASSETTE

QUANTITY: _____   TURNAROUND TIME (QUOTE): _____

REPLICATION ORDERS

SIDE ONE: TITLE _Servicing Your Ten-Speed Bicycle_

☐ CLV   ☐ CAV I   ☐ CAV LEVEL II
☐ CHAPTER STOPS   ☒ CAV III   ☐ PROGRAM
☐ AUTO STOPS   _N.A._   ☐ FLOW CHART

SIDE TWO: TITLE _____

☐ CLV   ☐ CAV I   ☐ CAV LEVEL II
☐ CHAPTER STOPS   ☐ CAV III   ☐ PROGRAM
☐ AUTO STOPS   ☐ FLOW CHART

QUANTITY _____

TURNAROUND TIME (Quote) _____

COMPACT DISC ORDERS

PROGRAM TITLES: _____

DISC LABELS: _____

ART WORK CONTENT: _____

☐ JEWEL BOX CASES
☐ BULK SHIPMENT

PLAYER TYPE

☒ SONY   MODEL: _LDP-1550_
☒ PIONEER   MODEL: _LD-V6xxx, LD-V4200, LD-V2200_
☐ OTHER   MODEL: _____

SHIPPING INSTRUCTIONS
ALL ORDERS FOB TROY MICHIGAN

☐ U.P.S.
☐ FEDERAL EXPRESS #
☐ STANDARD AIR

☐ AIR COURIER
COMPANY: _____
OTHER: _Best Way_

FOR ALL ORDERS
PLEASE COMPLETE THE FOLLOWING SECTION:

Please Give Smpte Time Code Numbers:

First Frame of Active Program: _00;02;00;01_

Last Frame of Active Program: _00;26;42;16_

Field Dominance:

_____ Field One   Mixed, Recorded Disc Master In: _____ 1 _____ 2

_X_ Field Two

Audio:

_____ Mono   _____ Stereo   _X_ Dual Independent   _____ None

_No_ Dolby Decoding Required

_No_ CX Encoding Required

Tape Channel One to Disc Channel   _X_ 1 _____ 2 _____ Both

Tape Channel Two to Disc Channel   _____ 1 _X_ 2 _____ Both

SPECIAL INSTRUCTIONS:

Custom labels will be sent from
Adams Printing Co. prior to 9/15.

PLEASE SHIP ORDER FORM ALONG WITH 1" C MASTER TAPE AND ART LAYOUT FORM
PROVIDED:

To: TECHNIDISC, INC.
2250 MEIJER DRIVE
TROY, MICHIGAN 48084
ATTN: CUSTOMER SERVICE DEPARTMENT

Figure 8-11 Disc Production Work Order

all audio for video is mixed and recorded **only** on channel 1.

If you look after these four items, no major problems should develop during the editing session that will need fixing later. There are some other details that will need to be completed on the Disc Production Work Order. These entries vary depending on the selected manufacturer. Their forms will guide you on special requirements or specifications.

LABELS AND PACKAGING

One last item to be concerned with is the labels for the disc, and the slip cases and other packaging that will be required. Most manufacturers will provide their own generic labels and slip cases, but these will display their names, not yours. If you want custom labels and packaging, you'll need to make arrangements to design them, create the "mechanicals" (camera ready copy with separations if needed), and get them printed and cut. The labels must be cut to precise specifications provided by the videodisc manufacturer. If you need guidance in selecting vendors to do this work, your videodisc manufacturer is a good source of advice.

Deliverables

Let's review the deliverable items that come from the Production Phase.

VIDEO MATERIALS

We've discussed several items that pertain to the video portion of the application:

*   The Master Videotape

    The Master Videotape should be recorded on broadcast quality tape, laid out according to manufacturer's specifications, encoded with non-drop S.M.P.T.E. time code, consistently edited on field 2 (or field 1) and recorded with dual independent audio tracks. It is submitted to the manufacturer with technical specifications provided on the Disc Production Work Order.

*   A DRAW Disc

    An inexpensive, directly recorded "one-off" disc copy used to begin early review and authoring before the replicated discs are available.

*   A Check Disc

    First replicated disc from the mastering process used for final review and approval to complete the entire replication run.

*   Label and Packaging Specifications

    Required with plenty of lead time if you want to use custom labels and packaging of the completed video materials.

OTHER MATERIALS

Although we haven't discussed them in detail in this chapter, you also should see to the completion of all printed materials that will accompany your application. The publication process takes from four to six weeks as a rule, so you should plan accordingly. You should also plan to have all computer graphics complete by the time the DRAW or check disc is available, so authoring can be finished in the least possible time.

CD-ROM materials should be submitted on diskettes, audio tapes or computer tapes in format specified by the manufacturer.

Evaluating the Deliverables

Of all the phases, Production is least suited to applying techniques of formative evaluation. With a full stage crew standing around, there is no time to give thoughtful consideration as to what production approach would be most effective to accomplish the application objectives. There will be times, of course, when such decisions must be made, but these occasions will be unplanned, and the decisions will be made quickly without great deliberation.

The one possible exception would be to take the rough cuts created during the off-line editing process for a quick review of the design team. In practice, this is rarely done unless for some reason, radical changes to the development plans were made during production.

It is not uncommon, however, for errors, omissions or opportunities for significant improvement to be discovered during the off-line or even the on-line editing process. In other kinds of video projects, it's too late to make these improvements. It would be much too expensive to go back and fix the errors or include the changes. In IVD, however, there is still another chance to improve the final product during the Authoring phase. Often, by resequencing the video or including new graphics produced by the computer, fixes can be accomplished that would be impossible in other media.

The major problem with making changes to the design in this fashion is to make sure that the documentation is kept up to date. Each change will affect the work of the graphic artists and authors. For this reason, it's not a bad idea to have the Super Storyboard Coordinator attend the final edit sessions with the master documentation, and perhaps the authors too. This will make it easier for them to understand the nature of the changes that are required, and to take notes on how they are to be accomplished.

A Last Word

There's no getting around it, Production is the most exciting and intensive phase of the project. It is this activity that attracts most Project Managers to undertake their assignments. It is usually fun, and when the master tape has been sent off for replication, it is one of the most rewarding moments in the project. It's a major milestone, and a good time to get the team together for a short celebration and recognition of a job well done. So far, so good.

If you haven't worked in video production before, you may be surprised at the dedication of the professionals to turning out a perfect product. The reason is simple—they know that each minor imperfection will be recorded forever, and will grow in magnitude over time. It's a good lesson to understand going in. Despite the pressures on time and budget, you should seldom, if ever, force the team to proceed past an unsolved problem unless you are convinced that it can be taken care of or eliminated in the authoring process.

The best approach during production, then, is to go in with a sound plan in complete detail, let the professionals do their work, and be available for quick decisions to help create the most perfect product possible. When the tape is "in the can," you'll probably be exhausted, but excited and ready to move on to the Authoring phase where everything will at last come together.

Chapter Nine

Authoring

Preview of the Authoring Phase

On the surface, authoring is the development phase between production and validation. It's that set of activities which merges the media elements with the application's logic to create the finished product — ready to be tested. If we dig a little deeper, authoring is much more. We'll see that the process is assisted by computer software products that we will call "authoring facilities." The concept and capability of an authoring facility goes beyond simply merging media elements. These software products can play a significant role in other project phases. The choice of an authoring facility influences design, development, and documentation.

The Authoring Phase includes three general activities:

1. "coding" — to integrate media elements, application logic, and transition techniques into a series of presentations.

2. "testing" — to try the application from an end user's perspective, uncover errors, and correct them.

3. "tuning" — to smooth and refine the presentations, logic, and interactions into a seamless and professional product.

Selecting an authoring facility requires knowledge of several different alternatives and their unique capabilities. We'll describe the alternatives. Then, for each one, we'll discuss the selection criteria, the phase considerations, and how it affects project activities.

One of your most far-reaching decisions as a Project Manager is the selection of an authoring facility. That decision must be made early in the project; that decision affects each succeeding development phase — including authoring.

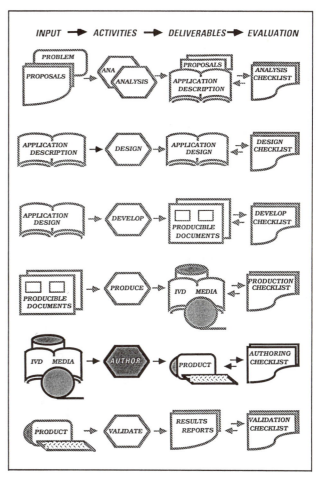

Figure 9-1 IVD Development Phases

Looking Over the Territory

What We're Trying to Accomplish

In this chapter, we'll try to shed some light on one of the most elusive concepts in multimedia development, the authoring process. As Project Manager, you may find yourself in the position of having to make or approve the selection of an authoring facility. Our focus will be to divide these authoring facilities into six general types, and discuss the advantages and disadvantages of each approach. We'll also describe the effect of the selection of the authoring facility on the rest of the project.

> **Note.** It is worth emphasizing that the selection of the authoring facility will affect project activities in many other phases besides authoring, and the activities of many people besides authors. When selecting a facility, it is much more important to understand these effects than it is to be overly concerned with technical functions.

Our goal is to provide you with sufficient background to recognize the tradeoffs between various types of authoring facilities, make sure that the facility selected is appropriate for your project requirements, and to understand how the authoring facility selection will affect the activities and skill needs in each project phase.

Goals and Deliverables of the Authoring Phase

As illustrated in Figure 9-2, the Authoring Phase has three general steps: coding, testing and tuning. The goal of the first step, coding, is to meld together all of the diverse media elements that have been developed and produced separately, and combine them into a single, integrated presenta-

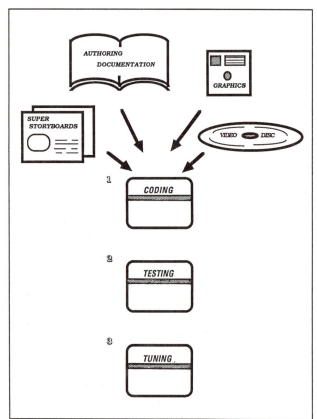

Figure 9-2 Authoring Phase Activities

tion. The way this is done in an interactive media application is to create a computer program that will control the delivery system to present the audio and visual elements, and will implement the logic of the application as depicted in the original documentation.

This computer program can be coded in several ways, depending upon the choice of authoring facility. The options range from having a highly skilled computer programmer write detailed code for each step, to using an authoring system that will provide the code based on input from subject matter experts who know very little about computers.

Whatever the source, the program will initially be created on a magnetic disk computer storage device. In this form, it can be easily modified to improve its effectiveness and correct errors. The second step in the Authoring Phase is testing. This requires setting up a comprehensive test plan to check each logical path that a user might take to be sure there are no errors, dead ends or circular paths with no escape. A successfully completed testing procedure should be as important a goal as the completion of the program itself. The third activity in the Authoring Phase is called "tuning." This is often done by the application designer working with the author. The objective is to make the application appear smooth and well paced. The timing of the events is adjusted, and the transition from one visual element to the next is made to be as seamless as possible. Tuning can make the critical difference in giving the application a professional look.

When coding, testing and tuning have been completed, the program is ready for validation. After any revisions or refinements, the final deliverable is the completed program on magnetic tape or disk, ready to be replicated and included in the material for distributing the application.

How Do We Get There?

We'll begin by describing the job of the author, and the purpose of the documentation that other team members provide to the author. We'll see that both the author's role and the documentation itself will vary depending upon the type of authoring facility selected.

Then we'll move on to describe six basic types of authoring facilities:

• General purpose languages,

• Authoring languages,

• Authoring systems,

- Timeline processors,

- Application shells,

- Hypermedia generators.

We'll define each of these, and consider their tradeoffs, advantages and disadvantages.

We'll also discuss several other kinds of ancillary software in this chapter that support project activities by providing services not included in the selected authoring facility itself. Also, we'll describe the effect and usage of each kind of facility in activities in other project phases, and what kinds of skills are necessary to perform them. Based on these factors, you should be in a better position to evaluate and approve the selection of an authoring facility for your project.

So What's New?

If you compare IVD to linear video projects, the entire subject of authoring and authoring facilities is new. If you come from a video background, you may not be comfortable with the entire idea of a presentation sequence controlled by the user through a computer program. Some of the terms and concepts may be outside of your prior experience, and seem rather difficult to grasp at first. If this is the case, you'll probably prefer to work with the higher level facilities such as authoring systems, timelines or hypermedia generators. These facilities are more application oriented, and require less detailed knowledge of computer operations. If you come from a data processing background, the computer concepts will be less formidable, but there will be a lot of new ideas to deal with. When implementing a data processing project, the choice of programming software is usually not difficult. We now have over three decades of experience in development of computer programming, and most institutions have settled on appropriate software long ago. IVD/multimedia, however, is a much newer field, and the decision is much harder. The relationship that has developed in the data processing industry between the systems analyst and programmer is well defined; in interactive media, the relationship between the instructional designer, development team, production team and author is much more complex, and is affected significantly by the choice of authoring facility.

Another factor in authoring is that the technology is rapidly developing, and new types of facilities can be expected to appear in the near future. As this book is written, hypermedia systems are just beginning to be widely used. More sophisticated author interfaces are being developed based on windowing and object-oriented programming. Work is being done in the areas of artificial intelligence, knowledge-based systems and expert systems. New hardware capabilities are being developed. All of these technologies will affect both authoring and presentation systems.

The conclusion is, therefore, that no matter what your prior background, there will be many new concepts concerning authoring facilities and the activities in the Authoring Phase. However, if you gain an understanding of the basic types of facilities and the capabilities and limitations of each, you should be able to evaluate the selection and manage the activities with confidence.

Authoring and Authoring Facilities

The Role of the Author

Let's begin by previewing the job done by the author, and the purpose of the authoring documentation. If you're new to IVD, you may even be a little confused by the word "Author." You could assume with some reason that this person is responsible for writing scripts or the text for graphic screens. No, the Author is responsible for creating the **computer program** that will control the presentation.

The word "Author" is left over from the early days of writing computer based training courses. At first, there were no Authoring Facilities available to make this job easy. If you wanted to write a course to run on a computer, you first had to learn the computer language. Thus, in the early days, there was little distinction between authoring and programming. Today, high-level Authoring Facilities have separated the two functions. Authors use high-level Authoring Facilities; programmers use detailed programming languages.

The work expected of the Author will vary depending upon the functions provided by the Authoring Facility, and whether the Author is responsible for developing certain parts of the application, such as text screens and graphics. In some projects, developers of content will be trained in the use of the Authoring Facility, and will use it to develop material much like the classic author of computer based training courses. In others, the development of all media elements will be left to specialists in writing, graphics, video and so on, and the Author is responsible for combining the individual elements into a smooth, polished integrated application — not a trivial task!

To accomplish this job, the authoring documentation must meet the needs of the tasks that the Author is responsible for. These tasks are in turn determined by the organization of the project, and the functions, features and services provided by the Authoring Facility. In one project, a detailed production flowchart and notes from the Application Designer may be sufficient. In another, the Author may need detailed instructions as to how all individual elements are to be presented. In all cases, the documentation provided should be designed to work hand in hand with the logic and functions of the authoring facility.

Selecting Authoring Facilities

Major Considerations

Six facilities

We'll discuss six kinds of authoring facilities that are commonly used (singularly or in combination) to create the programs for IVD presentations. They are:

1. **Authoring systems**

   High level computing systems that provide sophisticated services and "fill in the blank" templates for authors, thus relieving them of the need to have detailed programming skills.

2. **Application shells**

   A faster, less expensive way to implement an application by "plugging in" audio/visual elements into a program that provides a prepackaged design, structure and end-user interface.

3. **Hypermedia application generators**

   A recently implemented approach to recording information in small, related elements using various kinds of media, and providing flexible and logical user access to the elements through a system of cross references to other related information elements.

4. **Time line processors**

   A relatively new facility that is specifically designed for editing presentations of media elements in an IVD environment.

5. **Authoring languages**

   Languages with special functions and commands that were specifically designed to sup-

port computer based training and IVD/multimedia applications.

6. **General purpose languages**

   Languages that support computer systems in general, and were not specifically designed to support a computer based training or multimedia environment.

Each of these was designed to meet different purposes, support different kinds of applications, and support different authoring environments. Each one requires different types of skills and activities in the project team. Figure 9-3 shows the six kinds of authoring facilities mapped against selection criteria. This chapter will provide the details to fill in the matrix.

Select early

The authoring facility should be selected early in the project, no later than the beginning of high level design. The principal reason for this is that it will have significant impact on the design of the application. Early selection allows the design to be constructed in a way that is compatible with the capabilities of the selected facility. Moreover, if the capabilities are known beforehand, good designers can usually accomplish the objectives of the application without requiring functions not provided by the facility.

AUTHORING FACILITIES			
	SELECTION CRITERIA		
	DESIGN REQUIREMENTS VS FUNCTION	DELIVERY SYSTEM CONSIDERATIONS	DEVELOPMENT SKILLS AND RESOURCES
AUTHORING SYSTEMS			
APPLICATION SHELLS			
HYPERMEDIA APPLICATION GENERATORS			
TIMELINE PROCESSORS			
AUTHORING LANGUAGES			
GENERAL - PURPOSE LANGUAGES			

Figure 9-3 Selecting the Authoring Facility

Unfortunately, no simple formula exists for making an authoring facility selection. In addition to the above, many other factors in the project will be affected. These include the activities of the project team, when they actually use the authoring facility functions, and what ancillary software is needed. These factors will be discussed in the following sections.

SELECTION CRITERIA

Design requirements

Application design requirements are a key consideration. High level facilities, including authoring systems and time line processors, have their own set of capabilities and limitations. To achieve the productivity promised by these systems, it is necessary to take advantage of their capabilities, and to avoid designs that are precluded or made difficult by the limitations. Application designers should learn the authoring facility early in the design phase, and check the design as they go to be sure the structure and logic can be attained within its capabilities. If the application requires complex logic such as a system simulation, database manipulation or real time host communications, a language may be required.

> **Note.** A key point to consider is that **productivity** considerations should override **design** considerations when at all possible. Good designers should be able to meet their objectives in many ways, and specifically within the bounds of the chosen authoring facility. The higher level facilities provide greater productivity and should be selected unless it can be firmly demonstrated that a language approach is required.

Finally, it should be recognized that high level facilities were built with certain design functions in mind appropriate to certain generic kinds of applications. Most authoring systems were designed to support complex education courses requiring extensive testing activities and answer processing. Time line processors were designed to support multimedia information presentations. The application criteria themselves should guide selection toward the facility that was originally designed to support that kind of application.

Delivery system factors

The delivery system for the application is a second factor that affects the choice of authoring facility. If the application is one-time and stand-alone, any facility will do. If the application is part of a larger set, such as a curriculum at a learning center, the standards set by the chosen authoring system could be the deciding factor. If the application must interface with other programs, communications or data bases, the ability to interface with these programs would be a key factor in selecting a facility.

Another critical consideration is the license arrangement that will be needed to allow the application to be delivered to the host sites. This is especially true in higher level facilities in which the authoring package creates presentations that are run on delivery systems with a smaller program called a "presentation system." A Presentation System is a subset of the authoring system that will present the application, but not provide facilities for modification or further authoring. Some of these presentation systems are allowed to be distributed to any users without further payment of license fees. Others require that all user stations pay a separate license for each delivery system that will run the application. The license is usually much less than for the full authoring system, but if many copies of the application will be distributed, the cost and administrative effort required can be significant.

> **Note.** Check with the vendor of the authoring facility to see what license will be needed for the Presentation System on user delivery systems. If separate licensing is required, see if a "site license" can be purchased that will allow you to distribute to any system without further cost or administrative tracking of which systems are allowed to run the application.

Development skills and resources

Different facilities require different skill mixes. Lower level facilities, that is, general purpose and authoring languages, require the author to have computer programming skill. Higher level facilities don't require programming knowledge, but may require skill with other types of programs such as graphics packages or word processors. No matter what facility is used, however, the author must understand the design considerations it imposes. This will involve knowledge of the facility's design philosophy and capability, and clear communications with the application designer.

Project resources are also affected by the chosen facility. Productivity will be higher when higher level facilities are used by project personnel with the proper training. General purpose languages and authoring languages offer much flexibility in function and design, but as applications get larger and more complex, overall productivity will drop, and time to complete the project will increase as the number of lines of code increases.

PROJECT EFFECTS

Once selected, the authoring facility will have a significant effect on the development process. One consideration is the use of ancillary software by project team members — who uses it, and for what purpose. Secondly, the actual activities of the team members and skills required will be different in each phase depending on the authoring facility.

Ancillary software

The development process for interactive video can be made more productive by many kinds of software that can provide support over and above the authoring facility itself. Authoring systems usually contain most of the support required during all phases within themselves. Time line processors and languages have little or no support for design and development activity, and other programs must be employed in these early phases.

Types of ancillary software useful in the development process include:

- Outline processors,
- Text/word processors,
- Database managers,
- Graphics packages,
- Project management software,
- Spread sheet processors.

Another type of program that can be particularly useful is a Development Support System that has been especially designed to support development and production activities in IVD/multimedia projects. If the development methodology of your project matches the approach supported by one of these systems, the productivity gain can be remarkable.

Project activities

Many diverse skills are needed on an IVD/multimedia project. Activities performed by the people with these skills will vary when different authoring facilities are selected. Many authoring systems and hypermedia generators contain support features for most or all of the project team members. These features may include tools for designing course structure, creating graphics and text presentations, analyzing student responses, and so on. Thus, a powerful authoring system can be used in all phases by many team members, and contribute significantly to the overall productivity of the project. Other types of facilities may offer only minimal support for activities other than authoring, and they must be accomplished with other means. The one activity not usually affected by the authoring facility is video production. All of the facilities are based on the assumption that the video is complete and available on a disc for authoring. The development and production of the video still frames and motion segments is a major factor in creating the application, but it is done using traditional video production methods. It is done the same way no matter what authoring facility is used, and is therefore not a major consideration in authoring facility selection.

CONDUCTING A BENCHMARK TEST

If you are starting a new function for multimedia development in your organization, and have no compelling reason to select one specific facility over another, the benchmark test might be your best approach. After you have narrowed down the **types** of facilities that will meet your needs, you will still be faced with a bewildering number of choices of programs. The manufacturers of these programs will state that their facilities will provide all of the functions that you need, and in general, this will be true. The question of **how well** your needs are met is something else. Every facility has its own strengths and weaknesses, and what you need to know is how well they are matched to your specific requirements. The benchmark test is an effective way to find out. The idea is to take a small portion of your application and expand it into a detailed design document. Add to it the important design features that may come up in other areas. Use some existing videodisc material to simulate the video sections. Then, have each contending manufacturer create the application section under your observation. You should be able to get a very clear idea of the ease of learning, ease of use, documentation and functional power of the facility from this exercise. It will also avoid the trap of having the manufacturer create the demonstration out of elements that can be best accomplished with his own facility.

Considerations for Authoring Facilities

AUTHORING SYSTEMS

Design Considerations

Capabilities

Authoring systems are created with one objective in mind: to make it easier and more efficient for the designers and developers to create applications. They do this by removing the computer programmer from the loop. This gain in productivity comes at the expense of some loss of flexibility in design. Some authoring systems are quite rigid in their structure, and will produce applications that are very similar in design; others provide more latitude, which usually makes them more difficult to learn. You can expect, however, that any authoring system is going to reflect the creator's view of "good" application design, and will make it very easy to author applications that conform to this idea. To deviate from the standard design elements, however, will be more difficult or perhaps impossible. This is not to say that the productivity gains provided by a good authoring system are not worth the restrictions that may be placed on design. Most creators of authoring systems are competent educators, and their ideas of "good" design are likely to be quite sound. If your authoring staff goes along with the system, utilizes its capabilities and avoids its restrictions, you should expect them to author effective applications with maximum productivity. There are literally hundreds of authoring systems that have been written to support computer based training applications, and most of them have been extended to support IVD. Many others have been written with IVD and multimedia specifically in mind. It sometimes seems that more authoring systems have been written than applications. There are a few major areas that can be examined for any given authoring system to see if its capabilities match the needs of your application. They include:

- Structural design elements provided by the system,

- Screen design aids,

- Media elements supported,

- Capability to interface with a language,

- Capability to exit to another program,

- User controls and services,

- Graphic, video and audio development aids,

- Library maintenance utilities,

- Administrative reports for course and student records.

One especially valuable feature is called "WYSIWYG" coding. This is an acronym that stands for "What You See Is What You Get." (It's pronounced, "Wiz-e-wig.") It's an important concept in all kinds of computer application development, and authoring systems are no exception. In some systems, the author codes the application in some kind of descriptive manner, specifying what the user is going to see when the application runs. If the authoring system provides a WYSIWYG interface, the author works on screens that look much as they will when the user sees them. This avoids the unproductive necessity to code, then test, then recode to correct or modify.

Limitations

The limitations of an authoring system can be looked at as capabilities that the system doesn't have. If one or more of the capabilities listed above are particularly needed by your application, a system that doesn't provide them would be unacceptably restricting. Unfortunately, this is rarely a black and white decision. The promotional literature of most authoring systems will claim to have all of the listed capabilities and then some. When evaluating a specific system, you would need to consider your specific requirements and judge the suitability of the individual features against them. A benchmark test would be the best way to do this.

Development Skills and Resources

The main purpose of investing in an authoring system is to minimize the need for specialized skills for development, particularly in the programming area. A good system will allow the authors to concentrate on the objectives of the presentation, the subject matter content and effective use of the media. This means that their skills should lie in the areas of instructional design, subject matter familiarity and creativity with media presentations. It does **not** mean that the authoring task can be turned over to people with subject matter expertise alone, expecting the system to "take care of" presentation considerations.

If your project demands high quality, you will probably want to have specialized skills on your team in areas such as graphics design, video writing, instructional design and so on. In this case, you should pick an authoring system that supports the team concept, and allows the specialists to work in their areas without conflict with others. Some sys-

Figure 9-4   The author's work is as good as the authoring documentation

tems are designed with the premise that a single author will handle all aspects of the presentation, and may not lend themselves to a team approach.

Programming skills can be minimized by using a high level authoring system, but that doesn't mean they can be totally absent. The application is, after all, being implemented on a computer, and is based on the precepts of computer based training or in fact **is** computer based training. Your team will need someone to call on who is at least familiar with computer operations and logic. If language options or program exits are used, the programming skills to support them will need to be present.

Project Activities

An authoring system can make its maximum contribution to productivity if it can be used in all phases of application development. In the Design Phase, the Instructional Designer can use the system to record the general and detailed objectives, and layout the high level design of the activities without actually creating the specific content. Then, this outline can be added to in ever increasing detail. After peer reviews and expansion into a detailed design structure, the Development Phase activities can begin. Writers and artists can begin development of the elements, using the facilities of the system itself. Some systems will generate documentation from this input that will help make the Production Phase more efficient. If all of the development input has been captured in prior phases, the coding task of the Authoring Phase has been all but completed. Authoring can be limited to testing the application, and

tuning the presentation. The application thus developed can be used directly in the Validation Phase, and revisions accomplished as needed with minimum effort. Ideally, all information needed in the final presentation can be entered into the computer only once, and will become a part of the finished application.

The activities of the team in this scenario are highly integrated, efficiently organized and oriented toward a commonly understood goal. As a Project Manager, you could not ask for more. To achieve this result, however, you will need a team where every member understands the design philosophy imbedded in the authoring system itself, and how the Instructional Designer has adapted that philosophy to the specific design of the application. This requires excellent training, effective communications, and frequent meetings of the team to view the application as a whole. When used in this manner, an authoring system can be the standard that coalesces the individuals into a team. If it supports these activities well, it will be worth many times its cost.

APPLICATION SHELLS

Design Considerations

Capabilities

An application shell is a prefabricated program that is "coded" by simply supplying information about the specifics of the presentation by some easy method, such as filling in blanks. The design and structure of the presentation and the end-user interface is provided by the shell itself.

Various shells have been written over the years for use in computer based training systems. In one system, the author fills in such elements as question stems, expected right and wrong answers with appropriate responses to each, and responses to unanticipated answers. In another, the author fills in screens that provide objective statements, rules, examples, practice items and test items. It is fairly easy to convert these shell approaches to IVD by using video segments for various elements of the presentation.

A different example has been recently made available for accessing a visual data base. The visuals may consist of video segments, graphics, still frames, audio segments, etc. The application is created by arranging the visuals into an outline format. The descriptive text in the outline is used to automatically create menus to access the visuals.

In all of these cases, the creation of the application requires little more than content analysis, and the production of the elements. The design, structure and logic are provided by the shell. Authoring is done almost by rote, and little testing is required. The obvious benefit of this approach is to lower the time and cost of designing and authoring the application. Even if it is not planned to use the shell in the final presentation, it often provides an efficient approach to develop a prototype for concept testing.

Limitations

The obvious limitation of the application shell is its lack of flexibility in design. If the visual data doesn't fit a clean hierarchical structure, or if a trainer wishes to include some other activity than provided by the fill-in screens, the shell will probably make it difficult or impossible to accommodate the deviation. If several presentations are to be developed, use of a shell is likely to result in a look of sameness. There is some virtue in the consistency provided by this approach, but from the end user standpoint, predictability in media can lead to boredom. Often, the best approach is to use shells for prototyping, but let the designers have more freedom when developing the final presentations.

Development Skills and Resources

The most compelling reason of all to use a shell is that it reduces the requirement for specialized skills to the absolute minimum. Design considerations are virtually removed from the picture — the shell provides a ready-made design approach. Authoring skill is reduced to a "fill-in-the-blank" level. Nevertheless, if the final product is to have an acceptable quality, development and production skills will be as important as ever. Professional graphics, well-written scripts and high quality video will determine how the presentation looks and plays.

An exception to this can occur when using a generic video disc. These are discs that contain a collection of related visuals, such as medical slides or art portfolios. If you can find a disc with the content to suit your purpose, video production is no longer an issue. You can further reduce your development skill base to graphics capability, and if you are producing your own audio, to scripting and audio production.

In summary, the use of a shell can minimize design and authoring resources, and reduce the total amount of development by twenty to thirty percent. If this approach can do your whole job, it should be considered. Even if it won't, it can still be a valuable tool for prototyping your presentation.

Project Activities

The decision to use a shell will determine the nature of project activities to a great extent. The media requirements will be specified by the design of the shell. Project personnel will need to first understand the design, then shape the content to fit it. This may limit the bounds of artistic creativity, but can be highly efficient in getting a presentation finished with a minimum investment of time and resource.

HYPERMEDIA GENERATORS

Design Considerations

Capabilities

Early versions of hypermedia generators were based on text files, and in fact were often called "hypertext" applications. The idea was that whereas standard text files were linear in nature and had to be created and accessed in sequential mode, "hypertext" provided direct links from key words to other parts of the document (or other documents) that contained related material. Hypermedia generators have extended the basic ideas of hypertext to encompass any media presentation method available to the system. In addition to other text and graphic files, hypermedia applications may provide audio segments, video still frames or motion segments as well.

The basic concept of hypermedia design is simple, elegant and powerful. It is intuitively obvious to people who have been used to organizing their ideas on index cards. In fact, the best known program, Apple Corporation's HyperCard®, makes its screens look like stacks of index cards. The structure and organization are easy to grasp by those who record the information, as well as those who later use the application to access the information.

Limitations

Hypermedia generators serve a particular purpose, and are generally not suitable as full-function authoring systems. If the design of your application calls for simulation, drill and practice, testing or other kinds of rich interaction with the user, this kind of facility probably won't do the job. There is no reason, however, that these functions could not be designed into the hypermedia approach, and it is likely that future implementations of these facilities will grow in power.

The major concern in hypermedia applications is that the author may fail to give sufficient attention to the overall design. The program makes it easy to create links from one topic to another — at times, almost too easy. Complex networks of information can be built quickly in which the user can easily get lost.

Another consideration is that the presentations created by a particular hypermedia generator are going to look pretty much alike, whether they are dealing with the history of drama, or carburetor repair. This provides the blessing of standard user procedures across all presentations, but the curse of sameness in look and feel may lead to boredom. This may be avoided by using the basic screens and links to provide the structure of the application, but relying on graphics and audio-video elements to present the information. Another item to check is the capability for video display. Many hypermedia generators support only a two-screen system with computer text and graphics on one, and only video on the other. This has the advantage of providing more "real estate" for presenting material. There are several drawbacks, however. The system may require a larger "footprint" at the delivery site. The application must be designed carefully so the user knows which screen to look at all the time. The designer may have to repeat the video image in a computer graphic to allow annotation and pointing at specific items.

Development Skills and Resources

One of the most fascinating aspects of hypermedia generators is their ability to create entire usable applications with little intervention between the subject matter expert who records and organizes the information, and the user who accesses it. Many would question the quality of such instant applications, but the fact remains that in situations where there is a large quantity of needed information, and limited time and budget to create the application, hypermedia can do the job. For example, a major university transferred two years of a medical curriculum in a short time by having students transfer lecture notes that were then edited by the professors.

This "quick and dirty" approach may not appeal to you if application quality is an issue. Nevertheless, a hypermedia generator may be an extremely effective way to collect the input data you need from subject matter experts. The hypermedia information data base can then be structured and illustrated into a high quality presentation by experienced IVD developers.

It's also possible to create very elegant applications using the hypermedia design approach. As more users become familiar with the conventions and structure of hypermedia applications, this approach will have some definite advantages. Such applications will require talented artists, writers, and video producers like any other high quality presentation, but the hypermedia approach to design promises to be a very efficient paradigm for information access applications.

Project Activities

Like an authoring system, the hypermedia generator itself will be used in all of the development phases. In the Design Phase, the hypermedia generator provides the basis for the application design. In the Development Phase, the subject matter expert can provide the information elements on computer screens right from the beginning with little training. At this point, the subject matter expert can be excused while the designer cleans up the logic of the linkages, and improves the structure of the information. Graphic artists can then clean up and improve the graphic screens and illustrations, while video developers translate the elements that will be resident on the videodisc. At every step, the project personnel are working with a finished copy of the application as it has been developed to that point. Validation can be started with the original screens that the subject matter expert provides. Authoring becomes a process of testing and cleaning up the linkages, and tuning the finished product to make sure it flows clearly and smoothly. In summary, if the hypermedia approach to application design will meet your requirements, the project activities can be carried out with extremely high productivity. Every keystroke becomes part of the application as it stands at that point, and coding, testing and tuning are all done in a WYSIWYG environment.

TIME LINE PROCESSORS

Design Considerations

Capabilities

The time line processor is a unique form of authoring facility whose functions are specifically oriented to the special requirements of creating an interactive video presentation. An example of this type of facility is IBM Corporation's "InfoWindow Presentation System," or "IWPS." The basic idea of this approach is to present the author with a list of the media elements available in the system, and provide an easy way to invoke any one of them at any point on a "time line" which measures time from the beginning of the event. For example, a video segment could be started at time "0.0", and at time "3.2" seconds later, a graphic added, and at time "12.5" seconds, a graphic menu displayed with the touch screen activated.

Time line processors that have been created up to now are better described as media element editors than authoring systems, with which they are often confused. A time line processor is used **after** all the media elements have been created. Other software, such as text processors or graphic creation packages, are usually used during the phases of design, development and production. Then, the time line processor is used to tie together all of the individual elements into a single integrated presentation.

Limitations

Time line processors are a relatively new approach to creating interactive presentations, and do not have the long history in computer based training that affects the functions of authoring systems. The functions of time line processors tend to be oriented toward effective use of multimedia in presentations, and educational functions such as answer analysis, testing, student administration and so on have not been addressed (although there is no reason they could not be in the future). Application designs that depend on these kinds of functions may be difficult to implement. Providing such functions may require a programmer to code a program exit.

Development Skills and Resources

The time line processor is designed to support the team approach to IVD/multimedia development. The author is not expected to create media elements, but rather is expected to **integrate** the elements created by other specialists. The skills of designers, artists, writers and video producers are necessary to the project. The author who uses a time line processor is also a specialist with his or her own special brand of skill.

The author's skills are more akin to those possessed by a good video editor than they are like a programmer's or an author of computer based training. The time line processor provides functions for achieving smooth transitions between video pictures, segments and graphic screens. The author must have the technical skill to use them, which is easily obtained. The author must also have the artistic skill to use the techniques effectively, and this requires experience and visual imagination. This is a critical skill, since a poor author can take media elements produced to the highest quality standards and create a presentation that is badly timed, jerky and generally distracting to the user.

Project Activities

The application designer should be trained to know the capabilities and limitations of the time line processor before the detail design is attempted. This will save unpleasant surprises later during the authoring phase, and gain the maximum benefits from the presentation functions of the facility. Other than that, however, no team member uses the time line processor for any of the activity associated with design, development or production. Other ancillary programs are used such as text processors and graphics packages, but the time line processor itself is of little use until the media elements have been created.

Once the graphics, and perhaps the video are done, however, the time line processor can be used to create a preliminary version of the application very quickly. From the notes of the designer the time lines for each activity (or "event") can be keyed in quickly in a process that is little more than data entry. Once entered, the application can be tested, and the all-important tuning process begun. During tuning, the timing of the presentation and the transitions between elements can be tested and revised. Often, designers will oversee this activity or actually do it themselves if they are familiar with how to use the time line processor.

In summary, if the application's objective is to present material with the maximum effective use of media and ease of user control, the time line processor may provide the best results in the shortest time.

AUTHORING LANGUAGES

Design Considerations

Capabilities

Authoring languages provide extensive flexibility in application design. They impose no pre-designed logical structures or screen designs. The functions provided by the command set of the language are usually powerful enough to match any requirement set by the application designer.

Many proponents of authoring languages got their early training creating lessons in computer based training (CBT), using one of the many CBT languages available for small computers. Adding commands to one of these languages to control a videodisc player or CD-ROM drive is fairly easy, and the authors see no reason to give up their familiar techniques for more restrictive higher level facilities. In many cases, this is a reasonable position.

Authoring languages provide a command set that will allow exercising basic computer functions such as input, output and computation, as well as more powerful functions especially oriented to the requirements of computer based training. An example of the latter is the function of "answer analysis," a strategy used to judge student responses to questions that they enter via the keyboard. The responses are classified as "right," "expected wrong" or "unanticipated" by comparing them to author-provided answer lists. Most authoring languages provide for wide flexibility in responses, including misspellings, alternate forms of the answer, ignoring of extraneous words or phrases, or (if appropriate) ignoring use of upper and lower case letters. Other special functions include graphics display, use of different fonts and colors for text, creating and updating student records, and of course controlling other media devices attached to the system.

Some authoring languages have extremely large and varied sets of primitive commands, providing ultimate flexibility in design. Others have smaller sets of carefully chosen commands that serve most of the same functions, but are easier for a new author to learn.

Limitations

Although there are few limitations on design at the application level when using an authoring language, there may be some at the computing system level. Authoring languages are low level facilities when compared to authoring systems, but are fairly high level when compared to machine-level coding. An authoring language may not be able to control certain functions, or to provide the performance necessary for some applications.

Development Skills and Resources

The use of an authoring language demands the skill of a programmer. Higher level facilities benefit from authors who have some basic programming concepts, but authoring languages require actual knowledge of programming techniques, and a facility with writing computer code.

This is not to say that the author must be a computer science major capable of writing system code using modern structured languages. The authoring languages are based on simple primitive commands and educational functions that can be learned in a reasonable amount of time by anyone with a logical mind. However, techniques that programmers use, such as looping, conditional branching, subroutine calls and so on, must be understood to write an application in an authoring language.

A major consideration for these applications is that future maintenance must be performed by someone familiar with the language. Often, the only one who can efficiently figure out the coding techniques is the original author himself! This fact could make a Project Manager dependent on an individual for all future application modifications, and this one consideration has often swayed managers to select higher level, more easily maintained facilities.

Project Activities

When a language is used to implement a project, the activities are likely to be much less structured than when a team is creating elements to fit into the framework of a high level facility. The very tradition of languages is that applications were undertaken by individuals who performed all tasks from design through validation and answered to no one but themselves. Design is free form, and development begins immediately with writing of code. The media elements (other than video) are created by the code, along with the logic to present them. Once the video elements are folded into the presentation, it is essentially complete except for final tuning. The phases of development and authoring become one and the same. However, the tasks of code writing, testing and debugging require substantial effort, and you are not likely to have saved time through this approach to authoring.

GENERAL PURPOSE LANGUAGES

Design Considerations

Capabilites

There are virtually no design restrictions on an application implemented in a general purpose language other than the system and hardware itself. A skilled programmer can provide any function desired and optimize the performance of the presentation at the same time.

Figure 9-5 Programmer services provide ultimate flexibility in application design

Limitations

The principal limitation on design is the need for the designer to have access to a programmer with the requisite skills, and to be able to communicate the design to that programmer. Design and programming are two essentially different disciplines with their own thought processes and languages. Even if early communications are clear, it is common for designers to want to fine tune the presentation after it has been coded, and this revision can cause extensive recoding.

Another consideration is that more complex designs require more complex programming, with more time needed for coding, debugging and documenting. IVD/multimedia programming has proven to be more difficult than it appears, and schedule and cost overruns are a distinct possibility.

Thirdly, if application maintenance is a consideration, a substantial investment in documentation must be incurred, or a commitment made to having maintenance done by the original programmer, or more likely, both.

Development Skills and Resources

General purpose language implementation requires the services of skilled programmers. This facility should only be considered if these resources are already available.

Project Activities

Early in the development of IVD, general purpose languages were the only vehicle available for implementing these applications. Individuals with long experience in IVD often prefer to use general purpose languages now, because they are used to working in an environment with no restrictions imposed by a higher level authoring facility. These projects are often approached with a free-wheeling design session or brainstorming that is likely to produce an innovative approach to the content. Then the design is documented in the form of scripts and flowcharts, and turned over to the project personnel to produce the video and program the logic and graphic portion. The major difference in these kinds of projects is that the design team need not know nor design to the restrictions of an authoring facility, and that much of the development is actually implemented by the programmer. Therefore, communications between designer and programmer must be given extra careful attention.

Conclusions

The selection of an authoring facility is a critical decision in an IVD/multimedia project. It will have a major effect on design considerations, skill and resource requirements and project activities. It should be based on several factors:

- Productivity considerations that favor selection of the highest level of facility that will do the job.

- Design considerations for meeting application objectives and delivery system capabilities.

- Compatibility with other existing or planned applications that use or will need a particular type of facility.

- Skills and resources (including training time) needed to support a given facility.

- Requirements for future modifications and maintenance that would be more easily accomplished with a higher level facility.

- Cost of the authoring facility, and licensing considerations for the delivery system software.

The background presented in this chapter should be helpful in weighing these factors. The final selection of a specific package can then be made on the basis of price and function. As time goes on, however, the kinds of facilities available and the authoring techniques they support will become richer, and it will be necessary to follow the developments in the field. Applications such as artificial intelligence, expert and rule based systems, advanced hypermedia techniques, computer aided design, desktop publishing and so on will affect the design of authoring systems. Full-function development support systems that will generate production documentation along with the application code itself are in development, and available now for specific systems and applications.

The rich variety of facilities available now and in the future makes it possible to select the program that will provide the optimum and most productive support for your project. The wide choice makes for a difficult decision, however, and it won't get easier as new facilities are offered. As you're planning your project, provide for the time and resources to make an early and informed decision. If you're considering several facilities, create your own benchmark application segment that represents your design requirements, and test the capability of the different programs to implement them. Then, the facility you select can do its job of increasing the productivity of the whole team.

Deliverables

The one deliverable item from the Authoring Phase is a fully tested and documented program that will drive the application in the manner prescribed by the designer. The program is usually delivered on a set of master diskettes, or other machine readable format, that is replicatable by the manufacturer of the application. In applications with small numbers of delivery sites, the delivery program may be locally reproduced on individual small computers. In larger applications, the program will be replicated on to distribution media such as diskettes or CD-ROM.

The documentation is critical for future maintenance. If a high-level authoring facility was used, the system itself generally provides a good documentation set. If an authoring language or general purpose language was used, documentation should contain clear and complete descriptions of the design and structure, data record and file layouts, installation and run procedures, and error code listings. There should also be extensive comments and annotations in the source code listing.

The results of the testing should be documented as well to insure its completeness. A test plan should include installation and usage testing in addition to logical tests of every branch of the program. In large programs, this testing can involve many people over several days, so make sure these activities are included in your overall project plans.

Roles of the Project Manager

Managing the Creative Process

The authoring process can be just as creative as design and development, and is just as critical to the overall success of the project. Higher level facilities allow authors to concentrate more on presentation techniques than system considerations, but no facility can substitute for a skilled author in creating a high quality "look and feel."

As Project Manager, you need to seek out authors who can visualize and create high quality user interfaces, and who can understand and implement the designer's approach to the application objectives. When you see evidence of this creativity, make sure it gets the recognition it deserves. Authoring is the last chance to fine tune the application, and those who can do it well rate high praise indeed.

Managing the Business Process

The business side of authoring has to do with insuring that the productivity promised by the authoring facility is achieved. Computers are fascinating devices to those who program them, and IVD authors are no exception. They have motive and opportunity to exercise creativity, and if properly managed, this can be of great benefit to a project. However, if the author strays too far afield, and spends time embellishing the design or adding complex programming approaches that are interesting but not germane to the objectives, the schedule can slip before you know it.

A general rule on most programming projects is that it takes 50% of the time to get 90% complete, and 50% to finish the job. Final tuning, testing and debugging and completing the documentation always take more time than anticipated.

These factors should encourage you to keep careful track of the activities and progress of the authors. Frequent review of the work in process by the designer, and careful reporting of major milestones will help keep the authoring phase on track.

Evaluating the Deliverables

The Authoring phase provides the first opportunity to review the application as it will actually be presented. Using the check disc, each section can be evaluated by the designers, peers and members of the target audience. There is still time to act on their suggestions and smooth out the last wrinkles before the application is subjected to final validation.

A Last Word

Selection of an authoring facility is an important and complex decision. It will have a profound effect on the first project implemented, and will likely affect all other projects to follow. This in turn will influence the personnel and vendors that are hired, and even the kinds of projects that interactive video will be used for in future applications.

Careful consideration should be given to the factors we've discussed, including design requirements, delivery requirements and available skills. Higher level facilities should be given first choice in order to gain maximum productivity. In the absence of other compelling factors, a specific facility is best chosen on the basis of a benchmark test. Most importantly, the facility should be selected early in the project, and its functions should be fully understood by the application designer. If the design is constructed to use the capabilities of the selected facility to best advantage, and to avoid structures and functions that are difficult or impossible to achieve, authoring productivity should be high, and the project will have the best chance of achieving high quality with on-time, on-budget completion.

Chapter Ten

Validating the Application

Preview of the Validation Phase

Validation is the final phase in the development sequence. It's your formal proof that you've met the sponsor's original objectives, which were proposed back in the Planning Sessions. This chapter looks at why you should (or should not) conduct a validation, the extent of the activities, who's involved, and the procedures to follow.

Essentially, the validation process brings the product, the intended audience, and the eventual environment together under the watchful eye of a trained observer—someone who can confirm the application's success or uncover the problems that might decrease its effectiveness. A formal validation process consists of three major steps:

- **preparation for the validation ...** organizing the questions, securing the test audience, constructing the environment.

- **conducting the validation ...** observing the application, interviewing the audience, recording.

- **assessing the results ...** analyzing and organizing the validation findings into a formal report for your review and possible action.

After a successful validation of the application, it can be folded into the implementation activities that are already in progress.

Looking Over the Territory

At this point in the project, we have completed at least one copy of the entire application in a reviewable form. During the prior phases, we have taken every possible step to insure that the material we have created will accomplish the original objectives, but up to this time, we have not had the opportunity to put the whole package in the hands of our target audience and say, "Here, try it." In this chapter, we'll discuss how this "tryout" can be done in a way that will provide assurances that the application is ready to be released to the world in general. We'll discuss

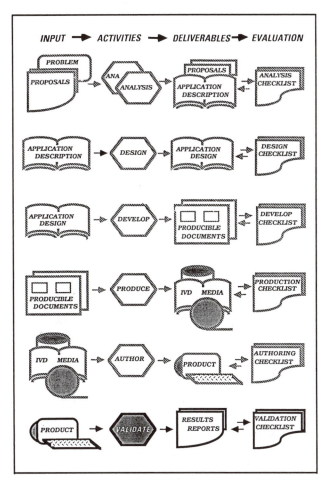

Figure 10-1 IVD Development Phases

the steps in preparing for the validation test, what to look for in the validation results, and how to remedy any shortcomings that may have been uncovered.

What We're Trying to Accomplish

There are three main questions to be asked during validation:

1. Did the sample target audience(s) achieve the objectives?

2. Did they like the application?

3. Is the application installable and usable?

The first question is usually answered by quantitative measurements. (Remember, if you have multiple audiences, the objectives may vary.) In training applications, a formal validation usually begins with a pre-test that measures where the students are before they begin, and a post-test that measures the results they obtained during the training. In some cases, it is important to follow up some months later with another test to measure long-term retention. In marketing applications, results like these would be measured through market research techniques.

The second question, about how they liked it, is usually investigated with a simple questionnaire. It's not to be expected, nor even desirable, that all users have a positive reaction. Users that don't fit the target audience profile may well not like the content. "It's too simple," "It's too complicated," "It doesn't cover what I'm interested in," are typical comments from this group. If the target audience liked it, statements like these from outside the target audience should not concern you.

The question about installability and usability are best answered by setting up a realistic environment. Staff it with the same kind of people that will install and administer the application. Observe them carefully to see if they run into trouble.

Normally, a validation will uncover areas that can be improved, and occasionally, outright errors that must be fixed. This data will provide you with a factual foundation for your decisions about revision and rework.

With a successful validation complete, the results recorded and the problems fixed, you can go forward into the implementation step with confidence that the application will do its job.

Deliverable Items

The output of the Validation Phase is twofold:

1. A Validation Report containing objective data that supports the contention that the application will (or won't) meet its goals.

2. A list of the recommended revisions or improvements that will make the application better.

This is a short list, but deceptively simple. There's a lot of preparation and activities to be done to complete these items.

So What's New?

Back when we discussed the Analysis Phase, we said, "It isn't that analysis is much different than other projects, but in interactive media there is likely to be more at stake." The same comment applies here. To have invested the substantial resources in the project that brought it this far, it must have been worth doing. Now it's worth insuring that the application has achieved its original goals and objectives.

The methodology for conducting the validation could be applied to any other user-directed medium. However, since this step is so often bypassed, and the methodology may be worth a refresher, we'll cover the major points in this chapter.

One important difference for some applications is the careful observation of the effect of the environment. You may need to go to some lengths to provide the same level of ambient noise and light and other distractions to be able to evaluate how the application will work in everyday conditions.

Another difference will be to observe how the users navigate through the application with only the screen to guide them. The screen is a narrow window into the rich logic of a typical presentation. If the application doesn't provide enough guide posts to keep them oriented to where they are and where they're going, the validation should reveal the problem. Such problems are usually fairly easy to fix, and can make all the difference in the success of the project.

How Do We Get There?

The detailed procedures depend on how seriously you plan to conduct a formal validation. In many cases there is simply not enough time or money, and in some cases there is not enough need to conduct a full scale validation. We'll spend some time discussing valid reasons **not** to conduct a validation. On the other hand, if you **are** planning to conduct a formal validation, there are several important steps to cover.

First, it is important to begin preparing the validation test in enough time to get all the arrangements made. It's almost as difficult to set up for a complete validation as it is to implement the application itself. You must:

• plan to recruit a suitable target audience sample that is big enough to give you valid results,

• get them all together at the same time and place,

• have the application ready for them to use,

along with all the administrative support and ancillary materials that will be there when the real application is implemented.

Second, the measurement instruments must be ready. Based on your preliminary analysis, you should have a fairly close idea of the objectives that your audiences are expected to achieve, or the attitudes that you wish them to develop. If your application is in training, it's likely that it contains a final test (which may be voluntary or required). Otherwise, you may have to construct a test just for the validation. It's just as important, however, to have a pre-test ready to measure the user's entry level knowledge and skills. Only by having this information will you be able to measure the effect of the application itself. In addition, you should prepare a questionnaire to evaluate each user's prior experience, need for the application content and attitudes toward training in general and this delivery system specifically.

With these preparations in place, you should be able to conduct a meaningful validation, evaluate the results, and take action to fix the problems uncovered. If you have carefully evaluated the application during the previous development phases, however, the problems should be minimized, and you should be able to approve it for release and implementation.

The Validation Phase: Approaches to Validation

As the road map in Figure 10-2 shows, there are several ways to approach the validation. A formal validation takes time, money and effort, and selecting the approach should be a reasonable business decision. Let's discuss three approaches:

- Conservative: Prototyping the application,

- Calculated Risk: Skipping the validation,

- Middle-of-the-Road: Formal validation with Mid-Course Corrections.

We'll cover the first two in this section, and spend the rest of the chapter on the formal validation process.

Prototyping the Application

Contracting with a vendor to produce a prototype of the final application is often a worthwhile investment. It accomplishes much more than just validating that the application is sound. It pulls together

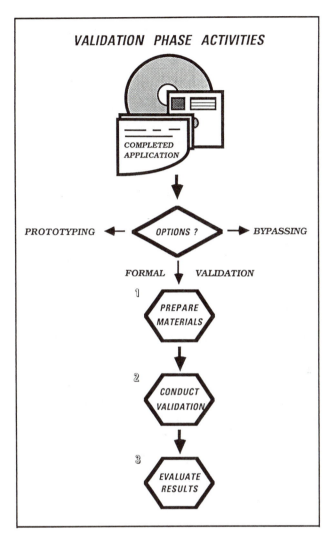

Figure 10-2 Validation Road Map

the entire team, rehearses the complete development process, and allows much better control of the final project. If the prototype content is carefully chosen, most of the developed material can be included in the final application, and most of the cost for the prototype can be recovered unless substantial revisions are required.

On the other hand, prototypes are expensive to build, and will almost certainly add time to the overall project. There is no economy of scale. That is to say, start-up costs cannot be spread over major activities because the tasks of the designers, writers and other producers are relatively small. This effect can be especially important in video production, and the cost per finished minute could be substantially higher than if the entire application's video were produced in one session.

A prototype should be considered in certain situations. It makes sense:

- if the project is important and expensive,
- if the application is new,
- if the vendor is unfamiliar,
- if time permits.

The extra cost will be money well spent to make sure that the final product's development will go smoothly and the result will be effective.

If you are familiar and comfortable with the vendor's work, and if you're both well acquainted with the genre of the application, it probably makes more sense to go right into full scale development.

Skipping the Validation

Most instructional designers would look askance at the proposition that the validation step be dropped altogether, but in the real world, it's sometimes necessary to take a calculated risk. There are several business realities that may lead you to this conclusion.

You may eventually find yourself in the enviable position that the success of the application is virtually assured when the development phases are complete. The risk of not validating is small enough so that the cost of validation is not worth it. This situation could occur when the development vendor is well known, and the application is well understood. If the same vendor has just produced Module 8 of a planned ten module application, and the earlier modules have all been successful, there is probably little risk involved in releasing the new module without a formal validation.

Occasionally, a company will use IVD for an important announcement or public access application where image is critical, and cost is not a consideration. The very best producers have been hired, the on-screen talent is chosen for national face-recognition, the video and graphic production has been done to the highest broadcast standards. With this kind of overkill, a validation may not be necessary — problems will probably be minimal, and who could afford to fix them anyway?

The most realistic cause for skipping validation is, however, that there is simply not enough time. As a Project Manager, you have no choice; the deadline is too short, and even with the tightest project scheduling, the application must be released without a test. Marketing applications are the most notorious in this regard. Managers of marketing programs are usually not aware of the difference in time requirements between interactive presentations and other media. Often the choice is to turn out a full product in 90 days, or not at all.

When faced with this situation, you must fasten your seat belt, and give it your best shot. Hire the best, most experienced vendors and team members you can afford. Insist that the design be kept simple, and based on proven techniques. Select the media elements that will be quickest to produce whenever possible, consistent with quality requirements. Keep your nights and weekends free. And be aware that despite the risks involved, many of the most effective IVD presentations ever produced were done under these trying conditions. Often, pressure is a catalyst to quality.

> **Note**: While skipping validation may be an option, the program testing process discussed in the chapter on Authoring should never be omitted.

Formal Validation

Now, let's consider a well-planned project that has left time in the schedule for a formal validation. As Project Manager of a new application, this should be your preferred approach. Preparation for validating the application should begin far in advance of the actual test. It's likely that different people will be involved in conducting the validation for two reasons. First, the skills of validation are different than those of development. Second, it makes good sense to have a more objective observer evaluate the effectiveness of the application than those who developed it. We'll call this function "The Validator." We'll discuss the tasks of the Validator in each step of the Validation Phase.

First, though, let's review the mid-course corrections that the developers should have applied throughout the project to arrive at the best possible product for validation.

MID-COURSE CORRECTIONS
The Validation Phase is not the time to begin evaluating the effectiveness of the application. In every phase (with the exception of Production) we have discussed evaluation techniques that should be employed as much as possible to insure the eventual

success of the project. In addition to the phase checklists, we've also suggested:

- Analysis Phase

  - Conduct market research and focus groups.

  - Interview subject matter experts to determine the right content.

  - Interview end users to determine their needs.

- Design Phase

  - Conduct peer reviews with other designers to evaluate the design.

  - Conduct structured walkthroughs of the detailed design with end users and management.

- Development Phase

  - Conduct paper simulations with scripts and graphic renditions with end users.

  - Use preliminary video tapes if available.

- Production Phase

  - No time here for pondering whether you're producing the right stuff.

- Authoring Phase

  - An excellent time to test application sections as they are completed with single end users, and make final design adjustments.

If you have made time for these mid-course evaluations and corrections, the probability is high that the final validation will pass with flying colors.

PREPARING FOR VALIDATION

During this stage, a validation plan is prepared that specifies where the validation will take place, and how the sample audience will be selected. The measurement instruments will also be prepared. These may include pre-tests, intermediate feedback and testing forms, post-tests for measuring attainment of the objectives, and subjective evaluations for measuring the level of acceptability.

The Validator's Role

1. Prepare and give a formal presentation explaining the items needed for the plan.

2. Develop the validation plan.

3. Develop the validation questionnaires, interview questions, focus-group guides or other appropriate support for the validation method(s) chosen.

CONDUCTING THE VALIDATION

This is the stage where the application is tested. The environment should be one or more actual sites where it will be implemented, or a close facsimile if this is impossible.

The Validator's Role

1. Conduct the validation in accordance with the validation plan.

2. Provide on-site personnel to resolve problems related to:

   a. Running the application.

   b. Resolving courseware errors.

3. Insure that participants complete interviews or questionnaires.

4. Review and summarize the validation results.

5. Prepare and give a formal presentation explaining the results.

EVALUATING THE RESULTS

There are two aspects of a validation that are important to you as Project Manager. First, you want to know whether the application accomplished its objectives with the end users. Second, you want to know how they liked it.

It turns out, however, that it is nearly impossible to achieve a consensus on these items. The reason is that your test audience will represent a varied cross section of the real target audience, and their reactions will vary according to several factors. If your test audience is large enough to represent a significant sample (as it should be), these variations can be expected, and moreover, should match up to the reactions of the entire target audience when the product is released.

Figure 10-3 illustrates the results that you should be looking for. It shows two curves, one for performance in meeting the objectives, and one that indicates the acceptance level of each participant. If your application validates successfully, you should find that the performance line and the acceptance curve map out like those shown here.

The sample audience is positioned on the bottom line according to their relative qualifications. In a training application, the qualifications would be determined by prior knowledge or experience. In a marketing application, the qualifications would relate to degree of interest or need for the information being presented.

The vertical line represents the level of performance and acceptance. The performance level in training may relate to post-test scores, or if mastery

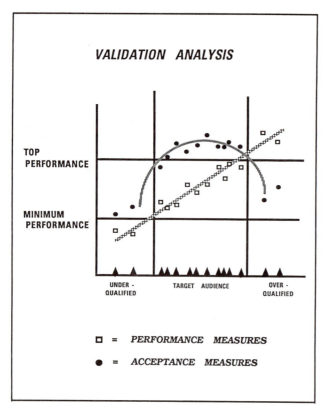

VALIDATION ANALYSIS

TOP PERFORMANCE

MINIMUM PERFORMANCE

UNDER-QUALIFIED   TARGET AUDIENCE   OVER-QUALIFIED

□ = *PERFORMANCE MEASURES*

● = *ACCEPTANCE MEASURES*

Figure 10-3 Validation Results

is required, time on task. The acceptance level is determined by an evaluation questionnaire. In marketing applications, both items are obtained by interview.

The application objectives fall within the shaded area, between the minimum and maximum expected performance, and the least and most qualified members of the target audience. The ideal performance line would fall as shown, with performance increasing as qualifications increase. (This shows, at least, that your application is not doing **harm** to the participants.)

The acceptance curve should look like the one shown. The application should not meet the needs of the under-qualified or disinterested audience, and there is no reason to expect them to like it. The over-qualified audience should find it too simple, too slow, or lacking in advanced details that they would be more interested in. The target audience members, however, should find the content relevant, and hopefully you will find that they liked the application activities.

In order to find these results, you must be able to define all of the input. The objectives and audience definition were set out during preliminary analysis. To position the participants along the base according to their qualifications, you must prepare a question-

naire beforehand to determine their background, and their need for the information in the application.

FIXING THE PROBLEMS

In this stage, the results of the validation are evaluated, final revisions are made, and the application is released for implementation. Video revisions are to be avoided if at all possible, of course. One of the major advantages of IVD/multimedia applications is that in most cases, needed revisions can be accomplished by modifying or creating graphics and reprogramming the logic. It is rare that well-planned video elements must be re-shot.

The Validator's Role

1. Based on validation results, prepare a revision plan.

2. Obtain approval of the revision plan.

3. Revise the application:

    a. Video revisions

        1) Annotate the SSB and video scripts with all approved revisions.

        2) Produce all approved revisions.

        3) Edit the revisions into the "master" video tape in videodisc format.

        4) If required for revalidation, produce another check disc.

    b. Audio revisions

        1) Annotate the SSB and scripts with all approved revisions.

        2) Implement all approved revisions.

        3) Incorporate the revised audio into the "master" video tape.

    c. Graphics revisions

        1) Annotate the SSB and graphics renditions with all approved revisions.

        2) Implement the revisions.

    d. Computer diskette revisions

        1) Annotate the SSBs and program documentations with all approved changes.

        2) Implement all approved revisions.

        3) Incorporate revised graphics.

        4) Perform a software check on the changed code to insure that the code executes.

5) Produce the "master" diskette(s).

e. Print revisions

1) Implement all approved revisions.

2) Produce camera-ready copies of all print pages changed.

f. Perform application checkout using revised materials.

4. Schedule a follow-up validation if needed.

Deliverables

At the beginning of this chapter, we listed two deliverable items for the Validation Phase:

1. A Validation Report on the observed effectiveness and acceptability of the application.

2. A list of the recommended modifications and improvements.

As we have seen, both of these documents can be extensive, and take a lot of time, effort and resource to compile.

Roles of the Project Manager

The Project Manager is usually not responsible for the validation itself, but must play a key role in providing the necessary resources. Here are the major items:

1. Identify validation site.

If possible, this site should be one of the planned host sites. If not, every effort should be made to match the environment as closely as possible, including the personnel.

2. Identify validation audience(s).

This could take a long time in some cases. When the application is implemented, you may expect the audience to arrive sporadically in small numbers over a long period of time. For the validation, you'll need to identify a significant sample and get them all together in one place at one time.

3. Procure and set up validation equipment.

This is not trivial either — it requires the same implementation as the actual applica-

tion, possibly before the complete delivery system is readily available.

4. Provide validation materials.

This will probably be locally reproduced copy, but should match the final material as closely as possible.

5. Provide "on-call" support for hardware/software problem resolution.

You're almost certainly going to run into problems here, so have your authors and technical support staff standing by.

6. Provide access to the appropriate material and personnel.

You'll need to negotiate with the management of the validation site to be sure that they can and will make the administrative help and materials available during the validation.

Managing the Creative Process

The key to this aspect is to make sure that the validation is conducted objectively, and the developers view the results as constructive input, not criticism. In the event that you must rely on the development staff to conduct the validation, be sure you review the validation instruments, tests, questionnaires and interview guides to be sure the results will be factual, and not colored by the hopes and expectations of the developers.

Managing the Business Process

We've already pointed out that validation costs time, money and effort. It's up to you to determine that the project is worth this final checkout, and that the resources are well spent if you decide to go ahead.

Of all of the Project Manager's roles in this phase, negotiating with the host site for the validation is the most critical, and should be based on sound business principles that benefit the host management. It's a good opportunity to test your selling strategy for all the host sites when the application is fully implemented.

Evaluating the Deliverables

The Validation Phase itself is devoted to making a final evaluation of the application; you have the task as Project Manager to evaluate the evaluation. You must make sure it is objective, adequate to judge success or failure, and provides feedback for fixing problems.

If your application is for training, the validation procedure is well known. A full and adequate validation should include a pre-test that tests the participant's knowledge of the final objectives, but is completely different than the tests included in the application itself. Normally, the application tests are used as the post-test to measure student performance.

Another type of deliverable for a training application is called an "Item Analysis." This data compares the results of each student on each question in every test or progress check. The performance on each item is compared against the student's overall performance to determine if the question is a good one. A question that everyone gets right is probably not useful. If everyone gets it wrong, it is probably not clear. If the slow students get it right, and the higher performers miss it, it definitely has a problem. If most students favor one wrong answer, there may be some misleading information in the preceding presentation. These and other judgments can be made from a complete item analysis, and a good validation should include this technique. One of the major advantages of Level Three presentations is that detailed information necessary for item analysis is easily gathered.

Marketing application validation is based on more subjective information (until the final sales figures for end users can be observed). It usually makes sense to work with the marketing department to get their OK on what information is relevant. Often, the validator for a marketing application is a professional market researcher.

A Last Word

Validation is an important process that is often cut out of a project for various reasons, some justified, but more often as a result of poor planning or execution of the project. Nevertheless, it deserves your maximum effort to make sure it is planned for and actually included. There are many reasons:

- It gives you the best chance to put out the best possible product.

- Because they know their work will be objectively measured, your team will be encouraged to apply their best efforts in development and production.

- If questions arise about the effectiveness of the application before or after implementation, solid validation results will be the best source of answers.

- Your own ability to manage and improve future projects will be enhanced by a full understanding of the strengths and weaknesses of past projects.

A complete validation is the capstone of a successful project, and a sign of the professionalism of the development team. The results will have long-lasting effects, and will be a significant factor in the advancement of your career and your ability to justify future projects. It will be worth all your time and effort to get a validation into the schedule, and to keep it there until it's done.

PART FOUR

Implementation and Management

With the successful completion of the development phases, the application is ready to be installed, and the project is nearing an end. We have two remaining topics to round out your project activities: implementation and management. Their single chapter coverage and placement at the end of the book are not meant to diminish their importance nor to assign them a clean-up role.

On the contrary, these two activities are critical to the entire project and occur in parallel with the development work. They're out of sight to everyone but you. You're managing two parallel efforts: development and implementation. The main part of this book has covered development; now we're ready to look at the implementation activities, and the management considerations for the project as a whole. These chapters will cover:

- **Implementation** ... this involves the planning, contracting, and monitoring of a completely different team—the vendors who will build the facilities, prepare the site, and install the product. Chapter 11 guides you through these important activities.

- **Management** ... this covers all of the aspects of leadership, control and accounting for the project. We'll briefly discuss all of these activities, but focus on two critical areas, scheduling and budgeting. Chapter 12 describes some tools and procedures that will help you stay on top of these tasks.

When you finish these two chapters at the end of the book, you'll see how their content must be applied starting back with the planning sessions at the beginning of the book and continuing through each and every step of the project. Indeed, now that you've reached the end, it's just the beginning.

Chapter Eleven

The Implementation Phase

Looking Over the Territory

What We're Trying to Accomplish

The Implementation Phase comprises all activities needed to prepare, deliver, install, and maintain the application in the actual sites. It involves activities separate from the development of the application itself, and is generally performed by in-house personnel and vendors other than the development team.

Implementation can be almost as complex in itself as the development phases. The work effort should commence as soon as the project is approved, and proceed in parallel with the development effort. This is especially true if the application will be installed in new sites. Planning and preparation can make the difference in the success of your application.

Three categories must be considered in implementation: physical installation, other systems and people. People are key to the success of the application. Implementation must consider not only their training, but also their attitudes. Preparing a positive attitude at the host sites is one of the most important, and most often overlooked factors in application implementation. The Implementation Phase has two periods:

1. Preparation

This includes physical planning, kiosk design and construction if needed, preparing for interfacing to other complementary systems or procedures, training, and preparation of an announcement plan.

2. Implementation

This includes delivery, physical installation, testing and setup for on-going maintenance and monitoring of the application.

Goals of Implementation

The goals of implementation include the following:

- Installation of the application in each host site, on schedule and without disruption of normal host site activities.

- Integration of the application into the daily routine of the host site and the other systems that may be affected by the new application.

- Readiness of host site personnel to accept the application and to provide administrative support.

- Activation of a plan to maintain the application and monitor its performance in meeting the objectives.

So What's New?

If you have had experience in installing a computer network, you will probably have an advantage over your compatriot who has only dealt with video networks. Computer networks usually comprise many of the same components as multimedia systems, and multimedia systems can be looked at as computer systems with additional peripheral devices that add media capability. A video network, on the other hand, is often installed by sending familiar video players to the sites, and having a duplication vendor send the tapes out.

Nevertheless, installing multimedia systems can involve complexities that are new to any Project Manager. The delivery devices are often placed in new areas where the personnel are not familiar with any kind of computer or system. The day-to-day administrative tasks of managing diskettes and compact discs, videodiscs and support materials must be planned. The operation and maintenance requirements will demand special training, and it will probably be worthwhile to spend some effort on preparing the attitude of the host site personnel to accept the new system. Finally, you'll need to make sure that the systems can be installed and kept operational by an organization that can diagnose and repair problems that arise either from video, CD-ROM or computer problems.

How Do We Get There?

Figure 11-1 indicates how the Implementation Phase fits into the overall project. Implementation is not a phase that follows the development phases; rather it is a separate process that goes on in parallel with them.

One reason for this is that implementation takes a great deal of planning and preparation. Often, the activities are time consuming. These preparations need to be complete as soon as the development phases are done, so that installation can proceed on a timely basis.

Another reason is that the people involved in implementation are different from those developing the application. Instead of instructional designers, artists and writers, implementation requires physical planning experts, carpenters, electricians, movers, and computer technicians. Only one function is required in both legs of the process — that's you, the Project Manager. If your project involves setting up a sizeable network of systems, you may need to consider adding an implementation manager to your team to handle these activities.

Preparation for implementation should begin at the same time that the development phases begin. This will provide the maximum slack time to handle any problems that come up. By the time the developers are ready to hand over the completed application for installation, the implementers will be ready to receive it.

The installation itself could take many directions, depending on the circumstances of the project. Adding a new application to learning centers that are already functioning effectively is a fairly simple procedure, while installing a completely new application in a nationwide network of standalones would require a major and well-coordinated effort. In this chapter, we'll assume the worst case and consider the various approaches to installing a network of applications.

Managing the Implementation Phase

Preparing for Implementation

As soon as the development phases are underway, you should begin planning for implementation. The first step will be to identify the actual firms or individuals who will be responsible for the various activities of implementation. Where will you find the architects, engineers and industrial designers to perform physical planning? Who will prepare the training for site personnel? Who will build the facilities? What other organizations must be contacted to prepare for integration with other systems that the application will affect?

All of these questions should be considered early in the project, and preparations be started as soon as possible. Let's look at them one at a time.

PHYSICAL PLANNING

Physical planning comprises the activities of getting ready to install the physical components of the system. It covers designing the floor space, providing electrical and communications facilities, air conditioning, lighting, sound engineering, security, and other similar factors that will be needed to support the system. If the system contains physically large units such as carrels or kiosks, access to the space should be considered. A complete set of drawings for each installation site should be made to insure that all necessary requirements have been met.

The kiosks or carrels themselves need to be designed carefully. The designs should consider the attractiveness of the installation and the human

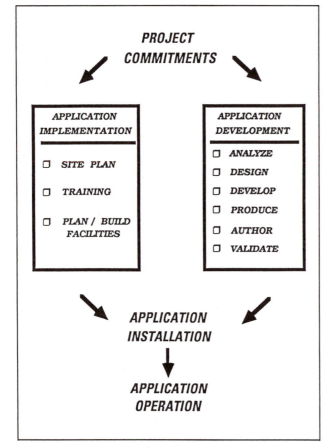

Figure 11-1 Implementation Activities

factors, along with technical factors such as fan requirements, power requirements and service access. If maximum up-time is a requirement, the installation should permit easy replacement of entire system units.

The specifications for the machines that will be installed can be obtained from the manufacturers, and this should be done as one of the first steps in implementation preparation.

There is usually a building or facilities engineer available at the host site that can provide much of the technical support you'll need, or know where to get it. Kiosk or carrel manufacturers can provide the help you'll need in the technical specifications as well as the esthetic considerations. Make these contacts early.

PERSONNEL TRAINING

Technical training

Training requirements for the site personnel will vary widely. In some cases, it will only consist of recognizing that the system has a problem and calling an "800" number to report it. In others, there may be special activities that require operating system skills such as start-up/shut-down, communications procedures, error diagnosis and so on. Training material for the initial installation (and for new personnel when turnover occurs) should be prepared early so it can be ready in time.

The "Roll Out" Plan

In addition to the technical and procedural training, you should also give thought to the announcement of the impending system installation itself. A good roll-out plan can mean the difference between a system that is practically ignored and one that is eagerly awaited and accepted. The announcement may be made with posters, brochures or site visits by project personnel. Excerpts from the application can be provided on video tape to heighten interest. The objective is to get the site personnel to anticipate the system and take pride of ownership when it arrives. This can only be accomplished by taking a long look at "what's in it for them" early in the preparation stage.

BUILDING FACILITIES

If this application is to be installed for the first time, the facilities that will house the equipment must be designed and built. Depending upon the environment that the application will run in, this may be fairly simple, or may be a major task.

Learning Environments

One common environment is the Learning Center. Several factors will be important to consider:

- Will the system be installed in existing carrels, or will the carrels be custom designed?

- Will more than one student interact with the system at the same time?

- Will the station be dedicated to IVD/multimedia activities, or will other activities take place at the same position?

- Will auxiliary materials be stored at the carrel or in a central library?

If the facility already exists, plans will have to be made to install the power, hide the cabling and provide service access. These items are easier to deal with if the carrel can be custom designed. Providing space for two or three users to get to the application at the same time is usually a plus, even if the materials weren't originally designed with multiple users in mind. Other considerations such as space and storage requirements should be carefully thought out ahead of time, and as much flexibility allowed as possible for future applications.

In some learning environments, the capability for large screen projection may be a factor. There are several manufacturers of projection equipment. They should be contacted early to determine the design requirements, and to make sure that your system is compatible with their projector.

Public Access Environments

If your application is to be installed in a public access environment, you will need to house it in a construction that has come to be commonly called a "kiosk." (The original meaning of "a three sided enclosure used to display and sell wares" has little relationship to the high-tech structures often used today.) There are many features and functions of the enclosure itself to be considered, so again, it's important to get started on the design as early as possible.

Some of the considerations that should be incorporated into kiosk design include:

- Power and communication requirements,

- Heat dispersion, ventilation and fans,

- Service access,

- Dealing with ambient light and noise,

- Security,

- Ability to move or ship the kiosk easily,

- Touch screen height and angle for the range of users,

- Need for a repeating monitor for public display,

- Need for privacy of the user,

- Need for storage and display of auxiliary materials,

- An attractive, appropriate appearance.

Clearly, meeting these requirements successfully will require the services of a professional organization with experience in constructing these housings. Your delivery system manufacturer can probably provide you with the names of several firms who have this expertise.

COORDINATING COMPLEMENTARY SYSTEMS

In preparing for the implementation of your application, it is advisable to consider what other systems might affect it, or how it might affect other systems. In this case, the word "system" should be taken in its broadest sense. For example, in a retail environment your application may provide a different way to conduct sales; it may well affect the activities of the current sales force and the way they have done their business heretofore. It is worth a great deal of thought and planning to make sure that the change is mutually beneficial, and that everyone perceives it that way.

There are three primary areas to consider:

- Human activities,

- Paper-based procedures,

- Machine-based procedures.

Human activities should consider what people do now in the area where the application will be installed, and what they will be required to do once it is installed. This may involve changes to their current activities, such as using a point-of-sale application as a sales aid, or new activities such as start-up/shut-down or other operational procedures. It's well to keep in mind that people have a natural resistance to change, and managers don't take kindly to additional time and skill requirements without a significant return for their effort. Books have been written on "Change Theory" that discuss the change process and the role of change agents. Some advanced reading in this area can pay large dividends.

Paper procedures might change due to the presence of the new intelligent terminal on the scene, or because of new reporting requirements used to monitor the new application. The new system should not be perceived as "just more paperwork."

Machine-based procedures will be affected if the application is on-line to a computer. This may be as minimal as simply putting an extra load on the system, or it may have significant effects on other programs and systems already in place. Whatever the effect, it will be worthwhile to discuss the situation with the Information Systems department, and perhaps to get a systems analyst involved to determine how the application can best be integrated into the operations.

Installing the Systems

THE INSTALLATION TEAM

When it comes time to actually install the application, you'll need to have a well-prepared team in place ready to accomplish the task. The nature of the team and the skills required will depend on many factors. These may include:

- Is this a first-time installation?

- Will site construction and wiring be required?

- What systems skills are available at the host site?

- How many host sites will be installed at once?

- How widespread are the host sites?

- Can the installations be staged over time?

- How much time is available to complete the whole job?

These factors will affect how you put the installation team together. You may use permanent employees, temporary employees, contracted personnel, or a combination of these. The initial installation of the system and its software is likely to be a one-time effort, so contracting the job or hiring temporary personnel may be the best approach. On the other hand, if system skills are available for installing and cabling the systems, and a clear procedure can be distributed with the system, contracting may not be necessary.

APPROACHES TO INSTALLATION

Once the installation team has been selected, you'll need to put together an installation plan that will be appropriate for your situation. There are three basic methods to choose from:

- Direct installation,

- "Flying squad,"

- Central assembly.

Direct Installation

This is the least expensive option. The individual system units are shipped directly to the sites, and are unpacked and assembled by local personnel. The process can be simplified by creating a custom set of instructions for the installation, with its checklist of parts and cabling directions. (The instructions provided by the system manufacturer are likely to be too general for effective use in a specific installation.) Once assembled, the installer must run system checkout diagnostics, load the operating system and other required programming to run the system, and load the application software. These procedures can be assisted with pre-written software routines that automatically perform most of the required tasks. Nevertheless, the local personnel will have to have some knowledge of the computer software systems and general hardware installation procedures. You may even want to **validate** the process and the instructions as you did with the application.

The "Flying Squad"

In this approach, the system components are shipped directly to the installation sites. Trained personnel from a central location visit each site in turn to unpack the system, and install the hardware and software. The installation team can also test the system, instruct the local personnel on operation and maintenance, and set up procedures for trouble recognition and reporting.

Central Assembly

The system components are shipped to a central site where they are assembled, loaded and tested. This may include installation in a kiosk. Then, the units are disassembled, repacked and shipped to the host sites. Alternatively, they may be shipped as a complete unit. The latter approach will probably require special handling and additional expense, but may avoid installation problems at the other end. This method is more efficient than assembling the system in individual sites, and also allows problems to be discovered and fixed before the actual installation. However, it requires extra shipping costs which may be substantial.

USABILITY EVALUATION

If you plan to have local personnel participate in installation and maintenance procedures, it may be worth the cost to subject those procedures to a formal usability evaluation. These evaluations are best done in facilities that have been especially designed for the purpose. The facilities include a testing room that can be equipped to match the set-up at the installation site, and an observation room with a one-way mirror. Video recorders and logging equipment are provided. The procedures to be tested are performed by a sample of people selected from the field that will actually have to use them later. The tests are conducted under the supervision of trained observers who assist the project personnel in evaluating the procedures and fixing the problems discovered.

These evaluations can cost $15,000 and up when performed in a professional usability laboratory. Nevertheless, they can provide a high degree of certainty that there are no "show-stoppers" that would have to be fixed later at a much greater cost in a large implementation project. If a smooth, on-time installation is a key requirement, a usability evaluation is well worth considering.

Deliverables

At the beginning of this chapter, we listed several goals of the implementation phase that should be accomplished as deliverable items. Let's review them:

- Installation of the application in each host site, on schedule and without disruption of normal host site activities.

- Integration of the application into the daily routine of the host site and the other systems that may be affected by the new application.

- Readiness of host site personnel to accept the application and to provide administrative support.

- Activation of a plan to maintain the application and monitor its performance in meeting the objectives.

It should be clear that delivering these items will require extensive planning that must begin early in the project.

Roles of the Project Manager

Managing the Creative Process

In the chapters that dealt with the development phases, we discussed the "creative process" in terms of the artistic approach involved in creating media. Implementation deals with different considerations and different types of people, but there is certainly plenty of room for creativity in all of its components.

Training, roll-out plans, and design and construction of the physical facility all require creative approaches to conception and problem solving. You may need this input more if your own creative talents lie in the artistic area rather than physical or systems engineering. You should seek and recognize the professionals who can bring this element to the implementation process.

Managing the Business Process

The business side of implementation is critical. There are several kinds of contracts to consider, cost out, and put in place. Some of them are one-time costs, such as learning center or kiosk design and system installation. Others represent on-going costs, such as system repair and maintenance, or retraining of new personnel. These costs should be recognized and included in the overall expenses when considering the original justification for the application.

The costs for installation should cover:

- Time and cost for the installation team,

- Cost for training materials and creating installation procedures,

- Cost for a usability evaluation,

- Cost for a central assembly site,

- Cost to prepare the host sites,

- Travel costs for the installation team,

- Shipping costs for the systems.

The on-going costs should include:

- Cost for floor space at the host site (utilities, rent, etc.),

- Cost for local administration and training,

- Cost for consumable material replacement,

- Cost for system repair and maintenance,

- Cost for operations (such as system time or communications lines).

Just gathering the data to make reasonable estimates for these costs is a challenge. At the risk of beating a dead horse, once again the advantages of beginning early in the project are clear.

Evaluating the Deliverables

The final results of the Implementation Phase will be easy to evaluate. Did the installation go smoothly, on time and on budget? This kind of Monday morning quarterbacking, however, will be of little use if things didn't go well.

The item to evaluate in implementation is the plan and the preparation steps, and the time to evaluate them is early on. By looking ahead now, you will be able to take every possible step to insure that the application does not risk encountering major problems just when a successful end is in sight.

A Last Word

Your involvement in planning for implementation captures much of the essence of the challenge of project management. Through most of this book, we have concentrated on managing the development phases, and indeed, most of your team and vendors will be concentrating on this process as an end in itself. In this chapter, we've addressed a whole set of activities going on in the background that the development team may not even be aware of. You, however, must be fully involved in scheduling, budgeting, controlling, and coordinating both development **and** implementation. If you can manage these two sides of the project effectively, you will have earned your title well.

We have covered most of the costs that will be incurred during implementation, but we have not attempted to quantify them. The variations between specific projects are too great to make this useful. The best way to plan in this area is to first determine the general requirements of your project. Then, contact the individuals or firms that can supply the services, and use their estimates for specific costs in your budget.

Finally, we have stressed the importance of an early start. This will avoid surprises as to schedules or costs, and insure that installation can be accomplished as soon as development is complete.

Under-estimating the magnitude of the Implementation Phase can be one of the major pitfalls in a project. With adequate planning and preparation, however, you can avoid the problems and complete the project in a smooth and professional manner. When this last step is done well, you will have accomplished both the sponsor's objectives, and your own goal of successful performance as a Project Manager.

Chapter Twelve

Managing the Project

Looking Over the Territory

What We're Trying to Accomplish

Throughout this book, we've discussed the knowledge and skills you need to manage an IVD/multimedia project, but we haven't talked about **managing** itself. In this chapter, we'll look at the management process, and the tools you need to keep the project on track.

The word "management" has many connotations, of course, and all of them are important in an interactive media project. You need to:

- Apply good management techniques to individuals and the team as a whole in the sense of leadership.

- Manage in the sense of providing and controlling resources.

- Provide guidance and make management decisions when conflicting needs have to be resolved.

- Manage the details of project activities to make sure you are progressing on time and on budget.

All of these areas are large topics in themselves, and many books are available that discuss them in detail. We won't attempt that here. In this chapter, we'll try to define a reasonable framework for organizing the information you'll need to manage these media projects, and discuss where and how the information can be obtained.

How Do We Get There?

The information needed to manage and control an IVD project is too voluminous to keep in your head. A good way to keep track of it is to maintain a Project Management Book with the relevant material kept up to date. Our approach will be to assume that such a book exists, divided into appropriate sections. We'll discuss the content of each section, and the sources and tools that apply. Naturally, you'll personalize and expand the book with your own tools and techniques.

So What's New?

Many of the considerations for project management are common to most other large projects. For the sake of completeness, we'll mention the kind of information you need to keep, but won't spend much time on it. The two areas whose contents are unique and critical to interactive media are scheduling and budgeting. We'll spend the bulk of the time on these two.

There is no simple, pat answer to the questions "How much does a multimedia project cost?" or, "How long will the project take?" There are just too many variables to consider. However, there are approaches that can be used to make preliminary estimates that will fall in the right ball park, and later, to make detailed budgets and schedules that you and your vendors should be able to live with and meet.

The Project Control Book

Personnel Assignments

The first section we'll discuss has all of the information you'll need about the personnel working on the project. You should have a list of exact names of your own people, and another list with the vendor's people. The master list should show their assignments, and how to get hold of them. The vendor list should also identify the immediate managers of the people working on the project. A letter of appreciation for individual effort to a manager can be effective in fostering good vendor relations.

For personnel on your own staff, a separate page with a full job description and performance plan is a good management tool. Of course, the individuals should have their own copy, and be fully aware of what they're expected to do, and how their performance will be evaluated. A periodic review of their contributions, and areas where improvements can be made should be a standard operating procedure. In Chapter Three of this book, we listed the roles that need to be assigned in the project, and this can serve as a starting point to get the list of personnel compiled for your project. Remember, there are two teams to be assembled, one for development and one for implementation.

Project Schedule

Dr. Elizabeth Wright, who has managed many major IVD projects over the years, says that "The real project manager should be the project schedule." If each major task and milestone is listed and scheduled, a frequent review by the team to update the status of their own tasks may be all that is needed to keep the project on track.

In this book, we've been discussing projects that are fairly large in scope. Projects of this size need to be scheduled in detail and followed closely as they progress. The best way to do this is to use a computer with project management software. There are many excellent programs available, and the chances are that you or your company is already using one or more of them to control other projects. If you're not familiar with using this software yourself, you may be able to find someone who can set it up for you. Otherwise, you'll need to identify someone (hopefully someone who is comfortable with using computers for other tasks) to get trained on using project management software. If you're not sure which package to use, visit a software store for some demonstrations and comparisons, or go through the reviews in computer magazines.

> **Note.** In the following paragraphs, we'll discuss how project management software works, and what information you'll need to provide as input. If you already understand this, you may want to skip the rest of this section.

Project management software works pretty much the same way, no matter which specific package you use in your organization. You begin by listing each task, and estimating the time that the task will take. You also list the dependencies of each task, that is, which tasks must be completed before others may begin. Then, you provide information on the resources, and perhaps the funds that each task will need. All of this data is entered into the project management program, and it will compute a consolidated schedule for the entire project. If (as is likely) the overall time of the project is too long, the program will point out areas where tasks can be restructured, or additional resources can be applied to bring the time down to an acceptable duration.

Your first job, then, is to create a list of project tasks or activities. A good way to approach this is to review the list of deliverables that we have suggested for each project phase. (You may also want to refer to the RFP outline in Appendix E of the Resource Section where the deliverable items have been listed by phase.) The list should also include "milestone" or "node" events, such as phase reviews.

The next step is to estimate the time that each activity will take to complete. Although it is easier to make estimates for small tasks than for the project as a whole, it is still not an exact science, and some programs will allow you to enter a range of times. The milestone events are identified in some appropriate way, such as giving them a time of zero. Get your vendors and specialists to help you make these estimates, and gain their agreement with your final numbers.

Now, each task must be put into sequence by listing all of the prior tasks that must be completed before it can begin. This isn't as bad as it sounds, because the project management software can keep track of the cumulative prior tasks; all you do is list the task that immediately precedes the current task.

A good way to approach sequencing is to draw a "PERT" chart. (This is a classic approach to project scheduling — it stands for "Project Evaluation and Review Technique.") You may want to start with a hand-drawn chart on a blackboard or large sheet of paper. After all the information is entered into the program, most project management software will print out a PERT chart as one of the reports.

The PERT chart shows the relationship between all tasks in diagrammatic form. For example, Figure 12-1 shows the tasks in the Design Phase.

Most tasks have one predecessor task. (The exception in the example is "Intermediate Budget" which has two.) When the chart is completed, times can be entered for each task, or zero time for the milestone events. When these times are entered, the program will determine the "critical path" — that is, the longest path through the tasks based on the times entered. The Critical Path represents the shortest time that the project can take, based on the information you've estimated.

In addition to the PERT chart, most project management packages will print out another report diagram called a "Gantt chart." This chart is based on a time line divided into days, weeks or months that runs along the top. Each task is depicted as a horizontal line, showing its start and stop dates. Tasks that run concurrently are shown as parallel lines. This report gives a clear picture of each task of the project over time, and what tasks are going on at each moment in time.

Other information may also be handled by the project management software. You may, for example, be able to specify the people assigned to each task. For each task, the program will look at who is assigned, and if that person is not available due to conflicting assignments, the start of the task will be delayed until the assigned person is free. Another function provided by some project management programs is to keep track of the budget for each task, and report project cost information.

Unless you are very experienced, and very exact in your first estimates, the project will probably look as if it will take too much time in the first pass. However, study of the critical path should show where the problems and bottlenecks are likely to occur. Tasks that are delayed because people aren't available can be accelerated by adding resources or reassigning responsibilities. Activities that stretch out too long may have to be broken up into pieces that can be done in parallel. Project management software can help you find these situations before they become problems, and help you construct a plan that will work.

After the plan has been put in place, the data can be updated with actual results as the project proceeds. At periodic meetings, the tasks that were supposed to have been completed can be reviewed, and estimated completion dates of tasks underway can be revised. The schedule provides an excellent control and communication vehicle. When this information is entered into the program, new reports can be generated that gauge whether the project is still on schedule. If slippage is occurring, it can be detected early and corrected before it becomes critical by adding resource or scheduling overtime.

The areas of the project that require the closest attention are programming and authoring. More projects that have failed to meet their target dates have stumbled here than in any other activity. The reason is that it is very difficult to estimate the effort needed to fix what appear to be a few minor

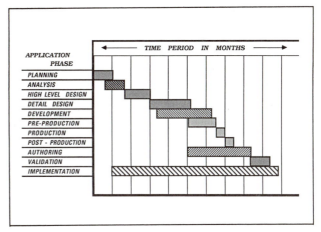

Figure 12-2 A Representative Gantt Chart

remaining bugs. The use of high level authoring facilities can help matters, but problems can still occur.

Note. Divide the authoring activity into two major parts: initial coding, and testing/debugging/tuning. Allocate equal time to both parts. Start initial coding as soon as possible, and if possible, leave slack time in the schedule to complete testing. If training is required, get it done early. Break down each activity into as many sub-tasks as possible, and watch the progress reports carefully. Don't get complacent if early progress seems rapid; programming projects often follow a pattern that 90% of the work seems to be completed in 50% of the time. That last 10% is always hard to come by.

If you're working with a vendor or another department, it's not unreasonable to expect them to implement a formal scheduling process, and to share the reports with you.

Keep in mind that you are managing two major processes, development and implementation. It's likely that you are the only one who is fully aware of

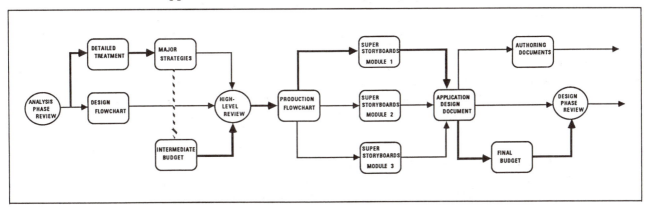

Figure 12-1 PERT Chart for Design Tasks

activities in both areas, and it's your responsibility to keep both legs on schedule, and making them meet on time.

In summary, use the project schedule as a management tool. Circulate copies to the team, and encourage them to follow their own tasks and bring them in on time. This should provide both an effective challenge, and a method for identifying schedule problems early enough to fix them before they impact the whole project.

Project Budget

It may not appear so, but the budget is easier to manage than the schedule. For one thing, cost overruns are most likely to occur when the schedule slips, and you need to add more labor costs in the form of people or overtime. Secondly, it is easier to get more money, or to rob from Peter to pay Paul than it is to manufacture more time. Nevertheless, the budget is the most visible evidence of your skill and competence as a project manager, and it has to be given careful attention.

The total project budget can be divided into two categories: development and implementation. They further break down as follows:

- Development costs
    - Training costs for developers,
    - Development system costs,
    - Labor, travel, supplies and services for each development phase.
- Implementation costs
    - Replication and distribution costs,
    - Delivery system costs,
    - Training costs for site personnel,
    - Kiosks or learning center installations,
    - Initial costs of installing systems,
    - On-going costs of maintenance.

As a project manager, you'll be most concerned with estimating the development costs. The implementation costs will be provided by various vendors who will present the cost figures by contract or bid. Development costs are more difficult to estimate, however, because there are so many variables brought in by design and quality considerations. In this section, we'll focus on estimating the budget for development.

A budget is a prediction of the actual costs that will be incurred. There are three times that this prediction can be made, each one providing a more accurate estimate. The three budgets are:

1. The Planning Budget — prepared during the planning process to estimate a ball park cost figure so that the project can be justified. (We started this process in Chapter Four.)

2. The Intermediate Budget — prepared during high-level design as a reasonableness test of affordability for the selected treatments and strategies.

3. The Final Budget — prepared from the detailed design document to specify the operating budget for all project activities.

We'll discuss each of these in turn, and provide some guidelines that should help you prepare budgets for your own project.

THE PLANNING BUDGET

When a project is first being considered, the cost must be estimated in order to determine whether it is justified. Of course, the estimate at this time is going to be very rough, but nevertheless, it must be made. There is simply no way to evaluate a project without some reasonable input as to its cost. In this section, we'll discuss how this can be done with at least enough accuracy to serve as data for a management decision to start work on the project.

The question, "How much does an IVD/multimedia project cost?" is similar to the question, "How much does a house cost?" The final and accurate answer will depend on thousands of factors that can't be judged without a lot more information. Nevertheless, insurance actuaries must deal with the house question every day. They handle it by using broad guidelines that give fairly close answers without knowing all the details, such as "Dollars per square foot multiplied by the approximate size of the planned house." We can do the same with IVD.

A useful unit for making preliminary cost estimates for multimedia projects is:

$$\frac{\text{Cost (in hundreds of thousand dollars)}}{\text{Total User Hours}}$$

This might look a little complicated at first, but it is not much different than "$/sq ft" (dollars per square foot). Note that "$/sq ft" is really a statement of the **quality** of the house. A house that costs $45 per square foot is constructed of a higher quality than one that costs $33 per square foot. Multiplying the quality unit measure by the size, say 3200 sq ft, will give a fairly good estimate of the cost of a house of that general quality and size.

Likewise, "Cost per total user hours" is a measure of the overall quality of an interactive media presentation. For simplicity, let's call this unit the "Q-factor" to remind us that it is a measure of quality. If we measure the cost in hundreds of thousands of dollars, the Q-factor will come out in small numbers for most industrial quality level presentations. Multiplying the Q-factor times the total hours of user time in the presentation will give us an approximate total cost. Let's look at a couple of examples.

Suppose we are considering a custom training project that we expect to provide three total hours of training. We believe that a Q-factor of 1.0 will give us adequate quality to meet our objectives. (We'll discuss how to pick Q-factors later, but this is a typical Q-factor for first-time industrial quality custom training projects.) A quick calculation tells us:

Q-factor (1.0) X $100,000 X Total User Hours (3) = $300,000

Now let's consider a custom point-of-sale application produced at a higher quality level Q-factor of 3.5. We don't expect customers to spend more than 5 minutes on the system, but in order to cover all the options, we plan to produce a total of 20 minutes of activity. The cost would be estimated as follows:

Q-factor (3.5) X $100,000 X Total User Hours (.33) = $115,500

As these examples show, if we can estimate the approximate total user time of the presentation, and if we can state the expected quality level in terms of Q-factor, we can come up with an approximate cost. As we'll see, you should be able to determine reasonable values for these factors during the planning process.

Q-factors for custom training presentations tend to run in the range from .5 to 1.5 for the first module produced. Presentations designed for public access and marketing run in the 2.5 to 5 range, and can be even higher in special cases. These Q-factors assume that all services are purchased from professional vendors at going rates. If some or all of the services can be obtained in-house, substantial savings might be realized.

One of the key factors that affects the variation in Q-factors for IVD projects is the quality of video production. A video-rich application, shot in a professional studio or on location, will push the cost toward the higher end of the range. If this quality of video is planned, the Q-factor should not be set at less than 1.0 for any type of application. If you will use a cast

of professional actors, the Q-factor will go up toward 3. If you plan to shoot on an exterior location, or use recognized talent, your Q-factor will get up into the range of 5. Rough estimates, to be sure, but experience bears them out.

Another key factor to note is the learning curve that will be encountered over the life of the project. The figures quoted so far are based on the premise of the first module of custom IVD. If this comprises the whole project, the estimates should stand. If the project consists of many modules of generally the same design, produced by the same team, the Q-factor should drop dramatically. There is not enough data available to be definitive about how fast the Q-factor will drop, but theoretically, the curve should look like the one shown in Figure 12-3.

During the first period, the team is learning the procedures and overcoming the problems that we have described in prior chapters. Once learned the cost per module drops as more are produced, and economies of scale can be realized. Finally, the team approaches maximum efficiency, and further cost reduction is prohibited by the fixed costs of production.

One major project has been estimated at a Q-factor of .1 for 600 hours of training — $10,000 development cost for a user hour. This implies a total project cost of six million dollars. Other factors were involved such as use of in-house video facilities, well justified in a project of this scope. With a learning curve developed to this point, it's easy to imagine the lessons being completed like pages off a printing

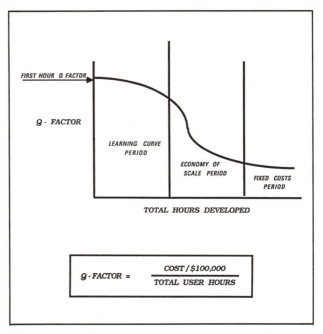

Figure 12-3 Learning Curve for the Q-Factor over Several Projects

press. Empirical results like these support the idea that interactive video can become a practical medium, even if the initial cost of entry is high.

In Chapter 4, we introduced the worksheet shown in Figure 12-4 as a means of preparing the estimated project cost for the Planning Session. Now that we have covered the activities represented by the various cost figures, it is worthwhile to review the form. You may want to copy Figure 12-4 and use it to make a preliminary budget for your own project. At this point, you should be able to estimate a reasonable total cost. Enter that figure into the lower right space for "100%" of the total. Then, apply the percentages we have shown for each item (or revise them to match your own estimates) and compute the line items for the development phases. Make your own estimates for implementation costs, as discussed in Chapter 11. These figures should be solid enough to take to your Planning Session.

THE INTERMEDIATE BUDGET

As the project proceeds into the Design Phase, a clearer picture of its probable cost begins to emerge. In Chapter 6, we discussed a set of matrices that could be used for design and evaluation of the treatment. We mentioned at that time that one of these

— the Media Strategy Matrix — could also be used to estimate the production cost of the presentation. Let's review that matrix again, this time concentrating on its use as a cost predictor. It's shown in Figure 12-5.

The matrix indicates the media planned for each major presentation topic. It provides a review of the media strategy, and a way to make sure that the use of higher quality, more expensive media treatment favors the higher priority topics. By ascribing costs to the individual media elements, the total cost can be arrived at. At this point, of course, we are only able to make reasonable estimates of how much of each type of media will be used, and how much each element will cost. A good designer should be able to come fairly close to the first estimate, however, and the production vendor should be able to provide the latter. As a rough starting point, we've provided typical costs for media elements produced by a professional outside vendor. They are listed in Figure 12-6.

These ranges are guidelines only, and could be more or less in certain situations. They provide a place to start, however. They also provide a way for you and a potential vendor to arrive at a reasonable agreement on the budget. If the vendor knows that you expect to pay, say, $2000 per finished minute for video, he can show you examples of his work at that level, and both of you will know what to expect.

When you have totalled the costs from the matrix, you have only computed the **production** costs for your budget estimate. There are still the costs of the other phases of analysis, design, development, authoring and so on. There are manufacturing and distribution costs to be included, and there is the vendor's overhead and profit to be added in. For the intermediate budget, the following rules of thumb can be applied:

1. Estimate total development costs by multiplying the production cost estimate by 2.

2. Add 30% to all out-of-house development costs to cover profit and overhead.

3. Add videodisc and CD-ROM mastering and replication costs. If you can't compute them closely, use a figure of $3000 for each disc side.

4. Add estimated costs for other components such as workbooks, brochures, packaging and so on.

It will probably be useful to get these estimates onto a computer spreadsheet program. As you talk to vendors, the estimates of media elements and their costs should become more refined, and the spreadsheet can help you hone the estimates quick-

IVD COST ESTIMATE WORKSHEET

DEVELOPMENT ESTIMATES

PHASE	DIRECT LABOR	SUPPLIES	TRAVEL	MATERIAL	SERVICES	TOTALS
ANALYSIS	5		2		1	8
DESIGN	10	1	2	1	1	15
DEVELOPMENT	10	1	2	1	1	15
PRODUCTION	5				40	45
AUTHORING	12					12
VALIDATION	3			2		5
TOTALS $ %	45	2	6	4	43	100%

IMPLEMENTATION ESTIMATES

	FIRST YEAR	SECOND YEAR	THIRD YEAR	FOURTH YEAR	FIFTH YEAR
DEVELOPMENT SYSTEM					
DELIVERY SYSTEM					
REPLICATION DISTRIBUTION					
CONSTRUCTION SITE PREPARATION					
INSTALLATION AND TRAINING					
OPERATIONS MAINTENANCE					

Figure 12-4 Planning Budget Worksheet

ly. If you go through this exercise in this level of detail, you can be confident that your intermediate budget is close enough to the final figures to use in planning your funding requirements.

THE FINAL BUDGET

When the first draft of the Design Document has been completed, all of the information is available to complete the final development budget. This can be combined with the final implementation budget to complete the final project budget. This is a detailed document that should be prepared on a computer spread sheet if at all possible. The project personnel involved in each phase should be listed and the labor and cost components spread out for each. This format will show the project cost that has been incurred at each phase milestone. At this point, the project has completed the Analysis Phase, and is well into the Design Phase. No more than 15 to 20 percent of

the total project budget should have been expended at this point — even less if no money was spent for market research. The major costs that will need tight control still lie ahead.

If you're working with an outside vendor, the phase breakdown of costs has an important advantage. It doesn't happen often, but it's not unheard of that the relationship may break down and the contract terminated before the project is complete. If this happens, the money due for the partial work can be clearly defined by the phases completed, and the ownership of the work in process will be clear as well.

The project management software that you have used for preparing the schedule should provide valuable input for budgeting. If you used the software to track resources and costs, many of the numbers you need will already be provided. At any rate, you should list the personnel involved by phase, and enter an estimated number of hours and hourly rate

PRESENTATION ID (*format type*)	HIGH-PRODUCTION MOTION VIDEO	INDUSTRIAL QUALITY MOTION VIDEO	HIGH-QUALITY COMPUTER GRAPHICS	SECOND TRACK AUDIO SEGMENTS	VIDEO STILL FRAMES	COMPUTER TEXT SCREENS	BUDGET ESTIMATES ($000)
			MEDIA STRATEGIES				
1 A (simulation)	5 minutes		20				21.0 k
2 A (game)	5		20				21.0
1 B	2		8				8.4
2 B	2		8				8.4
3 A	2		8				8.4
5 A	3		30				13.5
4 B	:30 sec.		25				3.3
6 B	:30		25				3.3
7 B	:30		25				3.3
8 A	:30		25	6 minutes	25		6.3
8 B	:30		20	6	20		6.0
1 C (tutorial)		1 minute		3		20	2.0
2 C		1 minute		3		20	2.0
9 A	:30		15	3	15		4.5
10 B	:30		20	4	20		5.5
	22:30	2 min.	250	25 min.	80	40	120,000

Figure 12-5 Media Matrix

```
                MEDIA  COST  ESTIMATES


       MEDIA CATEGORY                   ESTIMATE

    Industrial Studio Video ......... $ 600 - 1100 pfm*
    Professional Studio Video ........ 1500 - 2400 pfm
    Professional Location Video ....... 1800 - 2700 pfm
    Broadcast Quality Video .......... 2500 - 3500 pfm
    Commercial Quality Video ........ 3000 - 5000 pfm


    Professionally Narrated Audio ...... 600 per hour


    Original Illustrations ............... 100 - 250 per screen
    Card Art Illustrations .............. 60 - 200 per picture


    Original Studio Photographs ........ 50 - 150 per picture
    Original Location Photographs ...... 100 - 300 per picture
    Stock Photographs ................. 25 - 100 per photo


           * pfm = per finished minute
```

Figure 12-6 Media Cost Estimates

for each of them. Then list other activities that will require funding, such as business trips, telephone calls, shipping, copying and so on. Apply the following cost breakdown on your spreadsheet:

1. Hours X Rate = Direct Labor

2. Supplies

3. Travel

4. Materials

5. Services

When you get to the Production Phase, you can list video production as a single line item, based on the cost estimate from your Media Strategy worksheet. Clearly, an item of this magnitude needs a more detailed breakdown, and you'll want to prepare the video production budget separately. You'll probably want to work with your video producer to complete this part. There are all kinds of line items like "Set Construction," "Lighting," "Gaffers," "Audio tech" and so on. We discussed these functions in Chapter 8, but you'll probably need expert assistance to prepare the budget. You should expect, however, that the total costs will be in line with your estimate of "Dollars per finished minute" that you made in the Intermediate Budget.

When all costs have been sub-totalled by phase, a fixed percentage should be applied to account for overhead and profit. If cost overruns appear likely, you can work backwards to readjust the tasks and schedule.

Having finished the development budget, you can combine it with the implementation budget to complete the final project budget. This is a good time to review the estimates and actual expenditures for activities on the implementation side of the project.

Even the final budget, of course, is only an estimate of actual costs. As these costs are incurred, they need to be tracked. You'll probably have several opportunities to evaluate new creative ideas in design that will require reallocation of costs, or perhaps a request for additional funding. Complete and accurate accounting will play a critical role in evaluating such requests. The budget will provide you with a precise tool to make and manage these decisions, and to keep the project on its cost target as you go.

Approvals and Signoffs

The next tab in the Project Control Book should contain documentation of the approvals and signoffs that you have obtained at the completion of each phase. This can be a touchy and difficult area to manage. We have never met anyone who claims to **like** bureaucratic "official" procedures and formal signoff requirements. The need for them varies among organizations. When managing projects of this magnitude, however, these procedures can contribute real benefits to everyone involved. They can help the Project Manager avoid the common pitfalls that occur when necessary resources that have been committed are slow to come forth.

We have stressed the importance of the phase process, and your responsibility to make sure that "each phase has done its work" before continuing to the next. Carefully defined milestones in terms of specific deliverables, and formal signoff procedures can help you make sure phase evaluation is done properly. These procedures will keep your sponsoring executive interested and involved in the project by demonstrating progress, and insuring that the direction is in line with his or her goals.

A good mechanism for defining the signoff procedures is the vendor contract. In fact, most vendors will insist that such procedures are included, since it protects them from running afoul of internal organizational problems that they can't control. The contract should state that a formal signoff is required at the end of each phase to state that all deliverables have been completed and are acceptable. If this is stated in the contract, the sponsoring executive will have to sign off, and this will probably result in at least a brief review. These procedures can help maintain involvement, and possibly avoid unpleasant surprises down the road.

Other Records

In addition to the major sections above, the Project Control Book should contain tabs for other records that pertain to the project, and may be needed to provide explanations or audit trails later. Useful tabs include:

- Correspondence
- Accounting Documents
- Contracts and Agreements
- Miscellaneous Documents
- Personal Notes and Resources

A Last Word

The Project Control Book can become your most valuable ally in project management. Much like a time management notebook, it can almost take on a life of its own, seeming to take over managing you along with everything else. Like the time management book, this isn't necessarily bad. The contents of the book that we've described here cover all major aspects of the project, and if the book is up to date, it's a good bet that the project itself is up to date and progressing well.

SECTION TWO
PROJECT MANAGER'S RESOURCES

Appendix A

Checklists

Checklist for Evaluating the Analysis Phase

Analysis Documentation

BUSINESS CASE
- Have business goals, problems or opportunities that led to issuance of the RFP been explained?
- Have requirements and expectations of management, host site personnel and users for the application been presented?
- Has the problem category been defined? (Such as: instruction, marketing, or information/public access.)
- Have available resources been described?
- Have project constraints or limitations been explained?
- Has quantitative data for economic justification been included?

ENVIRONMENT
- Has a clear description of the planned application environment and its impact on the application design been provided? Environmental factors include:

  - Physical facilities and scheduling considerations.

  - Standard and auxiliary equipment required.

  - Application materials and complementary references.

  - Administrative personnel and procedures.

  - Personal considerations that influence the design.

AUDIENCE
- Has a clear, detailed description of the primary and secondary audiences been provided? These descriptions cover:

- Previous experiences.

- Current capabilities.

- Personal characteristics/demographics.

- Attitudes and interests.

TASK/NEEDS
- Has task or needs analysis data for the application been provided? Task analysis (describing tasks to be performed by end users) is usually associated with training applications. Needs analysis (perceived by or created for end users) is associated with marketing applications. This data should include:

  - Task/needs description.

  - Resources or tools required by end users.

  - Influences on or by other systems.

  - Input from end users, host site personnel, managers, and market research data (if available) is included.

CONTENT ANALYSIS
- Has the subject matter or content to be developed and its relative importance been specified?
- Has the content been purged of excess or irrelevant items?
- Can the specified content be covered effectively within the bounds of the planned materials?

OBJECTIVES
- Have the general objectives to be accomplished by this application been listed?
- Has a statement of requirements for the validation process been provided, including criteria for application success?

Request for Proposal (RFP) Contents

ADMINISTRATIVE

The document contains

- A cover letter with authorized signatures.
- A statement requiring complete proposals to conform to the RFP.
- Instructions for the delivery of the proposals including: time, place, and number of copies.
- Instructions for modifications, errors, and withdrawal of the RFP.
- Name, address, and telephone of the person designated to receive questions about the RFP.

CONTRACTUAL

The document

- Specifies the right to discontinue work on the part of either party with 30 days notification.
- Specifies the right to reject any or all proposals.
- Includes notification that false or misleading statements are grounds for proposal rejection.
- Retains the right to make addenda to the RFP.
- Provides for copyright and patent rights.
- Includes disclaimers for confidential information.

FINANCIAL

The document contains

- A schedule of percentage payments, usually listed by phase completion dates.
- Travel costs and per diem for subject matter experts.
- A statement removing your company or institution from responsibility for the cost of the proposal.
- Specification of the right to modify the budget according to changes in the scope of work.

SYSTEM DESCRIPTION

The document contains

- A complete list of the functional specifications of the hardware, including manufacturers' model numbers if already chosen.
- A detailed description of other requirements such as printed output, voice or data communications, etc.
- A description of the software requirements, including a list of licensed programs if known (operating systems, delivery system, etc.), and functional requirements of software to be written.

APPLICATION DESCRIPTION

The document contains

- All of the analysis data listed in the previous section.
- Any other relevant information needed to allow all bidders to have a fair opportunity to submit a complete and competitive proposal.

SCOPE OF EFFORT

The document contains

- A complete description of the work to be performed in each phase of the project, including:

  - A list of activities to be performed in the phase.

  - Specific responsibilities of the vendor and the contractor.

  - A list of work products to be delivered.

  - A statement of approvals required to complete the phase.

> **Note.** These checklists remind you to evaluate the critical factors of the application. As they are applied during this phase, you may have valid reasons why one or more factors have not been completed. The checklist insures that at least they have been considered. For those incomplete items without valid reasons you need to adopt a "what's wrong" procedure:
>
> - Describe what's missing, incomplete, or inaccurate.
>
> - Identify who/where the changes should be made.
>
> - Determine if additional resources are needed.
>
> - Monitor the re-work (and its impact on the project). Schedule an evaluation of the revised work.

Checklist for Evaluating High Level Design

Proposal Evaluation

ADMINISTRATIVE
− Has the proposal met the administrative requirements set forth in the RFP, including number of copies, time, authorized signatures?
− Has each of the requested deliverables been addressed?

FINANCIAL
− Have budget estimates been developed and documented?
− Are the budget allocations for each phase reasonable and appropriate for the production of the deliverables?
− Is the total price reasonable and competitive?

SCHEDULE
− Has a work plan and timetable for implementing each phase been described?
− Has the proposal defined the dates, personnel, resources, and responsibilities for each application deliverable?

PERSONNEL
− Are qualified personnel to perform each of the defined tasks listed?
− Does the proposal describe prior interactive media experience which demonstrates an ability to effectively manage and develop IVD/multimedia applications?

Preliminary Design Evaluation

GENERAL
− Has an overview of the problem(s) and the proposed solutions(s) been described?
− Do the application solutions substantially conform with the requirements of the RFP?
− Do the structure, treatment, and general strategies provide an effective solution to the problem(s)?
− Is the proposed solution imaginative and creative?

SPECIFIC
− Does the proposal describe each of the application development stages, the resources required, and the procedures to be followed? The explanations should outline how the vendor plans to:

• Collect, analyze, and validate the content.

• Work with subject matter experts and other users.

• Further develop application treatments and strategies.

• Format and develop storyboards and scripts.

• Develop documentation for production.

• Manage the production process.

• Test and evaluate the application.

• Maximize the delivery system technology while meeting the requirements of the application.

Authoring Facility Selection

At this point in the project, the authoring facility should be decided upon. Detail design should not be attempted without knowledge of system capabilities and limitations.
− Is the selected authoring facility appropriate for the application's needs?
− Has the design been constructed to accommodate the highest practicable level of authoring facility?
− Do changes or maintenance depend upon a single individual or organization?
− Can the application be maintained in-house?
− Have all charges for presentation software licenses been considered and detailed?
− Are the system-supplied and/or author-defined user interfaces, (e.g., Menu Designs, Control Icons) appropriate for the application, the audience, and the environment?
− If other applications are run at the site, will the user interface and administrative procedures be compatible?

NOTE: A description of authoring facilities is found in Chapter 9. They include:
• Spreadsheet/Timeline Processor.

• Hypermedia Generator.

• Authoring System.

• Application Shell.

• Authoring Language.

Checklist for Evaluating Detail Design

Overview

The following set of checklists is the most extensive in the entire project. You will find in the next section that the same checklists are used for the Development phase. The reason for this is that the factors considered in each phase are the same; in Design, the evaluation focus is on the plan to meet the goals; in Development the focus is on the execution of the plan. Of the two, however, it is much more critical to give attention to the Design Phase. A careful, complete review at this time can result in a cost effective, on-time implementation from this point on.

Analysis Data

The application design document incorporates data from the previous analysis activities. Verify that the following information is brought forward.

- A complete statement of the problem or opportunity.
- Application goals and objectives.
- Design parameters and constraints.
- Content analysis documentation.

Application Design Session

- Is the content properly presented and organized?
- Is the content presentation at a proper level of completeness and detail for the end user?
- Does the content presentation consider end user prerequisites and skill level?
- Is the content presentation matched to analysis phase requirements?
- Is the content accurately presented according to the sources identified in the analysis and design phase?
- Is the content presentation appropriate to the program's objectives?
- Is the content presented according to the time allocations approved in the Design Phase of the project?
- Is the content logically divided into topics and sub-topics corresponding to a menu/sub-menu structure (if appropriate) that can be grouped into disc sides?

- Are content and objective consistent with main topics having main objectives and sub-topics having intermediate objectives?

Design Documentation

THE FLOWCHART
- Does the flowchart have a legend at the beginning specifying the flowchart symbol used for each media choice (i.e., the symbol for motion video is specified, the symbol for computer text screen is specified, etc.)?
- Does the production flowchart clearly depict the logic and structure of the application, and show the media and content of each individual event?
- Does the production flowchart provide a means of locating the detailed development documentation for each event with labels and/or page numbers?

TREATMENT
- Is a clear and concise overview of the program provided?
- Are presentation methods and approaches described?
- Are story lines, themes, sub-themes included where appropriate?
- Are scene descriptions and sample scripts included where appropriate?
- Is the program described from the end user's point of view? How the user interacts? What the user sees?
- Are complete descriptions of proposed characters, shooting locations, and sets provided?
- Is the overall mood, style, texture, and intended effect of the program provided through sample scenarios or other descriptions?
- Have appropriate formats (mini-treatments) been selected for each event?

Strategies

STRUCTURE AND SEQUENCE
- Is the proposed structure and sequence appropriate and effective?
- Can the user select activities and pace the instruction according to individual needs?
- Is a conclusion or summary provided?
- Are tests provided when appropriate?
- Does the design provide smooth transitions and consistent development for all possible paths through the program?

– Does the design flowchart present a clear and concise framework or blueprint for the program?

MOTIVATION

– Does the design incorporate motivational techniques appropriate for the audience, environment and application?
– Is each segment of the program designed to capture the end user's attention when appropriate?
– Does the program use specific motivation techniques such as invoking curiosity, providing rewards, setting a challenge, creating a fantasy, depicting a role model, or using pleasing media?
– If used, is humor appropriate to the application, not offensive to any individual, and timeless relative to the life of the application?
– Are the motivational techniques used appropriate and cost justified, such as, using face recognition talent, animation, and location shooting?

MEDIA SELECTION

– Is media selection for each event appropriate to its purpose?
– Are time and disc capacity allocated to events according to the relative importance of the topics?
– Is the cost of the selected media and production technique appropriate for each event?
– Are production resources allocated to events according to their frequency of use, i.e., the most accessed paths through the program are allocated the most production monies when appropriate?
– Are media integrated to keep the user constantly engaged?
– Are media logically allocated according to the importance of the content and how it can best be learned?
– Are time estimates provided per videodisc side for allocating the available space to the content?
– Are time and storage estimates provided for audio and graphic files to be recorded on CD-ROM or magnetic disk files to make sure they are reasonable?

INTERACTION STRATEGIES

– Is the density of responses (i.e., how often the user interacts with the system) appropriate to the audience and application?
– Do responses require intellectual participation as opposed to thoughtless "paging" through the presentation?

– Is the level of user control appropriate to the application, the audience, and the environment?
– Are interactions planned which maximize the capabilities of the media and delivery system?
– Are appropriate instructional techniques (such as drill and practice or simulation) employed to achieve the stated learning objectives of the program?
– Are interactive functions well matched to the purpose of the presentation segments? Refer to the list of interactive functions in the Checklist for Detail Design.

1. INTERRUPTION: The user can interrupt the presentation to pause, resume, access menus, go to help, access a glossary, move backward and forward in a program for review and skipping.

2. PACING: At author-determined pause points, user can proceed when ready.

3. SELECTION: The program has a menu or linking structure that enables the user to select activities, content/subjects, desired presentation mode, and level of detail.

4. INPUT/FEEDBACK: The program has been designed to enable the user to receive feedback concerning correctness and appropriateness of responses, receive positive and negative feedback, and remediation when appropriate.

5. DIRECTION: The design provides for appropriate branching depending upon the prior responses of the user. For example, individualized tracking is designed for the novice, the expert, the student, and the teacher. A predetermined direction or track is provided for the user who has not indicated a tracking preference.

6. SIMULATION: The situation-determined responses are based on real-life.

ADULT LEARNING STRATEGIES

– Does the design effectively use principles of adult learning?
– Is a positive user attitude set from the start of the program?
– Is the user's mind actively involved with the presentation?
– Does the design allow the user complete freedom and control when appropriate?
– Does the design maintain interest by using a sufficient variety of media and presentation techniques?

- Does the design build on assumed prior knowledge, experience, and internal models of the audience?
- Are users always aware of where they are and where they are going in the program?
- In linear/branching structures, does the user know approximately how long a module should take, and how much remains to be done?
- Does the design provide the user a sense of progress?
- Can users validate their progress if they so desire?
- Is the level of difficulty appropriate for the target audience?

EVALUATION
- Is feedback effectively used to provide information to the user regarding the appropriateness of the user's response?
- Is feedback non-judgmental, positive, and pleasing?
- Does feedback provide information as to why the user's response was correct or not correct?
- Is negative feedback informative and tastefully used?
- Does remedial feedback present the content or question in a different way than it was originally presented?
- Is the remediation strategy worth the disc capacity and cost to produce it?
- Is a method for evaluating the user's performance and/or program effectiveness detailed?
- Is information collected to show whether learning has taken place as a result of the program?
- Is feedback to user responses immediate and appropriate?

Checklist for Evaluating the Development Phase

The following checklist is similar to that in the Design Phase. In design, you need to insure that all the application strategies are created; during development, you must verify that those same strategies have been documented completely for the production effort.

The Super Storyboard

- Is the SSB presented in enough detail to enable the reviewer to have a firm understanding of the program and to enable someone other than the creator to produce the program?
- Are the SSBs complete — specifying all branching, time estimates, shots, DVE's (digital video effects), graphics, use of character generated text, use of computer text, graphics text, and graphics art, props, touch areas, run times, and a page numbering scheme which corresponds to the needs of the authoring facility?

Content Analysis

These items pertain to changes in content that occurred during development. Normally, such changes should be minimal.
- Is the content properly presented and organized?
- Is the content presentation at a proper level of completeness and detail for the end user?
- Does the content presentation consider end user prerequisites and skill level?
- Is the content presentation matched to analysis phase requirements?
- Is the content presentation appropriate to program's objectives?
- Is the content accurately presented according to the sources identified in the analysis and design phase?
- Is the content presented according to the time allocations approved in the design phase of the project?
- Is the content logically divided into topics and sub-topics corresponding to a menu/sub-menu structure (if appropriate) that can be grouped into disc sides?
- Are content and objectives consistent with main topics having main objectives and sub-topics having intermediate objectives?

Goals, Objectives, and Intended Outcomes

- Is it clear from the Super Storyboard that the goals of the program will be met?
- Is it clear from the Super Storyboard that the objectives of the program will be met?
- Is it clear from the Super Storyboard that the learner is informed of the objectives?

Treatment

- Has the treatment specified in the Design Document been effectively, creatively, and efficiently executed in the Super Storyboard? (Refer to Treatment criteria specified in the Detail Design Checklist.)

Strategies

STRUCTURE AND SEQUENCE
- In general, does the sequence of activities seem reasonable?
- Can the user select activities and pace the instruction according to individual needs?
- Is a conclusion or summary provided?
- Is a test provided when appropriate?
- In the Super Storyboard, is it evident that transitions are smooth and logical for all possible paths through the program?

MOTIVATION
- Does the Super Storyboard incorporate motivational techniques appropriate for the audience, environment and application?
- Is each segment of the program designed to capture the end user's attention when appropriate?
- Does the program use specific motivational techniques such as: invoking curiosity, providing rewards, setting a challenge, creating a fantasy, depicting a role model, or using pleasing media?
- If used, is humor appropriate to the application, not offensive to any individual, and timeless relative to the life of the application?
- Are the motivational techniques used appropriate and cost justified, such as using face recognition talent, animation, and location shooting?
- Is it evident from the Super Storyboard that media techniques have been used that end users will find interesting and therefore motivating?

MEDIA SELECTION
- Is media selection for each event appropriate to its purpose?
- Is it evident from the Super Storyboard that time and disc capacity are allocated to events according to the relative importance of the topics?
- Is the cost of the selected media and production technique appropriate for each event?
- Are production resources allocated to events according to their frequency of use, i.e., the most accessed paths through the program are allocated the most production monies when appropriate?
- Are media integrated to keep the user constantly engaged?
- Are media selected to take advantage of the user's best channel of learning?
- Are text screens well designed and formatted for ease of reading? (For example, visual indicators or icons used where appropriate, text layouts in natural phrases.)
- Has the appropriate type size and style been selected for the particular needs of the target audience?
- Is the design of graphics consistent with other graphics appearing in the printed and packaging material?
- Is it evident from the Super Storyboard that time estimates for allocating the videodisc media to the content approved in the Design Phase have been adhered to in the Development Phase?

INTERACTION STRATEGIES
- Is the density of responses (i.e., how often the user interacts with the system) appropriate to the audience and application?
- Do responses require intellectual participating as opposed to thoughtless "paging" through the presentation?
- Is the level of user control appropriate to the application, the audience, and the environment?
- Are interactions planned which maximize the capabilities of the media and delivery system?
- Are appropriate instructional techniques (such as drill and practice or simulation) employed to achieve the stated learning objectives of the program?
- Are interactive functions well matched to the purpose of the presentation segments? Are interactive functions well matched to the purpose of the presentation segments? Refer to the list of interactive functions in the checklist for Detail Design.

ADULT LEARNING STRATEGIES

- Does the design effectively use principles of adult learning?
- Is a positive user attitude set from the start of the program?
- Is the user's mind actively involved with the presentation?
- Does the design allow the user complete freedom and control when appropriate?
- Does the design maintain interest by using a sufficient variety of media and presentation techniques?
- Does the design build on assumed prior knowledge, experience, and internal models of the audience?
- Are users always aware of where they are and where they are going in the program?
- In linear/branching structures, does the user know approximately how long a module should take, and how much remains to be done?
- Does the design provide the user a sense of progress?
- Can users validate their progress if they so desire?
- Is the level of difficulty appropriate for the target audience?

EVALUATION

- Is feedback effectively used to provide information to the user regarding the appropriateness of the user's response?
- Is feedback non-judgmental, positive, and pleasing?
- Does feedback provide information as to why the user's response was correct or not correct?
- Is negative feedback informative and tastefully used?
- Does remedial feedback present the content or question in a different way than it was originally presented?
- Is the remediation strategy worth the disc capacity and cost to produce it?
- Is a method for evaluating the user's performance and/or program effectiveness detailed?
- Is information collected to show whether learning has taken place as a result of the program?
- Is feedback to user responses immediate and appropriate?
- Has a data collection method been included for the application (marketing, instructional, or information)?

Treatment Review

- Are sentence length, structure, and vocabulary appropriate for the target audience?
- For text screens, are words correctly spelled, and standard grammar and punctuation used?
- Are screens neat, attractive, and well spaced?
- Are screens displaying instructional text formatted for easy reading and learning retention?
- Does talent narration use proper grammar and conventional language?
- Has talent been properly cast?
- Are sets realistic and interesting?
- Are action sequences believable?
- Are the dramatic sequences appropriate and logical to meet the program's objectives?
- Is the integration of the media smooth, continuous, and nondistracting to the viewer?

The following guidelines are highly dependent on the nature and purpose of the application, and must be applied loosely with individual good judgment:

- As a general rule, are there no more than five video stills or computer frames in a row before the user is involved in some kind of interaction?
- As a general rule, are motion segments usually no longer than one minute before the user is involved in some kind of interaction?
- As a general rule, are computer text screens double spaced with lines centered?
- As a general rule, are menus kept to one screen or frame?
- As a general rule, are menus and introduction screens or frames formatted the same for easy identification by the user?

Video Segments

- Does visual material accompany and amplify each key point?
- Does each sentence make a direct contribution to the message?
- Are video segments as short as possible while still achieving their objective?
- Are user-selected topics explicitly acknowledged?
- Is it obvious to the end user how to quit, repeat, or move on?
- Is there a smooth transition between different user-selected segments?

Audio, Music, Special Effects

- Is the audio written for the ear?
  - Smooth phrasing

  - Easily pronounceable words

  - Speaking (not reading) vocabulary

- Do the audio/special effects coincide with visual material?
- Do special effects contribute to the application message?
- Is background music appropriate; does it add any value?

Computer Graphics

- Are they correct? Spelling, grammar, technical accuracy?
- Are they consistent? Colors, fonts, art style, purpose?
- Are they easily processed by the user?

  - Five or fewer major points

  - Natural breaks and spacing

  - Readable fonts

  - Logical screen arrangements for reading

  - Unambiguous icons

- Does accompanying audio match the graphics' words and order?
- Does the highlighting support the message?

Touch Areas

- Has sufficient room been allocated for the touch areas?
- Have colors been planned to support visual acknowledgments?
- Is the shape of the visual target matched to the touch areas?
- Do touch areas extend vertically to avoid parallax errors?

Remaining Producible Documentation

- Is a method of computerizing the details of production variables evident in order to save time and money?
- Are the graphics presented in such a way that a computer graphics artist can easily follow them?

- Is there a Storyboard, script, or shot list entry for every video element in the SSB and production flowchart?
- Does the authoring documentation follow the form and conventions appropriate to the authoring facility, and may it be passed to the author without further explanations?

Checklist for Evaluating the Production Phase

Super Storyboard

- Have all criteria specified for evaluating the Super Storyboard been adhered to in the off-line and on-line videotapes?

Production Media

VIDEO
- Is the talent pleasing, appropriate, and well suited to the role?
- Does the talent add to the overall effectiveness of the program?
- Is picture quality well defined and distinct with no bleeding, streaking, and blurring?
- Is color realistic, consistent, and of high quality?
- Are all visuals (e.g., figures, charts, pictures, photographs, which will be used in the videotape) formatted according to television aspect ratio?
- For text screens, are words correctly spelled, and standard grammar and punctuation used?
- Are screens neat, attractive, and well spaced?
- Are screens displaying instructional text formatted for easy reading and learning retention?
- Does talent narration use proper grammar and conventional syntax?
- Are sets realistic and interesting?
- Are action sequences believable?
- Are the dramatic sequences appropriate and logical to meet the program's objectives?

AUDIO
- Is all talent narration pleasing and does it add to the overall effectiveness of the program?
- Are audio tracks clear and free of distortion and extraneous noise?
- Is the narration and all talent voices pleasing and easily understood?

– Are all technical terms pronounced and inflected properly?

– Is the music pleasing, effective, and appropriately used?

– Are other audio effects appropriate and supportive?

DISC MASTERING AND REPLICATION

– Does the master tape conform to all standards of format and editing of the manufacturer?

– Have all tapes been encoded with non-drop S.M.P.T.E. time code?

– Has a protection master been dubbed before sending the tape to the manufacturer?

– Is the information on the Disc Production Work Order provided by the Disc Manufacturer complete and accurate?

– Have all labeling and packaging instructions, mechanicals (camera-ready copy for the printer) and materials been arranged for?

COMPUTER GRAPHICS

– Have all screens been checked for technical accuracy, spelling, and standard grammar?

– Do all screens have a consistent style?

– Are text screens formatted for easy reading and retention?

– Is the amount of information limited and attractively presented?

– Are all fonts easily read?

– Are colors attractive and not over-used on a single screen?

– Are icons and user instructions clear and unambiguous?

– Are screens to be used with touch areas properly laid out:

• Sufficient room is present to place touch areas.

• Parallax errors minimized by using tall touch areas.

• The shape of touch targets matches the rectangular shape of touch areas.

• Colors and shapes are chosen to support various kinds of touch acknowledgment.

– Are screens to be used as overlays matched to video picture, with allowance for small variations in alignment from one system to another?

PRINT MATERIALS

– Is the layout pleasing and does it add to the overall understanding of the material.

– Has the material been edited for misspellings and inappropriate words or graphics?

– Are the camera-ready materials of high quality?

– Are print media well designed and formatted for ease of reading? (For example, visuals and indicators or icons have been used where appropriate.)

– Have the appropriate type sizes and styles been selected for the particular needs of the target audience?

– Has all necessary information been provided on the disc and diskette labels as well as the disc jackets (e.g. titles, copyrights, confidentiality)? Are they accurate?

Checklist for Evaluating the Authoring Phase

– Does the designer fully understand the capabilities and limitations of the selected authoring facility?

– Has the author had proper training and time to become productive in the use of the authoring facility prior to beginning the authoring phase?

– Have arrangements been made to provide systems, software and technical support to authors?

– Have all necessary licenses for authoring, presentation, and other required software systems been obtained?

– Are all graphics complete, identified, and accessible through the authoring facility?

– Have arrangements been made to deliver a videodisc to the author? Has a disc map that identifies the frame number of all video elements been completed?

– Have arrangements been made to provide a check disc or other method for authoring elements that will be delivered on CD-ROM?

– Is the authoring documentation complete, unambiguous, and fully understood by the author?

– If more than one author is involved, have plans been made for system integration and testing?

– Are systems and people available for testing and debugging the completed application?

– Has enough time been allocated for all authoring activities including coding, testing, and tuning?

Checklist for Evaluating the Validation Phase

- Is the validation plan complete, including all test and measurement instruments? Are these instruments representative of the application objectives?
- Are plans for obtaining a sample audience in place? Will they be truly representative of the target audience? Will there be enough users or students to provide significant results?
- Is the validation site the same as or representative of the host sites?
- Are personnel at the validation site prepared to participate in the validation?
- Have enough time and resources been allocated to accomplish the final revision?

Checklist for Evaluating Implementation Activities

- Has technical information for planning and installation been obtained from the system manufacturer?

- Is the physical plan complete, including site access, floor plan, equipment access, electrical service, communications lines, proper lighting, and other requirements such as air conditioning?
- Is the announcement plan effective and complementary to other communications received at the host site?
- Is training for site personnel complete and effective? Has it been tested and validated?
- Are kiosks or carrels well designed and constructed? Has provision been made for equipment access and cooling? Have arrangements been made for delivery and access to sites?
- Have all other systems or procedures that the application could affect been considered, and plans made for integration?
- Has an installation schedule and team been put in place? Are the installers completely trained?
- Have site personnel been trained to perform all maintenance including start-up, operation and shut-down procedures, replenishment of consumable support items, on-site preventative maintenance, trouble analysis and reporting and other procedures needed to maintain the application on a continuing basis?
- Are procedures in place for collecting monitoring data for the application?

Appendix B

Super Storyboard Form

The document that has been defined as the "Super Storyboard" in the text serves the purpose of depicting all media elements of an event, and showing their relationship to each other. The forms used are unique to each developing organization, and often unique to each project. Whatever form is used, it must provide adequate information to produce each media element that will be available in the delivery system.

In this appendix, we have provided two copies of the form used in the text. It is particularly useful for interactive video projects that are delivered on systems that have the capability for graphic overlay of the video picture, and user control by defined touch or pointing areas. It can be easily modified for use with systems that also provide graphic and/or audio elements from CD-ROM.

If this form will serve the purpose for your project, you have permission to remove the second copy for reproduction in whatever quantity you need to document your application.

Super Story Board

	LAST REVISION		EVENT	SEQ
	DATE/TIME	INIT.		

C O M P O S I T E

SCENE/SHOT ID: | AUDIO TRACK:

AUDIO/PRODUCTION NOTES:

TIMING/Read: | Cumulative:

G R A P H I C S

10

20

GRAPHIC ID: | TOOL: | MODE:

INSTRUCTIONS:

C O N T R O L

10

20

REFERENCE/LABEL:

AUTHOR DOCUMENTATION:

NOTES:

VIDEO:		DOCUMENTS UPDATED:									
SHOT	DESCRIPTION		STILL	SET/LDC	PROPS	TALENT	ON/VO	DVE	VIDEO GRAPHIC	PC GRAPHIC	OVRLY
1											
2											
3											
4											
5											

MASTER TAPE TIME CODE		RUN TIME		CHECK DISC FRAMES	FINAL DISC FRAMES
IN:	OUT:	ACTUAL:	CUMULATIVE:		

Appendix C

Application Design Matrices

Once the application's presentations are identified and their treatments are designed, your next concern is how those treatments will be carried out. These decisions involve the more detailed design strategies for media, motivation, interactions, and so on. Evaluating these different factors for multiple presentations can be a demanding task.

To help you with this part of the evaluation process, we've created a set of design matrices — one for each of the six strategies we described in Chapter Six. Their main purpose is to visualize and assess where your resources are about to be spent. Here's how you might apply these matrices:

- Pick one of the design strategies to be evaluated.
- List each presentation (with its designated format or treatment) in priority order from top to bottom on the form.
- Identify the methods being used to support each presentation.
- Assess the distribution of these methods across the form:

- Are the most expensive/sophisticated methods applied to the high-priority presentations?

- Do the selected methods support and complement the chosen format?

- Have viable strategies been overlooked?

- Are the chosen strategies within the project resources?

- Repeat the process for each of the six design strategies.

Initially, you may be thinking, "More forms! More paperwork!" The matrix approach, however, can save you time and concern later. Design is one of the more elusive aspects of the application you have to evaluate. There is a need to make the process less subjective and more tangible. The matrices can help you "see" design decisions and their impact early in the cycle — before development starts. Thus, your evaluation and approval to proceed to expend significant time and effort can be based on a fully considered foundation.

MEDIA STRATEGIES

PRESENTATION ID *(format type)*	HIGH PRODUCTION MOTION VIDEO	INDUSTRIAL QUALITY MOTION VIDEO	HIGH QUALITY COMPUTER GRAPHICS	AUDIO SEGMENTS	VIDEO STILL FRAMES	COMPUTER TEXT SCREENS

PRESENTATION ID *(format type)*		MOTIVATIONAL STRATEGIES
FANTASY		
ROLE MODELS		
REWARD		
CHALLENGE		
CURIOSITY		

MOTIVATIONAL STRATEGIES

MEDIA RELATED

PRESENTATION ID *(format type)*	HIGH PRODUCTION VALUE	LOCATION SHOOTING	FACE RECOGNITION	ANIMATION	PUPPETRY	

PRESENTATION ID *(format type)*	SIMULATION	DIRECTION	INPUT WITH FEEDBACK	SELECTION	PACING	INTERRUPTION	

INTERACTION STRATEGIES

PRESENTATION ID *(format type)*	ALTERNATE MEDIA	PROGRESS VALIDATION	PROGRESS MARKING	POSITIONING	FREE USER CONTROL	

ADULT LEARNING STRATEGIES

		SIMULATION	NETWORK	CRITERION REFERENCED	ADVANCED ORGANIZER	LINEAR BRANCHED TUTORIAL	OPEN HIERARCHY	CLOSED HIERARCHY
SEQUENCE / STRUCTURE STRATEGIES	*PRESENTATION ID (format type)*							

EVALUATION STRATEGIES

	EVALUATION LEVEL →				TYPE OF FEEDBACK				PRESENTATION ID (format type)
	SINGLE ITEMS	GROUPED ITEMS	ALL ITEMS		REQUIRED / VOLUNTARY	INFORMATIVE	REINFORCING	DIAGNOSTIC	

Appendix D

Components of Multimedia Documentation

Introduction

Documentation is the most reliable means of communications among the team members of an IVD/multimedia project. In this appendix we'll examine the various kinds of documentation needed to describe the design of an application. We'll see that many different forms and formats are needed, each serving a distinct purpose. Our goal is to provide you and the development team with a consolidated overview of the development process. In general, the purpose of each different format is to describe a specific set of work products to the specialized professionals who will produce them. The work products may be photographs, graphics, video segments, etc. The reason for using different formats is to communicate the specifications in a form that is most efficient for the specialist to use in producing them. Taken together, the complete set may thus be called **Producible Documentation**.

Producible documentation is perhaps the most important factor in the success of an interactive media project. Its role is to insure that each media element required in the final application can be created exactly as designed so that it will fit with every other element as planned. Also, it must allow the production specialist to create it without having to return to the designer or developer time after time to seek clarification. To accomplish this role, Producible Documentation must meet three criteria:

1. It must be **clear.**
2. It must be **consistent.**
3. It must be **complete.**

Let's expand upon these items. Producible Documentation must be:

- CLEAR ...so that everyone on the team understands what the final product will look like, and what their particular piece of it must contribute.

- CONSISTENT ... so that every individual element will match properly with every other element it is associated with.

- COMPLETE ... so that every element needed in the final application will be created and made available.

As Project Manager, you should make every effort to insure that your team and your vendor are creating documentation that meets these criteria. However, there is an even more important consideration that should command even more attention. That is the management of **changes**.

The nature of IVD/multimedia is to use many media elements in combination to communicate the message of the designer. It is not surprising, therefore, that the documentation of all of the elements is highly interrelated. A seemingly minor change to one element may affect several others, and those changes affect others yet. Every change in an element means a change in its documentation, or it is likely not to get produced correctly. There is no more important task in your role as Project Manager than to insure that procedures are in place and enforced to insure that changes are made in such a way as to preserve the integrity of the documentation.

In this appendix we'll look at several forms of documentation, discuss what formats they may appear in, and how they are related to all of the other forms used to describe the production requirements of the application. The forms include:

- The Design Flowchart.

- The Production Flowchart.

- A set of composite descriptions of each event in the application (called a "Super Storyboard").

- Development Documentation.

Depending upon the types of media elements called for in the application design, Development Documentation may consist of some or all of the following:

- Scripts or storyboards for the video producer.

- Scripts for the audio producer.

- Shot lists for preparing video still frames.

- Renditions of video art and card art.

- Renditions of graphics to be stored on the computer.

Already it should be obvious that developing this documentation and keeping up with it will be one of the major tasks of the project team. As their leader, you'll need to be able to read, evaluate and comment on all forms of documentation they produce. We have covered the evaluation criteria in the main body of the book. In this appendix, we'll provide a brief description of the content, purpose, and form of each major type of documentation. This will provide a background for you and a structured plan for the development team. Hopefully, this will be adequate to help you understand the documents and to improve team inter-communications. If you still have questions, however, take the time to have them answered by your designers and developers. If the documents aren't clear to you, they probably aren't clear to everyone else, and documentation that isn't clear will surely lead to trouble. On the other hand, if you insure that all documentation is clear, consistent and complete, and that changes are carefully managed, you should find that the expensive Production Phase will proceed smoothly, on schedule, on budget, and with a minimum of unpleasant surprises.

The General Approach

The sequence for developing IVD/multimedia documentation varies from one individual to another. A lot seems to depend on the individual's prior background. Those with data processing or computer based training experience tend to create logical flowcharts of the application and proceed from there; those with video background often choose to develop a storyboard or script of the activities first and then draw a flow chart to depict what they've done. Every project will have at least a flowchart and an audio/video script or storyboard. The other forms of documentation will be added as needed, depending on the project complexity and experience of the production team. As part of the development model, we're going to suggest an approach that is most representative of the many projects we've worked with over the years. It is based on starting with the flow chart, and developing detailed documentation from that foundation. The approach is borrowed from a successful technique used in developing data processing applications called "top down" development. The first steps are very general and high level. Each succeeding step describes the application in

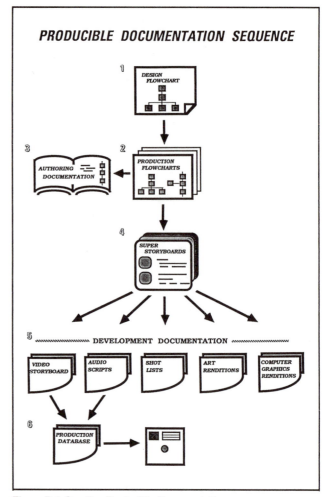

Figure D-1 Creating Producible Documentation

finer detail, and with more specialized documentation.

If this sequence doesn't seem natural to you, be aware that many successful projects have been developed using other approaches. The main point is that when you have completed your development, the documentation must be complete, consistent and clear in order to support the activities in the Production Phase.

The steps we recommend are as follows:

- Draw a **Design Flowchart** that depicts the major sections of the application and their logical relationship to each other.
- Draw a **Production Flowchart** that depicts the detailed steps, media content and logic of (eventually) every event in the application.
- Prepare **Author Documentation** based on the logic of the Production Flowchart and the information required by the author to implement the application on the system.

- Prepare a **"Super Storyboard"** that describes all of the media content, user interactions and system responses for each event of the application.
- Prepare **Development Documentation** for all individual media elements of each event in the format required by the producers of those elements.
- Extract a **Production Database** from the documentation that will help keep track of individual elements and allow efficient production.

This is a formidable list. Depending on your background, a lot of it might be new. Even if you have multimedia experience you may not recognize some of the names used here, because there is no established set of names or forms of documentation in the industry. What you *will* find is that everyone who develops these applications uses some kind of forms that accomplish the purpose of the steps we've listed. As we look at each one in detail, we'll cover what's in them and what they're used for. You'll be able to recognize any kind of IVD/multimedia documents, no matter what they look like or what they're called.

So What's New?

Documentation is probably the most important single factor that differentiates an interactive media project from other kinds. The differences arise from several factors:

- One key document, the "Super Storyboard," is unique.
- Most other documents, though not unique to IVD/multimedia, use terminology and additional information that is different from their standard counterparts.
- This documentation requires complex interrelationships between dissimilar documents that doesn't happen in other projects.
- The documents must provide clear communications between developers with completely different backgrounds.
- The level of detail is exceptionally minute, and seemingly minor omissions can require expensive corrections to be made during production.
- Changes to one part of the documentation multiply their effects to many other parts and must be managed with extreme care.

The bottom line is that no matter what your prior background outside of this technology, many documentation considerations will be new to you,

and will occupy a major part of your time and effort. If you're working with a vendor, you should be aware of the importance of this task, and be alert to make sure it is being looked after properly. If you're responsible for managing all or part of application development, you'll need to impress your team with the importance of **creating** and **maintaining** precise documentation down to a minute level of detail. You'll need to establish control procedures that make sure you have a firm handle on all elements of the documentation.

The Super Storyboard Coordinator

If your project has substantial complexity, it will probably be to your advantage to assign the role of "Super Storyboard Coordinator" to an individual who can be trusted to manage a great volume of detail. This person's task will be to keep the master copy of the Super Storyboard up to date, and to be sure that the subsidiary documents are consistent with it. In large projects, this role can become a full time job for one person.

Creating Producible Documentation

In this appendix, we're going to look at some examples of forms that can be used to create Producible Documentation. You may elect to use the formats we describe here in your project, but you should be aware that there are no standard forms for any of them. Especially if you are working with professionals with prior experience, you are likely to encounter different ways to document the various elements of the application. What we show you here will represent a **composite** of many types of documentation we have encountered over many years of experience. If you understand the **information** contained in each form we discuss, you should have no trouble dealing with other forms that are designed to accomplish the same purposes.

So, using the model we have proposed, let's look at some examples. We'll spend most of our time on the two types of documents that have unique features in IVD/multimedia documentation, the flowcharts and the Super Storyboard. To present the examples, we have constructed documents for an application that addresses the maintenance of a ten-speed bicycle. The content should be reasonably familiar to most of us, and the structure is applicable to many kinds of IVD presentations in training, education or marketing.

1

The Design Flowchart

The Design Flowchart represents the structure of the application in its most general form. It's likely to begin as a rough sketch of the major topics or activities identified during Content Analysis. The blocks and symbols that represent those activities are laid out in a way that describes the logical relationships between them. Generally, the relationship will be sequential, hierarchical or a mixture of both.

Some designers will flesh out the Design Flowchart with notes pertaining to audience, general objectives or other information that will help reviewers understand the application, and how it will accomplish its purposes.

As a working document, the Design Flowchart will probably be used only in the very first stages of design. Once this very high level snapshot of the application is agreed upon, the designers quickly move on to the construction of more detailed documents.

The Production Flowchart

The Production Flowchart is the fundamental document for detailed design of the application. It depicts the logical structure in finer detail, of course, but it provides much more information. Most designers represent the major types of media that will be used in each element by the shape of the block. Labels on each block provide names required for authoring, and for identifying the elements as they are produced. The proximity of the blocks on the flowchart provides a guide for efficient layout of the video material on the disc. The Production Flowchart is vital to all members of the project team, and care must be taken to be sure it is accurate, up to date and accessible.

HOW TO READ IT

If you have a background in computing and data processing, the flowchart will seem to be a natural means of describing the logic of the application; only the use of media symbols will be new. If you are unfamiliar with flowcharting, however, the chances are you'll be able to make sense of the flowchart by simply inspecting it and following the flow lines.

When the computer that controls a multimedia application is used to perform data processing functions or decisions, the standard symbols used in

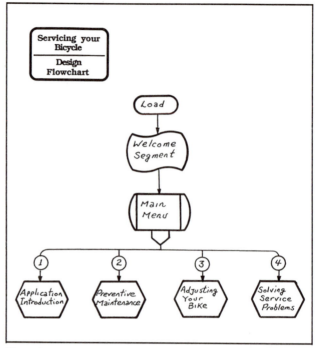

Figure D-2 The Design Flowchart

computer flowcharts may appear in the Production Flowchart along with other event symbols. The more common type of symbol, however, is the media element. Let's look at these in more detail.

MEDIA SYMBOLS

Media symbols represent two key types of information:

1. The **kind of media** used to present an element of the application,

2. The method used to **advance** the application from one event to another.

Figure D-3 shows a portion of a Production Flowchart. It uses symbols that depict the media elements available in interactive video applications. The symbols represent such elements as motion video, video still frames, graphic screens presented by the computer, graphic screens overlayed on video frames, and digital audio segments.

Most designers will indicate the kind of media to be used in an element by the shape of the block. There are no rigid standards used by all designers, so it is important to have a symbol glossary attached to the flowchart. There are no rigid standards used by all designers, so it is important to have a symbol glossary attached to the flowchart, as shown in Figure D-4.

Most of the media symbols have another symbol attached that indicates how the program advances from that point. These "advancing symbols" indicate such mechanisms as timeouts, keyboard entry or

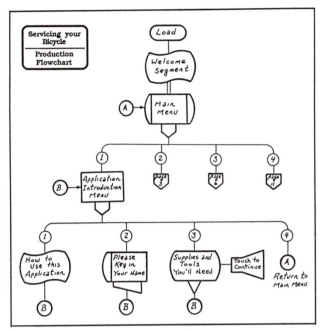

Figure D-3 Portion of Production Flowchart

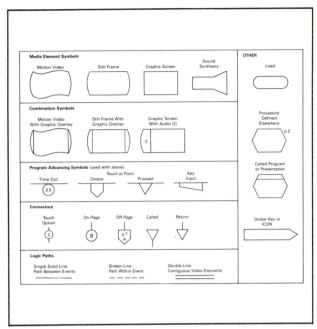

Figure D-4 Media Symbols and Advancing Symbols

user pointing with a touchscreen or mouse. (If no advancing symbol is used, it means that the application proceeds immediately to the next event without pausing.) The symbols may be easily created by using a special flowchart template like the one shown in Figure D-5, or approximated from similar symbols on standard programming flowchart symbols.

Note: This template may be obtained from the IBM Corporation. It can be purchased by calling IBM and asking for it by its form number, GX60-0104.

An actual Production Flowchart would probably contain even more information than shown in our sample. In a real application, the flowchart would show labels to identify each logical point in the structure, so the programmer or author can identify where to go to when the program takes a branch. It might also identify each media element with a label as a means of identifying it during production, and specifying where it goes in the program. Once you become familiar with how to read and assimilate

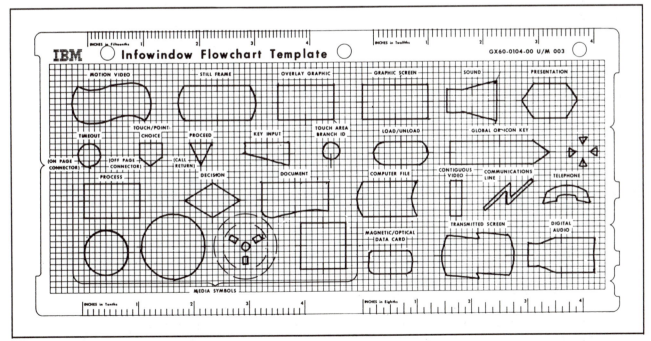

Figure D-5 Level Three Flowchart Template

these symbols and labels, the Production Flowchart offers a wealth of information.

When a flowchart is drawn in this way, it becomes easy to inspect it and get a good idea of "what's going on" at any point in the application. A video producer can quickly pick out all of the "curvy" symbols that indicate motion video. A graphic artist can pick out the graphic screens, and the elements that require graphics to be overlaid on a video picture by scanning for rectangular symbols. An instructional designer can review the structure, logic and media strategy all at once. The Production Flowchart is truly the picture worth more than a thousand words in describing and defining the application.

Now we'll take a look at more detailed documentation that is developed from the information contained in the Production Flowchart.

3

The Authoring Documentation

Because the logic of the presentation is so clearly depicted in the Production Flowchart, it becomes the main source of information for preparing the authoring documentation. This documentation will take on many forms, depending upon the type of authoring facility that will be used to control the sequence of the presentation. It may be as simple as filling out a set of uncomplicated forms, or it may require the full documentation for a complex programming language. Typical authoring documentation includes controls, optional paths, number and sequence of events. The various types of authoring facilities are discussed in Chapter 9, *Authoring*.

4

The Super Storyboard

In the latter half of the 1970's, a few pioneers in interactive video wrestled with the problem of how programs were developed for the new medium. The ones that had computer backgrounds recognized that a flowchart of some kind was useful, and those with video backgrounds used scripts and storyboards to create the video material, but there were no set standards or methods for depicting how **all** of the various elements would come together into a single combined program. Some way of doing this was

necessary, however, and this necessity was the mother of many individual inventions of documentation formats that served the purpose.

The documents that were created to describe the applications took on many forms. Most of them provided a layout that allowed the designer to sketch a drawing of what the screen contained at every point in the presentation. The forms would vary according to the type of system being used — two screen, one screen, or one screen with graphics overlaid on video. The forms would also contain other relevant information such as the audio script, production notes, notes about the graphics, the branching logic, and so on. These forms looked very different from project to project, but the information they contained, and the purpose of consolidating the relationships of all of the media elements was much the same.

These documents were also called by different names. Those with instructional design backgrounds tended to call them "Design Documents" or "Detailed Design Documents." Video producers called them "Scripts" or "Storyboards." Computer programmers would come up with names like "Logical Scenarios." To this day, various vendors call them by various names, and no standard exists.

The problem with many of these names is that they are the same as other documents that are also needed to create a full set of Producible Documentation. Therefore, in this book we have referred to the combined presentation description as the "Super Storyboard." Be warned that this name is used by very few multimedia producers; nonetheless, as you review the documentation for a given project, you are almost certain to encounter a document that serves this purpose, whatever it is called.

Another fact to be aware of is that there is not a standard form for Super Storyboards, and not likely to be. The reason is that each project has its own requirements set by the hardware authoring and delivery system that is to be used, and the software that is used to develop and author the application. The information requirements dictated by these requirements determine the form of the documentation, not the other way around. Forms are cheap to design and copy, so it is not uncommon for a development organization to design new forms for each project.

With those points in mind, let's look at a Super Storyboard (SSB) form we have designed. It represents a composite of the best ideas we have seen working with many developers of multimedia applications over the years. All of the information found in other forms of SSB's are included in it. If you are in a situation where you need to select a form of SSB for your project, we have included a full page copy of

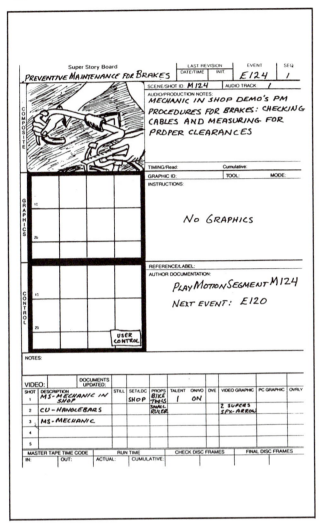

Figure D-6 Super Storyboard for a Video Event

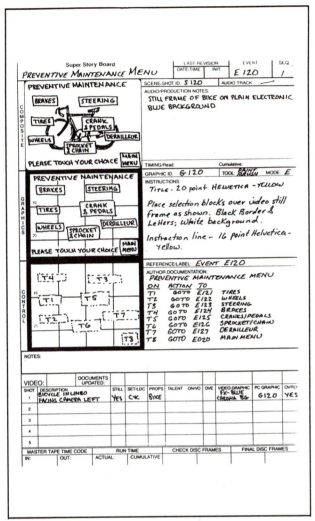

Figure D-7 Super Storyboard for a Menu Event

it in Appendix B, which you are at liberty to use or modify.

Figure D-6 shows a completed SSB for a video event from the bicycle maintenance application. The top section shows a sketch of the video scene, along with a general description of content on which the writer will base the accompanying video storyboard. The Graphics section notes that there are no graphics to be created for this event. The Control section merely states where to go next after the video segment has been played. This is all simple and straightforward. The information in the bottom section will be used to construct the Production Database which we'll discuss later.

Figure D-7 shows an SSB for a menu event. In contrast to the video event, this SSB carries a great deal of information. In the top Composite section, we see that a picture of a bicycle is overlaid with several choice buttons that allow the user to access various preventive maintenance procedures. Looking at this picture of the screen, there is no way to

tell what visual information comes from the videodisc, and what is generated and overlayed by the computer. This example shows why we have chosen to divide our form into three sections. The Graphics section below makes explicit that all of the words and buttons on the screen are to be created with computer graphics. Only the picture of the bicycle itself is to come from video.

The Control section shows how the touch (or mouse) areas are to be defined. The Author Documentation to the right lists each touch area, and specifies where the application will branch to when the area is touched.

The SSB is a valuable document in itself. By showing the composite of all media elements, the video director can see how to position and size the bicycle picture, the graphic artist can see how to position the buttons, and the author can relate the touch areas to the visual display.

The SSB also generates a need for further, specific documentation. The two examples we have looked at have called for several media elements. These elements need to be added to the lists for development documentation, and checked off as they are created or changed. Specifically:

– From the SSB for Event "E124" (Figure D-6):
  • Video Segment "M124" — a video storyboard will be required.

– From the SSB for Event "E120" (Figure D-7):
  • Video Still Frame "S120" — this will need to be added to the appropriate shot list for art work, video graphics, photo or studio shot, depending upon how it is to be produced.
  • Graphic "G120" — a graphic rendition will have to be provided for the computer graphic artist.

In the case of the graphic rendition, a copy of the SSB itself will suffice, since it has all the necessary information for the graphic artist. It will also serve as good documentation for the shot list. The video segment will need a separate script or storyboard to be written.

Thus, the Super Storyboard is a key linkpin to all project documentation. It generates the requirements and specifies the content of all the development documentation to follow. It has to be kept up to date, with one master copy representing the current status of the project. If you use a development support system that allows the documentation to be kept in a computer, this job can be made easier. No matter how it is kept, however, it is a critical foundation for keeping the development effort on track.

5

Development Documentation

As valuable as the Super Storyboard is for relating all of the media elements to each other, it is not adequate to use for production of the elements themselves. There is a lot of information that is extraneous to the needs of a specific producer, and other information that is missing. This can be especially true if your SSB has only one place to depict all of the visual display, and the separation of video and graphic information is not clear.

Development documentation tends to look like standard documentation for the particular media that it relates to. This is as it should be. Its purpose is to document the specific content of each element, and it is best to use formats familiar to the individual specialist producer of that kind of media. Let's look over the list of the different kinds of development documentation that might be required.

VIDEO STORYBOARDS

Video storyboards have been around for a long time. They contain three types of information:

• A depiction of the visual display.

• An exact description of the words and sounds to be produced.

• Production notes including camera moves, special effects, graphics to be added and so on.

Some writers prefer the storyboard format that provides these three sets of information in parallel columns. The visual content may be depicted by sketches, or described in words. Other writers, especially those with a film background, will write a script in linear, narrative form. The audio content is written with full margins, and visual and production notes are indented. Whether your writer uses storyboard format or writes "film style," you should be able to read and review the scripts and understand exactly what is to be produced. Your review and approval of these documents should be a key, ongoing part of the Development phase.

AUDIO SCRIPTS

An audio script for an interactive application is a different document than a traditional audio script written for a tape or broadcast medium. In traditional formats, the audio is written for, and spoken for the ear alone. In IVD, the audio is usually written as voice-over support for graphic screens. In sophisticated applications, these graphics may be shown as a series of screens, or animated. Therefore, the audio script serves a function similar to a voice-over script for a narrator for a video segment. For this reason, many writers will use the same storyboard format that they use for their video segments.

The most common approach for audio used with graphics is to record it on the second audio track of the videodisc. If the audio-over-graphics events are closely associated with video segments, the producer may want to go to the trouble of editing the second audio track so that the audio segments are close to the associated video. At the least, the producer must watch the 30 minute limit of available capacity on the second track. A good place to keep this record is on the Super Storyboard in the "Read time/Cumulative time" space. The same considerations apply to

CD-ROM, but the greater capacity makes this medium less restrictive.

Audio is often the forgotten medium in IVD, and sometimes a producer can give short shrift to production quality issues. As broadcast television has begun to give more attention to audio quality, IVD/multimedia producers are starting to follow suit, with good results. Audio carries a major part of the information in an application, and it well deserves the same care and attention in its planning and documentation that the visual media are given. As digital and CD audio become more widely used, the additional capacity will make it even more important.

SHOT LISTS FOR STILL FRAMES

A Still Frame is defined as a single video picture planned by the developer to be shown as a single frame. The video player shows the same frame over and over, one of tens of thousands of frames that can be recorded on a videodisc. If your application plans to make use of this facility, careful and extensive documentation is required. Still frames on videodisc are used for two main purposes. The first is as a production element in the presentation. These frames are often used as menus themselves, or more often, backgrounds for graphic menus. They may be used as backgrounds for text information screens, or used to carry the information themselves in a visual form. They may be used singly, or shown in a sequence of different frames, advanced by system timing or (usually better) a user-initiated signal to proceed. The second common use of still frames is a visual data base that the user may search around in with some kind of browsing interface or index. Many "generic" discs of this kind have been made with collections of paintings, specimens, slides, drawings and so on.

The documentation requirements for these two uses are different. In the first case, the still frames are chosen or created especially for the presentation. Their documentation must relate each individual still frame to the rest of the media elements in the presentation, via the Super Storyboard, scripts, and other documents that we've been discussing. In the case of visual databases, the individual frames usually don't need to be related to other elements. The collections tend to be large, however, and careful matching of the location of each frame to its indexing information must be assured.

Single video frames can also be converted to digital computer files, and stored on CD-ROM. These files can be compressed to make the storage more efficient. The number of frames that can be stored varies widely, depending upon the quality of the image, and the sophistication of the compression

method. The considerations for preparing the shot lists are the same.

Once the shot lists are compiled, and the shots assembled, there is a major production activity required to get them transferred to the videodisc or CD-ROM. If the number of elements is large, the physical handling of the media itself can become a major task. Getting slides from a library, into carousels, onto the master video tape and back into the library in the same, known order requires the most careful planning and handling. If you plan to include more than a hundred or so still frames, it will be worth the attention to plan ahead of time, and if possible, use a computer data base during production to help keep track of everything.

ART RENDITIONS

If still frames produced from card art or video graphics are to be used in the application, a detailed rendition must be provided for each one on the shot list. They should be identified as stills on the Super Storyboard, and labelled as such. If graphics are used in conjunction with them, the information that is graphic and the information that is video must be clearly differentiated. If the shots are to be photographed, careful directions (including computer graphic considerations) must be provided. (The three-section format of the SSB suggested in the case study is well suited to this purpose.)

COMPUTER GRAPHIC RENDITIONS

The last documentation items we'll look at are the renditions for the computer graphics. These elements are so important in IVD/multimedia applications that they are normally documented right on the Super Storyboard itself. Most SSB's provide all the information needed by the graphic artist (who is sometimes also the author). If the delivery system allows overlay graphics, the most important consideration is to provide absolute clarity as to what is to be in the video picture, and what is to be added by the computer graphic artist.

An important item on the SSB is the label of the graphic. This label will be used by the graphic artist when the screen is created to store and retrieve it from the graphic library. The author will use it to call for the display of the graphic during presentation. The project administrator will include it in the graphic production list to make sure that all needed graphics have been produced. A good convention to use is that graphic labels should be related to the events in which they appear. For example, in our previous SSB's, we assigned the label "G120" to the graphic used in the event labelled "E120."

6

Production Database

The Production Database is a set of information derived mostly from the SSB's and Video Storyboards that aids the video producer in managing an efficient production schedule. It's becoming common to keep such information in a computer data base that can be sorted into lists for various purposes.

A handy place to collect this information is provided at the bottom of the SSB form shown in Figure D-8. For each shot in the video segment, the required components can be identified such as the studio set or location, the "talent" (actors) that are in the shot or providing voice-over (V.O.) narration, props, graphics and so on. If Digital Video Effects (DVE's) are required in post editing, it can be noted. When this information is keyed into a data base, much useful information can be extracted. For example, a list of all shots to be taken on a single studio set can be listed out and produced at the same time, no matter what the sequence will be in the final presentation. All scenes with certain actors can be shot on the same days, avoiding extra cost. A prop list can be generated for the stage manager, and so on. The shooting of short individual segments for IVD is a more complex process than shooting one linear tape, and the production data base can be an excellent tool for making sure that the process proceeds smoothly.

Deliverable Items for Project Documentation

Let's review the list of documents that we have discussed in this module:

- A high level Design Flowchart.

- A detailed Production Flowchart.

- A set of composite descriptions of each event in the application (called a "Super Storyboard").

- Documentation for the author.

- Scripts or storyboards for the video producer.

- Scripts for the audio producer.

- Shot lists for preparing video still frames.

- Renditions of video art and card art.

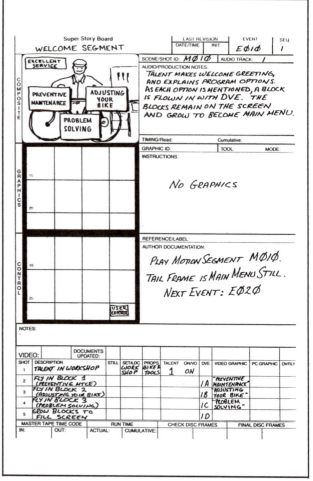

Figure D-8 Production Information from the SSB

- Renditions of graphics to be stored on the computer.

As you look over this list, you should have a reasonably clear idea of what information is provided by each individual item, and how each item relates to the others in the list.

Using Computers in Documentation

The complexity of IVD/multimedia documentation makes it almost mandatory to use a computer to keep up with it. It would be especially valuable to use an integrated system specifically designed for this purpose. At the time of this writing, only a few attempts have been made to produce such systems. Of those, most are proprietary systems used by vendors. A few are available on the market, and if the systematized approach of one of them matches the requirements of your project, you should consider using it.

If you don't use an integrated system, you'll probably want to keep track of the project using several individual software packages. These would include a project manager for managing the schedule, a spreadsheet processor to manage budgets, a data base processor to keep track of individual elements of project documentation, a word processor to produce scripts, etc.

Appendix E

Writing the RFP

The RFP Process

The key to obtaining good proposals is to write a good RFP. In this appendix we'll discuss the components of a good RFP, but there is more to consider than just the RFP itself. When you issue an RFP, you're beginning the first step of a legal process that will result in a binding contract between you and the selected vendor. Legal considerations aside, you want to be sure that the process you follow achieves several objectives. These include:

- Providing a creative design proposal that is relevant to your sponsor's goals.
- Paying the lowest amount of money that will still achieve a quality final product.
- Setting up a project plan that will achieve the results in the least practical amount of time.
- Specifying a phase process that will allow you to maintain adequate control of the project.
- Getting enough responses to allow competitive comparisons without inundating yourself with too many proposals to consider fairly.
- Being scrupulously honest, ethical and impartial with the responding vendors.

The following steps should help you achieve these objectives.

Pre-screen potential vendors

There are many qualified vendors who can produce excellent IVD/multimedia applications at reasonable cost. Before you make a decision to send out an RFP, you should make every effort to narrow the list of potential vendors down to a manageable size. Your criteria should include prior experience with the type of application you're considering, subject matter knowledge and geographical proximity. There are many sources to find lists of potential vendors.

They include:

- Industry magazines, yearbooks and trade publications.

- Lists of vendors provided by equipment manufacturers.
- Lists of vendors provided by videodisc replication companies.
- Exhibit halls at trade shows and conventions.

If your project is a major effort, site visits to potential vendors to see their organizations and prior works can be well worth the effort and expense.

Choose between Bid or Sole Vendor approach

There are many arguments to be made on both sides of the questions of whether to send out an RFP for competitive bids. If your company or institution has not undertaken a multimedia project before this, competitive proposals can provide insight as to various possible approaches to the application and a firmer idea of the lowest reasonable price to expect. On the other hand, if prior experience or the pre-screening process has led you to conclude that one vendor is the best qualified, the project should be let out on a sole vendor process.

It is the tradition of this industry that the expense of preparing proposals is borne by the vendor. This expense is usually not trivial. A well thought-out proposal is in fact a detailed analysis and high-level design for the project. If the reality of the situation is that a specific vendor has an inside track for some reason, fair treatment dictates that you should issue a sole vendor contract instead of a competitive RFP. When an RFP is issued in these circumstances (perhaps to satisfy a requirement of your purchasing practices) the vendors say that the RFP is "wired." Companies that become known in the industry for this practice may find it difficult to obtain good responses to future RFP's.

Write a quality RFP

The RFP should provide as much information as possible about the application. All of the analysis data you have collected to this point should be included. The results to be achieved and the criteria for measuring the success of the application should be spelled out as exactly as possible. The terms and conditions of the contract should also be worked out with your legal counsel and included in the RFP. The better your lawyers understand the application and your objectives, the better the RFP and the shorter the time to get it approved.

Be sure that the phase process of the project that you expect to follow is described in detail. The deliverable items should be specified, and defined clearly. If you intend to split the development contract into two parts, design and final delivery, state this clearly. If you expect the vendor to produce a prototype for approval, define the requirement in the RFP.

It's a good idea to provide some guidelines as to what you expect the project to cost. You should specify such items as the expected user time on system, number of disc sides, expected dollars per finished minute for video production, and limits for the total cost of the project. These guidelines are **not** likely to increase the final price you pay if they are reasonable to begin with. Vendors realize that they will enhance their chances by providing the low bid. On the other hand, they will have a firmer idea of the quality versus price trade-off you expect, and you will benefit by receiving proposals that will be more easily compared.

Invite a reasonable number of responses

There is benefit to both you and the vendor community for limiting the number of bids you request. From the vendor's point of view, it is only fair that the effort to write the proposal should have a reasonable chance for acceptance. A one-out-of-ten shot would be unreasonable for all but the largest, most expensive projects. From your point of view, you should not request more bids than you have resource to review. The proposals will probably be thick and detailed for large projects, and they will take time and skill to evaluate. To get a competitive set of responses, you should probably send out at least three RFP's, but a decision to send out more than this should be carefully weighed.

Provide additional information fairly

Vendors are likely to need more information as they prepare their responses, and you should make any non-proprietary data easily available. On the other hand, if one vendor asks for an important item of data not provided in the RFP, it's not your responsibility to provide it to other vendors unless they ask.

Make a decision you can live with

Decisions to select one vendor over another should be made as objectively as possible, but in the final analysis, many subjective factors will come into play. Your analysis should naturally include considerations of low price bid, quality of proposal, credentials of people assigned to the project, prior experience and financial soundness. At the same time, you will be living with the selected vendor and yourself a long time. Make sure you select someone you feel you can work with, and that you have been fair and equitable to all bidders. Then make the decision and get on with the project.

Structure of the RFP

A well structured RFP should contain certain elements to make it clear and complete. Here is an overview of a suggested structure that will achieve these objectives:

1. The Request For Proposal
    a. Introduction and Overview of Requirements
    b. Rules Governing Competition
    c. Instructions for Proposal Preparation
    d. Criteria for Proposal Evaluation

2. Appendix A — Application Design Requirements
    a. Delivery System Description
    b. Price and Quality Guidelines

3. Appendix B — Application Definition
    a. Analysis Information
    b. Content Specification

4. Appendix C — Scope of Effort
    a. Deliverable Items for Each Phase
    b. Review and Approval Procedures

5. Appendix D — Support to be Provided
    a. In-house Project Support and Facilities
    b. Access to Subject Matter Expertise

The following section expands upon the content of these items.

Contents of the RFP

The Request For Proposal

INTRODUCTION AND OVERVIEW OF REQUIREMENTS

This section should contain a succinct statement of the goals and objectives of the application, an approximate sizing of the project, and a list of action dates for proposal submission and project completion.

RULES GOVERNING COMPETITION

This section spells out the competitive rules so the vendor can be assured that the proposal will be considered fairly.

INSTRUCTIONS FOR PROPOSAL PREPARATION

This section describes the format and other requirements for submitting the RFP. Here is a recommended format:

1. A table of contents.
2. An overview and proposal summary.
3. An application design proposal including a design flowchart, treatment, and discussion of major strategies to be employed.
4. A statement agreeing to the development model proposed by you in the appendix dealing with the scope of effort, or an explanation of variances preferred by the vendor to conform to their usual procedures.
5. An identification of the project personnel to be assigned by name, and a summary of their qualifications and experience.
6. A work plan for meeting the required schedule dates.
7. A description of the resources required to be provided by you in order to meet the dates in the work plan (e.g., access to subject matter experts).
8. A schedule of costs broken down by phase and item, such as:
   - Direct labor
   - Supplies
   - Travel
   - Materials
   - Services
   - Overhead

CRITERIA FOR PROPOSAL EVALUATION

This section lays out the major criteria upon which the proposal will be evaluated. It is fair to list your criteria for judging submissions, including:

- The qualifications and experience of the assigned personnel.
- The quality and number of previous applications delivered by the vendor.
- The creativity and quality of the treatment and design proposed in meeting the goals and objectives set forth in the RFP.
- The ability and experience of the vendor relating to the subject matter of the application.
- The reasonableness of the total cost proposed, and whether it is equal to or lower than the cost proposed by other equally qualified vendors.

Appendix A — Application Design Requirements

DELIVERY SYSTEM DESCRIPTION

This section describes the functional requirements of the hardware and software. If a system has been chosen or committed to, it is so stated; otherwise, a detailed list of requirements for the development and delivery systems is provided, along with requirements for installation, administration, training, maintenance and service.

PRICE AND QUALITY GUIDELINES

This is one of the most critical sections in the RFP for both you and the vendor. It sets a level playing field for all vendors to compete on. It establishes you as a knowledgeable potential customer who understands the cost of IVD, and who expects a quality product for the price.

The price is dependent upon the quality expected, and the volume of material to be delivered. Therefore, this section should provide an estimate of the total user time on system for the application. If the application is a conversion from an existing course of instruction, the length of the present course and the expected length of the presentation should be stated. If the application deals with marketing or information, the expected average user time should be estimated along with the total user time for **all** activities included in the application. The number of disc sides expected to support the application should be stated.

A particularly useful guideline to provide is the expected quality level of the video stated in terms of dollars per finished minute of production. This not only sets the level of expectation for the video, but also indicates the quality level expected for all of the other media elements.

You can also point out in this section that these guidelines are provided for information only, and that favorable attention will be given to creative designs and treatments that accomplish the application objectives in especially effective ways within the production cost guidelines, or achieve the objectives with lower costs, or both.

Appendix B — Application Definition

ANALYSIS INFORMATION

This appendix provides a complete description of the application itself. It should contain all of the analysis information that you and your staff have compiled up to this point.

CONTENT SPECIFICATION

Based on the analysis information, a list of objectives should be included, and a content analysis of the topics to be included on the disc.

Appendix C — Scope of Effort

In the first section of this book, we've described deliverable items to be provided during each phase of the development model. We have pointed out that the names of these items, and indeed, the structure of the phases themselves vary from vendor to vendor. You may prefer other names for deliverables or different descriptions of the phase process yourself. These considerations aside, it makes good sense to write the Scope of Effort of the RFP with these things in mind:

1. Describe each phase of the project in terms of the specific documents and products to be delivered by the vendor.

2. Describe the contents of each document or product in detail so there will be no confusion due to terminology or semantics.

Here is a complete list of the items we have listed in this book by phase:

ANALYSIS

An *Application Description Document,* containing:
1. Application goals.

2. General treatment description (themes, story lines, characters, visuals, etc.).

3. User objectives/benefits.

4. Audience analysis.

5. Task/needs analysis for target audience.

6. Environment analysis.

7. Content analysis.
   a. Objective listing (and hierarchy).
   b. Content outline (major topics).

8. High-level application flowchart.

9. Treatment description and strategic approach.

10. Authoring facilities description and rationale.

DESIGN

An *Application Design Document* containing:
1. For all presentations:
   a. Detailed description of overall treatment (themes, story lines, characters, visual content, etc.).
   b. Expanded content outline (all major topics and sub-topics).
   c. Expanded application flowchart.
   d. Application strategy, structure, and sequence of presentations and events.
   e. Interaction strategy.
   f. Media selection matrix.
   g. Disc Layout by time and topic.
   h. Sample storyboards.
   i. User time on system estimates.

2. For instructional presentations or segments:
   a. Expanded objective hierarchy including all terminal and enabling objectives.
   b. Objective/content matrix.
   c. Testing strategy.

DEVELOPMENT

The work product will be a complete set of producible documentation containing (but not limited to) the following development items:

1. Design (high level) and production (detail) flowcharts.

2. Super Storyboards.

3. Video scripts/storyboards.

4. Video shot lists.

5. Audio scripts.

6. Graphic renditions.

7. Authoring documentation.

8. Programming documentation.

9. A production data base that can be used to schedule production activities in the most efficient sequence.

PRODUCTION

Video Production

Video production will be accomplished in three steps: pre-production, production, and post-production. Deliverable items include:

1. Pre-Production
   a. Production team list.
   b. Production plan.
   c. Shooting schedule.
   d. Final production budget.
   e. Cast list, with tapes of selected cast members.

2. Production
   a. Copy of any changed storyboards.
   b. Unedited video master tapes.

3. Post-Production
   a. A copy of the planned master tape, edited in off-line format for review.
   b. Videodisc master tape (1" type-C, Beta-Max or other broadcast quality format), edited according to manufacturer's specifications.
   c. Authoring and Validation video check disc(s) (or DRAW discs, if appropriate).
   d. Disc layout Map.

Audio Production

This section pertains to audio production that is not associated with video shoots, such as audio segments recorded independently on videodisc track 2, CD-ROM or other audio files.

1. Copy of any audio script changes.
2. Edited master audio tape.
   Note: If this audio is to be recorded on a videodisc track, it should be recorded on the videodisc master tape. If it is to reside on CD-ROM, it should be edited to meet the manufacturer's specifications.

PC Graphics Production

1. Diskettes with the original libraries of PC graphics.

2. Diskettes with the PC graphics converted into the form required by the Authoring Facility.

3. Documentation for identifying and locating graphics for subsequent processing, keyed to the Super Storyboards.

Print Production

1. Camera-ready copies of all print materials.

AUTHORING

This specifies items comprising a fully-tested, fully-documented running application, including:

1. Copy of software check plan.

2. Annotated copy of storyboards and application flowchart.

3. Validation diskette "master(s)" with videodiscs.

VALIDATION

Note: These items may be conducted in-house, or by another vendor.

1. Preparation
   a. Validation plan.
   b. Validation questionnaires and support materials.

2. Validation
   a. Summary of validation results.
   b. List of recommended revisions.

3. Post-Validation
   a. All revised application documentation.
   b. Revised final "master" videotape.
   c. Check disc(s), if required.
   d. Revised computer diskette "master(s)".
   e. Revised camera-ready "master(s)" of all print materials.

IMPLEMENTATION

Note: This activity would usually not be bid to the development vendor, unless you are requesting a "turn key" bid.

1. Implementation Preparation
   a. A complete physical installation plan for each host site specifying floor space, wiring, access, lighting and all other information needed to install the application.

b. A complete set of code and procedures for installing, initiating and maintaining the host site systems, with necessary printed instructions and documentation.

c. A complete set of announcement materials and instructions for using and disseminating them.

d. A complete training package for site personnel, including support materials for instructors or administrators.

e. A complete housing for the system (i.e. kiosk, carrel, etc.) delivered to each host site, ready for installation of equipment and application software.

f. All necessary documentation needed to integrate the application into other related or complementary systems.

2. Implementation

a. A fully installed and tested application working in each site.

b. A full set of administrative and maintenance documentation at each site, with personnel trained in their use to the satisfaction of site managers.

c. An operating system (on-line and/or off-line) for recording and evaluating monitoring data.

Experienced vendors should have no trouble recognizing the content and purpose of the various documents we have described here. They may, however, have a legitimate reason for preferring their own formats, names and order of creation. If their staff has grown up using a particular approach to IVD/multimedia development, it would not be efficient to change that approach just to fit the requirements of an RFP. Therefore, the RFP should contain a clause that permits a bidder to propose a different development model, providing that the purpose and content of each deliverable item is clearly and completely described.

REVIEW AND APPROVAL PROCEDURES

For each phase, the requirements for review and approval should be specifically stated. You should reserve the right to accept the deliverables with written approval at major milestones before work proceeds in the next phase.

Appendix D — Support to Be Provided

IN-HOUSE PROJECT SUPPORT AND FACILITIES

This section specifies the items that you intend to provide yourself, or produce with in-house services or other vendors. Naturally, their cost is not to be included in the bid. Such items might include:

- Access to computing facilities for development systems, including hardware and software required.

- Training of vendor authors for a previously selected authoring facility.

- Access to equipment and/or services for word processing, copying and publication of printed materials.

- Working space and secretarial support for vendor personnel.

- Use of in-house video production services.

- Access to existing audio-visual materials.

- Services required to support validation activities.

- Services required to support implementation activities.

Clearly, this list will vary with each project. It provides an opportunity to shave some significant costs from the project if items like these are available.

ACCESS TO SUBJECT MATTER EXPERTISE

If your project requires special expertise that is to be provided or is only available from within your own organization, you should specify that this support will be given. There are very few vendors who haven't been burned by the lack of access to subject matter experts at critical times in prior projects. If they are wise, they will insist that this access will be specified as a condition of the contract. If you make the commitment in the RFP, the vendors will be much more likely to submit serious proposals.

A Last Word

A clear and complete RFP demonstrates to potential vendors that you will be a knowledgeable and competent partner in the project. This will help attract the best vendors, and get the relationship started on the right foot.

Time spent in writing a good RFP will save time in the long run. If your analysis and requirements information is comprehensive and specific, the proposals you receive should be the same, and while the choice may not be easy, the information you base it on will be complete and definitive. If your quality and cost expectations are stated clearly and are reasonable, the bid prices should be fairly close, and you will be able to give full consideration to all facets of the proposals without undue attention to money alone.

Finally, be sure that you bend over backwards to treat all bidders as you would like to be treated in their position. Respect confidentiality, evaluate fairly, and make your decision quickly. In most cases, it is appropriate to explain the reasons for your selection to all vendors. They'll appreciate your businesslike approach, and will be likely to respond even more effectively to your future RFPs.

Appendix F

References and Publications for the IVD Project Manager

Ambron, S. & Hooper, K. *Interactive Multimedia.* Redmond, WA: Microsoft Press, 1988.

Arwady, J. and Gayeski, D. *Using Video: Interactive and Linear Designs.* Englewood Cliffs, NJ: Educational Technology Publications, 1989.

Crowell, P. *Authoring Systems.* Westport, CT: Meckler Corp., 1988.

Evans, A. and Milheim, W. *Selected Bibliography: Interactive Video.* Englewood Cliffs, NJ: Educational Technology Publications, 1987.

The Educational Technology Anthology Series (Volume 1) *Interactive Video.* Englewood Cliffs, NJ: Educational Technology Publications, 1989.

Iuppa, N. *A Practical Guide to Interactive Video Design.* White Plains, NY: Knowledge Industry Publications, 1984.

Luther, A. *Digital Video in the PC Environment.* New York, NY: McGraw-Hill Book Co., 1989.

Oberlin, S. and Cox, J. *CD-ROM Yearbook 1989-90.* Redmond, WA: Microsoft Press, 1989.

Parsloe, E. *Interactive Video.* Cheshire, U.K.: Sigma Technical Press, 1983.

Pettersson, R. *Visuals for Information: Research and Practice.* Englewood Cliffs, NJ: Educational Technology Publications, 1989.

Ropiequet, S. *Optical Publishing.* Redmond, WA: Microsoft Press, 1987.

Schwier, D. *Interactive Video.* Englewood Cliffs, NJ: Educational Technology Publications, 1987.

Sherman, C. *The CD-ROM Handbook.* New York, NY: McGraw-Hill Book Co., 1989.

Van Deusen, R. *Practical AV/Video Budgeting.* White Plains, NY: Knowledge Industry Publications, 1984.

Videodisc and Related Technologies: A Glossary of Terms. Falls Church, VA: Videodisc Monitor, 1988.

Wiegant, I. *Professional Video Production.* White Plains, NY: Knowledge Industry Publications, 1985.

Zemke, R. and Kramlinger, T. *Figuring Things Out.* Reading, MA: Addison-Wesley, 1982.

Appendix G

Glossary

Acknowledgment. The audio or visual acknowledgment given to a user upon the successful touching of an active element or icon on the screen.

ADO. AMPEX Digital Optics; a device for creating digital video effects (DVE's).

AFTRA. American Federation of TV and Radio Artists.

Analysis. The examination of an application in terms of its program content, goals, and objectives, audience needs and treatment of content material.

APA Graphics. All Points Addressable graphics. Graphics that can be addressed to any point on the screen. Each pixel is identified by its own specific address. (See Bit-Mapped Graphics.)

Application. Training/education, marketing or public access presentations are the most common applications using interactive videodisc/multimedia technology.

ASCAP. American Society of Composers, Authors, and Publishers.

ASCII. American Standard Code for Information Interchange. The standard code that is used for information transfer between data processing systems. It is the most common format for PC files.

Aspect Ratio. Ratio of picture height to width (video is 3:4).

Assemble Edit. Adding a video segment to the end of a tape. (See also: Insert Edit.)

A-Time Code. A time code track used to address audio segments on a CD-audio disc.

Audience Analysis. A complete description of the intended users of an application — including demographics, attitudes, skills and education.

Audio. Sound portion of a video signal, or sound used to annotate still frames or graphics. (See also Audio Track.)

Audio Buffer. A computer memory device used to store digital audio and play it back. Used in video players to provide still frame audio (sound over still).

Audio Mixer. A device that allows the simultaneous combining and blending of several sound inputs into one or two outputs.

Audio Segment. A contiguous set of frames from an audio track of a videodisc or CD-ROM. It may or may not be associated with a video segment.

Audio Track. The section of a videodisc frame that contains the sound signal. A system with two audio tracks can have either stereo sound or two independent sound tracks.

Author. A person who creates a presentation using an authoring system.

Authoring. A structured approach to combining all media elements within an interactive videodisc or multimedia program, assisted by computer software designed for this purpose.

Authoring Facility. A generic name for the means used by the author to control a presentation. See also Authoring Language, Authoring System, Time Line Processor, and Hypermedia Generator.

Author Profile. A computer file for an authoring facility that maintains information about the author and the system configuration for a presentation.

Authoring Language. A high level computer programming facility with natural language or mnemonic commands specifically designed to implement CBT or interactive videodisc applications.

Authoring System. A collection of authoring programs that allows users without computer programming skills to prepare videodisc application presentations.

Available Light. The amount of light normally present in the environment.

Back Light. Light directed on the back of the subject to be photographed that helps define the outline against the background.

BASIC Language. A widely used programming language that uses English-like statements and mathematical notations. BASIC can be used to develop multimedia programs.

Betamax. Sony 1-hour 1/2-inch videocassette recorder.

Bit-Mapped Graphics. A form of graphics that are addressed and accessible on a bit-by-bit (pixel) basis, thereby making all points on the monitor display directly addressable. Same as APA graphics.

Blanking. Electronically cutting off the video signal. For example, during the time it takes for a videodisc to search from one sequence to another, the video image is turned off resulting in a blank screen.

Blocking. Establishing of positions and movements for talent on the set.

Bookmark. A marker left in a presentation or program that enables the system to return to that event at a later time.

Boom. A long arm or device used to suspend a microphone or camera over the action.

Branching. The options available at a decision point in a program or presentation.

Burnt-in Time Code. Time Code displayed in a visible window on a videotape.(See Window Dub.)

Byte. A unit of computer memory used to store numeric or character information.Usually, memory size is stated as "nK" bytes, where "nK" represents the number of 1024 byte memory segments (e.g., 640K bytes).

"C" Language. A powerful language used by sophisticated programmers for general purposes, including complex interactive media programs.

CAI. Computer Assisted Instruction. (Also see CBT.)

Carrel. A student work station in a learning resource center.

Card. A computer board with printed circuitry and components that plugs into the computer's system board to provide a special feature or function. Also called an adapter (card).

CAV. Constant Angular Velocity (1800 RPM); the format for interactive videodiscs that allows access to single, specific frames. (See also CLV.)

CBT. Computer-based training (also CAI).

CD-Audio. An audio format recorded on 12 cm. optical discs that offers high quality sound reproduction. Because it is a consumer technology, it is very inexpensive. Some videodisc players use this format to provide two additional audio tracks on a 12-inch videodisc.

CD-I. Compact Disc - Interactive. A CD format that provides interleaved data, audio and video information on a CD. It is designed for inexpensive, standalone players, probably for the consumer or school market.

CD-ROM. Compact Disc - Read only Memory. A format for recording data on 12 cm. optical discs.

CD-ROM XA. CD-ROM eXtended Architecture. A format for recording compressed digital audio at lower qualities, allowing capacity to increase from four to nineteen hours on a single CD.

Chapter. A segment of a Level One videodisc that can be automatically accessed by searching to a chapter stop.

Chapter Stop. A code embedded on a videodisc that enables a Level One player to locate chapters.

Character. An individual byte of information. Characters may be text, graphic, control code, or ASCII.

Character Generator. A device that electronically produces alphanumeric characters for reproduction on a video display.

Check Disc. A videodisc produced prior to quantity replication to evaluate the video material and confirm the accuracy of the interactive program design.

Chroma-Keying. Replacing a certain color in a video picture with another scene, allowing effects to be created such as inserting live talent shot against a colored background into another background.

CLV. Constant Linear Velocity; the format for one hour linear videodiscs and CD-ROM discs. May be used in interactive applications in systems with a video frame buffer.

Color Bars. A series of colored bars or calibrated signal that is used as a reference for brightness, contrast, color intensity, and correct color balance. Usually generated electronically.

Computer Edit System. A video editing system, controlled by a computer and interfaced to several playback and record machines. This type of system is capable of making precise frame-accurate edits.

Contrast Ratio. The degree of difference or ratio between the light and dark areas of the scene.

Control Track. The portion of tape continuing the speed control pulses (sync track).

Control Track Pulses. Speed control pulses created by the VTR.

Courseware. A complete set of materials necessary to take a course. This would include videodiscs, CD-ROMs, computer programs to run the course and any other materials, such as workbooks, charts, diskettes, etc.

Cropping. The cutting off of picture elements by the camera framing.

CRT. Cathode Ray Tube. The vacuum tube used in all TV sets and computer monitors.

CU. Close-up. Notation used on video scripts.

Cue. A signal to commence an event. It can be a hand signal, or an electronic signal recorded on tape.

Cursor. A movable point of light on a display monitor that usually indicates where the next character or pixel is to be entered, deleted, or replaced.

Cursor Keys. The central keys of the numeric keypad, which control the movement of the cursor on the display screen, sometimes referred to as the arrow keys.

Custom Application. An application designed or performed according to an individual user's need (as opposed to generic).

Cut. Stop action or make an edit.

Debug. To remove logical errors from a program or application.

Decibel. A subjective measure of sound volume or strength.

Default. A value or condition assumed by the system, unless specifically overridden.

Definition. The degree of detail or sharpness in a TV picture.

Design. Creating a document that details the actual treatment of the application complete with presentation methods, story line, instructional strategies, flowcharts, and other important details that provide a clear picture of the final product.

Development. Refers to the phase of implementation when documents such as storyboards, production flowcharts, talent scripts, graphics lists, production lists, and authoring outlines are created. The input to this phase is the detail design document.

Digital Audio. A method of encoding an audio signal as a series of digits that can be stored in various media such as computer files, optical discs, or videotape. Playback is accomplished through an audio buffer.

Digital Video. A video signal that has been converted to a series of digits that can be stored in, and manipulated by a computer.

Directory. A specific, named section of disk or CD-ROM memory that contains the names and locations of specific files.

Disc. A generic name for optical recording media (as opposed to "disk" which refers to magnetic recording media).

Disc Production Work Order. The form containing technical specifications of a master tape required for submission of a replication order.

Disk. A magnetic storage device for a computer. See Diskette or Hard Disk.

Diskette. A thin, flexible magnetic disk in a semi-rigid protective jacket. Used to store and retrieve data. Synonymous with Flexible Disk and Floppy Diskette.

Dissolve. The gradual fading in of one picture while other fades out.

Dolly. The movement of a camera toward or away from an object. Also a wheeled apparatus on which the camera is mounted.

DOS. Disk Operating System. Software that manages data transfer, program execution, and access to peripheral devices.

DRAW Disc. (Direct Read After Write) — A less expensive videodisc produced directly from a videotape, one copy at a time. Usually used to check program material and author applications before replicated discs are available.

Drive. A device that stores and retrieves data.

Driver. A computer program segment that controls peripheral devices and drives.

Dropout. A loss of picture signal during tape playback — displays as a black or white streak in the monitor. Breakdown of tape coating.

Drop Frame Time Code. A non-sequential time code used to keep tape time code matched to real time. Must not be used in tapes intended for videodisc mastering.

Dual Mode Disc. A 12 cm. optical disc containing both CD-ROM data and CD-Audio. (Also, Mixed-Mode Disc.)

Dub. Tape-to-tape transfer.

Dubbing. The duplication of a videotape or the addition of new audio information to the tape.

DVE. Digital Video Effects, such as a squeeze-zoom or fly-in of one video picture into another. Once limited to video studio production, is now available on personal computers using digital video cards.

DVI. Digital Video Interactive. A format for recording compressed, digital video on a compact disc, providing up to 72 minutes of full motion video, or about 5000 still frames.

ECU. Extreme Close-up. Notation used on video scripts.

Edited Master. Original copy of edited program.

Editing. The process of building a master tape from work tapes with original footage and other sources such as film, slides, character generators, etc.

EDL. Edit Decision List; information prepared in an off-line edit session to make the on-line edit more efficient.

EFP. Electronic Field Production — using portable video equipment on location.

EGA. Enhanced Graphics Adapter. A computer graphics format that provides 16 colors (see VGA).

EIDS. Electronic Instructional Delivery System. A specification for an IVD device widely used in military training.

Element. A media, graphic or logic component of an event.

End Frame. The last frame, and associated frame number, of a video or audio segment. (Also called a tail frame.)

End-User. The individual who interacts with the completed application.

ENG. Electronic News Gathering.

Environment Analysis. A complete description of the physical installation and surroundings of an application, including people and other related systems.

Event. A segment of a presentation that is either a menu or choice frame, or the elements that are presented after a user interaction has occurred, until the next interaction is required.

Exit. See User Exit.

Fade. A gradual change in the picture brightness or sound level.

Fade to Black. The picture is faded out until the screen is dark.

Field. An NTSC video scan of the screen at 1/60 of a second constituting one-half of a complete video frame. Two fields equal one video frame, with each scanning alternate lines. (See Frame.)

Field Dominance. A term used in video editing to indicate the field in the frame that editing operations are performed on, and in disc manufacture to indicate which field the frame number starts on. Normally, the master tape and disc should have the same field dominance.

File. Information such as data, text, or a program that is stored as a unit under a specific file name.

Film Chain. An optical system whereby an image from a film or slide projector is transferred to a video camera for use in a television system.

First Generation. The original recording or master tape.

Flicker. A phenomenon that occurs in a videodisc freeze frame when both video fields are not identically matched, thus creating two different pictures alternating every 1/60 of a second.

Flexible Disk. See Diskette.

Floppy Diskette. See Diskette.

Flowchart. A graphic outline of a presentation that documents all aspects of each event.

Fly-in. A DVE where one picture "flies" into another.

Footage. The total number of running feet of motion picture film or videotape used, measured in minutes and seconds.

Format. (1) The arrangement or layout of graphics screens, touch points, or text (2) The arrangement of data on a data storage device (3) The physical and electronic form of information or videotape or videodisc. (See also Interactive Format.)

Formative Evaluation. A continuing process of improving intermediate materials and procedures directed toward meeting the objectives of the program. (See Summative Evaluation.)

Frame. A complete TV picture of 525 horizontal lines which is composed of 2 scanned fields of 262-1/2 lines each. One complete TV frame is scanned in 1/30th of a second. (See Field.)

Frame Buffer. See Video Frame Buffer.

Frame Number. The location of each frame on the videodisc. Frames are numbered sequentially from one to 54,000 per side, and can be accessed individually.

Frame Rate. The speed at which the frames are scanned — 30 frames a second for video; 24 frames a second in standard film.

Freeze Frame. A single frame from a motion sequence that is stopped. (See Still Frame.)

F-Stop. A calibration on the lens that indicates the width of the opening of the lens iris.

Full Frame Time Code. A standardized (Society of Motion Picture and Television Engineers) method of address coding for a videotape. It gives an accurate frame count rather than an accurate clock time. Sometimes called "non-drop time code."

Function Key. A key, or combination of keys, used to perform a specific function.

FX. Special effects in video.

Gaffer. Person who works on a production crew, building and striking sets, and providing general assistance to the director.

Gaffer Tape. Duct tape used for various purposes on a video set.

Gain. The level of signal amplification.

Generation. The number of copies away from the original.

Generic Application. Something that is not specific to one organization or group and appeals to a broad market.

Generic Videodisc. Videodisc that contains a collection of images that may be used as media elements in individual applications.

Glitch. Any picture distortion.

Graphic. Any pictorial representation of information.

Graphics (PC). Text or pictorial artwork created with computer-generated graphics software and then stored on the PC hard disk or CD-ROM. Types of graphics include: Image (Bit Mapped), Vector, Sprite.

Graphics (Video). Text or pictorial artwork created by a variety of means, such as, electronic graphics equipment or computer-generated graphics software, recorded on tape and pressed onto the videodiscs.

Graphic Screen. A graphic that is displayed on a monitor.

Graphics Mode. One of several states of the display. The mode determines the resolution and color content of the graphic screen.

Graphics Tablet. A sensitive board on which computer-generated graphics can be designed using a hand-held input device like a graphics pen to draw freehand, create shapes, and transmit instructions.

Gray Scale. The various shades of gray in a TV picture which correspond to color, varying from 0 (pure black) to 10 (maximum white).

Grip. Person who moves cables, hangs lights, etc.

Hard Disk. A rigid magnetic disk within a computer. The storage capacity is much greater than a flexible diskette, typically ten megabytes or more.

Hardware. The electronic and mechanical components of a system.

Head. An electromagnetic device that records or retrieves information from videotape or magnetic computer tapes or disks. An optical head reads data from an optical disc.

Head Frame. See Start Frame.

High Sierra. An informal name for CD-ROM data format. See ISO-9660.

IATSE. International Association of Theatrical and Stage Employees.

Icon. The graphics window associated with a function to be performed — usually appears as a graphic picture that suggests the function.

Image Graphics. See Bit-Mapped Graphics.

Implementation. The phase in which the application is installed.

Information Window. A window (small area on the screen) that provides prompting, or other information, for the author or user.

Informative Feedback. In instructional applications, indicating to the user if a response is correct or not. (See Remedial Feedback.)

InfoWindow. The hardware and software that comprise the IBM integrated interactive videodisc system.

Insert Edit. Video/audio segments inserted into a tape already having control track.

Instructional Designer. An individual who designs the instructional strategy and content flow of an interactive videodisc program based on specific objectives and application analyses.

Intermediate Materials. All those media selected for assembly onto the videodisc premaster — for example: 16mm film, video tape, 35mm slides, etc.

IPS. Inches Per Second — tape speed.

Interaction. The active participation and involvement of a user in directing his/her own movement through an application program by making choices, answering questions or controlling the system.

Interactive Format. A treatment for a specific activity or episode of an application. (See Treatment.)

Interactive Video. A convergence of video and computer technology. A user has control over a coordinated video program and computer program through the user's actions, choices, and decisions which affects how the program unfolds.

ISO-9660. A widely accepted format for recording data on CD-ROM. Sometimes called by the nickname "High Sierra."

Isolation. Technique of recording one camera on one VTR, another camera on separate VTR, then editing two tapes together.

IVD. Interactive Videodisc.

K or Kb. Kilobyte; 1024 bytes. (See Byte.)

Keying. Laying one video picture over another by electronic methods.

Key Light. The light used for primary illumination of a scene.

Keypad. A remote-control device for Level One or Level Two players.

Kiosk. A self-contained, free-standing unit used to house an interactive videodisc system. Usually designed for use in public access environments.

Laser. Light Amplification by Stimulation of Emission of Radiation. A laser uses high energy atoms to produce an intense beam of light. On a laser videodisc or CD-ROM, the laser is used to read the picture and sound information.

Laser Videodisc. An optically read disc that uses laser light to read the information from the disc. Also referred to as LaserDisc or Optical Reflective Videodisc.

Lavalier Mike. A small microphone worn around the neck.

Level. The average intensity of an audio or video source.

Level Zero Videodisc Applications. Linear video transferred to a disc.

Level One Videodisc Applications. Interactive applications based on manual keypad functions, picture stops and chapter stops.

Level Two Videodisc Applications. Interactive applications controlled by keypad and the videodisc player's internal computer. The control program is recorded on the videodisc itself.

Level Three Videodisc Applications. Interactive applications controlled by an external computer that uses the videodisc player as a peripheral device. This is the form of videodisc presentation primarily addressed in this book.

Level Four (and up) Videodisc Applications. Terms used by promoters of various advanced technology approaches to videodisc. Generally, no agreement exists as to precise meaning.

Light Level. The intensity of the light measured in foot candles.

Linear Video. A sequence of motion footage played from start to finish without stops or branching—like a movie.

Lip Sync. The process whereby the picture of a person's lips matches the sound of his voice.

Live. The process of transmitting a program the instant it is taking place.

Log File. A computer file used to record application activity.

Logging. Recording activity information at presentation time in the log file.

Long Lens. A telephoto lens.

Long Shot (LS). A shot from a great distance.

Macro Lens. A lens that is capable of close-up focusing.

Mastering. A real-time process in which the premaster video tape is used to create a glass master disc that will be replicated into the final videodiscs.

Master Tape. The edited and final version of the video tape which can be used to create a master videodisc.

Matte. An effect or device which blocks out an adjacent signal or light — used for keying one picture over another.

Mechanicals. Graphic art materials in camera ready form.

Media. Material or technical means of artistic communication using forms such as, film, art, voice, computer programming, etc.

Medium Shot (MS). The camera view between a close-up and a long shot.

Memory. The area within the computer which stores recorded information, either permanently or temporarily. Usually measured in terms of nK (e.g., 640K) where K represents one 1024 byte segment, or n "megs" which represents a megabyte, or 1024K bytes.

Menu. A list of choices presented on the screen.

Mixer. A device that combines and blends two or more audio or video signals.

Mode. (1) A set of functions grouped together that create a specific method for accomplishing a task. Debug mode, for instance, is a set of functions that create a specific method for capturing and correcting errors in the authoring of a presentation (2) In graphics, a code identifying the complexity of resolution and colors available in a graphics screen.

Moiré. Herringbone interference patterns in a TV picture. Often occurs when sets, artwork, or clothing contains narrow or closely spaced lines.

Monitor. A TV set without receiving circuitry that is used primarily to display video signals.

Monitor/Receiver. A dual function standard TV receiver and monitor.

Monochrome. Black and white.

Motion Segment. See Video Segment.

Mouse. A hand-held electronic device used to facilitate cursor movement and information entry into a PC.

MS. Medium Shot. Notation used on video scripts.

Multimedia. Once used to refer to computer controlled sound/slide presentations; now used as a generic term for sound and image-based applications delivered with a variety of technologies.

NAPLPS. The North American Presentation Level Protocol Syntax. A protocol used for display and communications of text and graphics in a videotex system. It is a form of vector graphics.

Needs Analysis. In marketing applications, a description of existing, perceived, or created needs of the intended user.

Noise. Random undesirable picture or sound interference.

Non-Drop Frame Time Code. A standardized (Society of Motion Picture and Television Engineers) method of address coding for a videotape. It gives an accurate frame count rather than an accurate clock time. Sometimes called full-frame time code.

NTSC. National TV Standards Committee — USA color TV signal standard. American and Japanese videodiscs are recorded using an NTSC signal.

Off-Line Editing. Editing prior to on-line editing. Straight edits only without special effects, or preparing edit decisions lists for the on-line editing sessions.

On-Line Editing. Editing done in an edit studio with original tapes and special effects.

Open Architecture. A system design philosophy which makes it possible to use graphics, text, or data from other, non-related systems or devices.

Optical Reflective Disc. A designation of the method by which data encoded on an optical disc is read by reflecting the laser beam off a shiny surface. Also called Reflective Disc.

Overlay. The capability to superimpose computer-generated graphics and text over motion video or video stills.

Palette. The available colors for a graphics screen; some or all of them may be displayed at one time, depending upon the graphics system.

Pan. The movement of the camera horizontally.

Paper Edit. The process of preparing an Edit Decision List on paper prior to post production. (See EDL, Off-Line Editing.)

Pedestel. A camera mounting device that allows easy up and down movement as well as horizontal movement. Used as a verb to mean moving the camera up or down.

PEL. See Picture Element.

Peripherals. A device that is controlled by the computer but physically independent of it; for example, the computer keyboard, printer, videodisc player, and CD-ROM drive.

PCM-1630. A device manufactured by Sony Corporation that records digital audio on a 3/4-inch video cassette. Used in preparing audio for CD-audio mastering.

Picture Element. The smallest illuminated area on a monitor, represented as a point with a specific color and/or intensity level. Sometimes referred to as a PEL or Pixel.

Picture Stop. An instruction to the videodisc player to halt a motion sequence on a predetermined frame. Picture stops are encoded directly onto the videodisc. They are used in Level One applications.

Pixel. See Picture Element.

Pop-Up Window. A window that appears in response to the entry of data.

Portapack. A portable video system.

Portfolio. A series of timed video stills, producing a "slide show" effect.

Post Production. The editing phase of TV program production.

Premastering. The process of assembly, evaluation, revision, and coding of intermediate materials. A premaster is the fully coded videotape used for the videodisc mastering process.

Pre-Production. Preparation activity that occurs prior to actual shooting.

Pre-Roll. The process of backing-up tapes and VTRs in preparation for an edit so that the VTR can get up to speed.

Presentation. The assembled series of events run by a user.

Presentation System. A system that manages the execution of an interactive video program. Usually associated with a specific authoring system, but licensed separately.

Production. The phase when the film or video footage is actually shot and recorded, and graphics are produced in final form.

Protection Master. A copy of the edited master tape made immediately after post-production is complete to provide back-up if the master tape is damaged in subsequent processing.

Pull-Down Window. A window that appears on a computer screen in response to user entries. It is often used to contain further menu choices.

Quadraplex. A 2-inch video tape recorder that used four rotating heads to record and play back video. Once the broadcast quality standard, it is now being replaced with 1-inch and 3/4-inch formats.

Quartz Lighting. Very bright and efficient lighting.

Random Access. The ability to access information by direct address as opposed to a linear search of data.

Raw Footage. Unedited tape footage.

Real Estate. A slang term for the space available on the videodisc or CD-ROM.

Record. The contents of a specific field or file.

Reflective Disc. See Optical Reflective Disc.

Registration. The overlapping of the red, blue, and green signals to form a correctly colored image. Also, the matching of the position of a computer generated graphic overlayed on a video picture.

Remedial Feedback. In an instructional application, explaining to a user why a particular response was wrong. (See Informative Feedback.)

Remote. Any program originating outside the studio.

Replication. The process of reproduction of videodiscs or CD-ROMs.

Resolution. The amount of resolvable detail in a picture. Picture clarity determined by number of scan lines per frame, or number of horizontal picture elements (PELS) on a line.

RGB. (Red, Green, Blue) A computer color display output signal with separately controlled red, green, and blue signals resulting in a high quality color screen.

RGB Monitor. A computer display that uses an RGB signal, allowing display of high resolution, color graphic screens.

Room Noise. Ambient noise recorded in a studio to facilitate later audio editing without a noticeable difference in sound quality.

Root Directory. The primary listing of files and sub-directories on a disk.

RS-232C. A standard serial interface that connects a computer and its peripheral devices.

SAG. Screen Actors Guild.

Saturation. The intensity of the color.

Search. The capability to instruct the videodisc player to move forward or backward to a specific frame location from any point on the same side of the videodisc.

Segue. (Pronounced seg-way) A transition from one program segment to another in video or audio.

SFX. Sound effects. A notation used on audio/video scripts.

Shooting Ratio. The amount of tape recorded relative to the amount of tape actually used.

Shot List. A list of illustrations to be produced by a single method, such as 35mm photographs. In IVD context, the list will be used to produce still frames.

Signal. Information transposed into electrical impulses.

Signal-To-Noise Ratio. The amount of visible "snow or noise" in a given picture relative to the actual picture signal. The higher the signal-to-noise ratio, the better the picture.

Single Picture Segment. A video picture that doesn't have motion, but runs at normal frame rate so that sound or voice-over from the videodisc audio track can be used.

Slow Motion. The ability to move forward or backward through a moving video sequence at a slower than normal speed.

SMPTE. The Society of Motion Picture and Television Engineers. A standards-setting committee.

SMPTE Time Code. An 8 digit code used for individual frame identification of the form: HH:MM:SS:FF (hours, minutes, seconds, frame numbers).

Software. The programs, routines, languages, procedures, and other non-hardware information that actually make the computer run.

Sound Synthesis. A device that produces human speech sounds and special effects for user-prompting and presentation enhancement.

Special Effects Generator (SEG). A video-mixing device that allows switching between several cameras and a variety of special effects such as dissolves, fades, inserts, wipes, etc.

Speech Chip. Synthetic vocalization of words and sounds stored on a microchip and used primarily to prompt the viewer.

Spread Sheet. (1) A type of chart comprised of rows and columns that is utilized for the storage and manipulation of data. (2) A screen display used in a time line processor to control and synchronize the individual elements of an event.

Sprite Graphics. A small graphics picture that can be moved independently around the screen, producing animated effects.

Squeeze-Zoom. A DVE where one picture is reduced in size and displayed with a full screen picture.

Start Frame. The first frame number of a video or audio segment. (Also called a Head Frame.)

Step. To advance one frame forward or reverse.

Still Frame. Still material, including photographs, graphics, pages, etc., designed and presented as a single videodisc frame.

Still Frame Audio. A feature available with some videodisc players that allows digital audio to be played from an audio buffer while displaying a still frame.

Storyboard. Documentation for video production that contains the audio script, and a complete description of the visual content, often in the form of pictures or sketches.

Stringer. Freelance person.

Sub-Directory. A directory associated with, and subordinate to, a higher directory.

Summative Evaluation. A formal measurement of the effectiveness of a completed application. (See Formative Evaluation.)

Super Storyboard. Documentation that describes all audio, video, graphic, and logical control elements for an interactive videodisc application.

Switcher. A video switching and mixing device. (Also called a "Switcher-Fader.")

Sync. Synchronization; the timing pulses that drive the TV scanning system.

System Prompting. Feedback for a user or author that is controlled by the system.

Tail Frame. See End Frame.

Tally Light. An indicator lamp on the camera which shows when recording from the camera is being done.

Task Analysis. Documentation of performance measures required in a given job.

Tearing. A picture condition when the image is displaced horizontally, usually caused by sync problems.

Technical Evaluation. A standard evaluation of the video tape premaster, performed at the completion of the premastering process, which measures the video signal and tests each edit.

Text Editor. A computer program designed to manipulate text.

Tight Shot. Close-up.

Tilt. A camera move made by swinging the camera in a vertical arc.

Time Base Corrector. A device that electronically corrects the mechanical and electronic errors created by a VTR.

Time Code. The frame address code recorded on videotape. (See SMPTE Time Code.)

Time Code Generator. An electronic device that creates a special address or time code to be recorded on the tape.

Time Line Processor. A type of authoring facility that displays events as elements on a spread sheet which depicts time from the start of that event.

Timeout. A situation in which user response must occur within a given time, or a default branch of the program is executed.

Touch Acknowledgment. The visual or aural feedback given to the user upon system acceptance of a touch to an active touch area.

Touch Areas. Areas of a touch screen that are activated to accept user input.

Touch Points. See Touch Areas.

Touch Screen. A display screen of a monitor that can sense a pressure touch, and report its location to the computer system.

Track. The path on a magnetic medium on which information is recorded.

Tracking. The position of the video head over the recorded signal on the videotape, or videodiscs.

Transition. The smooth passage from one screen to another. Techniques used include fades, dissolves, wipes, and cuts.

Transparency. The facility that allows a selected color in an overlay graphic screen to be designated transparent in order to show a video image or sequence behind it.

Treatment. Narrative description of the way a subject will be treated and a program will look when completed.

Truck. The lateral movement of the camera dolly or pedestal.

U-Matic. Sony Trademark name which refers to 3/4-inch videocassette format VTRs.

Underscan. The display of the entire TV image on a monitor, out to the edges not normally seen.

User. The person who utilizes a presentation. (Also called End-User.)

User Contact-Hour. A unit used to measure the total "length" of an interactive presentation, if all material provided were accessed. It is based on length of video, number of graphics and still frames, and logical complexity of the application.

User Control. One or more designated touch areas on the screen that provide on-screen user aids. Some examples could be help, pause, resume, glossary, stop, go back, go forward, etc. Often activated by touching an icon or control word.

User-Friendly. Interfaces with the user that are informative, easy to understand, and require little or no computer or programming experience.

User Exit. (1) A pre-programmed facility that allows a user to exit from an interactive presentation to other computer programs. (2) Any off-line program to which interpreter passes temporary control during the execution of a presentation.

User Time-on-System. An estimated time that the **average** user will spend at one session using the application. It is used in predicting system utilization percentage.

Validation. The process of gathering data to determine if the presentation/course meets the objectives and goals as originally described.

VCR. Video Cassette Recorder.

Vector Graphics. Graphics drawn at presentation time as specified by a stored set of commands called "Vectors."

VGA. Video Graphics Array. A computer graphics format that provides 256 colors. (See EGA.)

Video. Picture Information

Video Frame Buffer. A device that can capture, store, and display a single video frame, using a large, fast bank of computer memory.

Videocassette. A reel of videotape in a closed plastic container.

Videodisc. Video signal recorded on a disc. The most common format in the United States and Japan is an NTSC signal recorded on the optical-reflective format.

Videodisc Map. A chart that contains information (start and end frame numbers, audio track specifications, etc.) for each video and audio segment to be used in a presentation.

Video Gain. The amplitude of the video signal.

Video Levels. Chroma and luminance (color and brightness) levels measured on a scope.

Video Segment. A specific set of videodisc frames, usually containing sound and motion, played as one element.

Videotex. A system for storing graphic information in a host system that is transmitted over telephone lines or television signals. Often, graphics are vector type, stored in NAPLPS format. (See NAPLPS and Vector Graphics.)

Voice-Over (VO). A spoken message or narrative added to the picture.

VTR. Video Tape Recorder.

VU Meter. Volume Unit meter; measures sound level on an audio channel. Usually seen on the audio mixer.

WYSIWYG. "What You See Is What You Get." A feature of software development and coding programs that allows the coder to see the screens as the end user will see them — as they are being coded. A desirable feature in authoring facilities.

Wide Angle Lens. A lens with a very wide angle of view.

Window. A portion of a display device that is dedicated to a particular action, such as pop-up windows that are used to program options for specific elements of the spread sheet. (See also Information Window.)

Window Dub. A 3/4-inch or 1/2-inch tape copy of a production tape with time code displayed in a visible window, used in preparing for post-production.

Wipe (Graphics). A transition that specifies how a graphics screen appears as it replaces the present visual display.

Wipe (Video). A special effect whereby one image "pushes" another image off the screen. Produced by a special effects generator, wipes can take on many shapes and forms.

Zoom Lens. A lens that is capable of varying its image from long shot to close up and serving as several lenses at once.

Index

W

ABOUT THE AUTHORS

The authors have extensive background in all facets of the instructional design, development, production, and delivery process of interactive video/multimedia applications. They have created courses in print, videotape, and videodisc, and participated in multimedia projects working with many vendors. After observing the development process for several years, they designed and conducted a comprehensive hands-on workshop for Project Managers of interactive video/multimedia applications. This book consolidates that workshop material and the successful strategies used in over 100 multimedia projects.

Dr. Robert E. Bergman earned his Ph.D. in Instructional Technology at Georgia State University. During his 25 years at IBM Corporation, he held a variety of education assignments -- teaching IBM customers, developing instructor guides, training the trainers, and designing self-paced, multimedia courses. Just prior to retiring from IBM, Dr. Bergman was responsible for the design, development and delivery of author training on IBM's InfoWindow software product: Learning System/1. He is currently Associate Professor of Business Information Systems at Southeastern Massachusetts University teaching courses in performance technology and information systems.

Thomas V. Moore recently retired from IBM after a career of 27 years, primarily in educational assignments. These included teaching and instructional development using a variety of media. In the early 1970's, he managed the video facility that produced IBM's marketing division video tapes. He also participated in development of computer based instruction projects and interactive classrooms delivered via satellite links. He has accumulated over 15 years of experience in videodisc and multimedia technology. He developed and managed many projects, giving special attention to devising practical development and authoring techniques. Over the years, he has evolved effective, cost-justified approaches to managing projects that use advanced technologies for training, marketing and human communications.

The authors are continuing their research and consulting activities in interactive multimedia.